MW00795208

Also by Ayja Bounous

Shaped by Snow: Defending the Future of Winter

Junior Bounous

Junior Bounous and the Joys of Skiing

A biography

by Ayja Bounous

ISBN: 979-8-9867735-0-6 (Paperback)
LCCN: 2022915970

Edited by Madeleine Brown
Book design by Madeleine Brown
Cover design by Phillip Brown
Front cover photo by Fred Lindholm
Back cover photo courtesy of Snowbird archives

Interior photographs printed with permission from Fred Lindholm, James Kay Photography, Tyler Rye Photography, Snowbird, and the Special Collections of the J. Willard Marriott Library at the University of Utah

Printed by Paragon Press Inc., in the United States of America

First printing edition 2022

Published by Bounous Enterprises LLC

ayjabounous.com

To my parents. Your unwavering support has allowed me to pursue my lifelong dream of becoming an author, and for that I will be forever grateful.

Ayja Bounous

To the lady I followed all over the world, my sweetheart Maxine, who was a wonderful woman with whom to raise a family.

To my father, for braving a new country to make a life for himself, for teaching me the value of work hard, and for cultivating a piece of land that would become my home and livelihood.

To my mother, for showing me unconditional love, and for gifting me my first pair of skis.

To my sons, Barry and Steve. It has been a great pleasure to watch both of you continue my legacy in the ski industry and pave your own paths in life. Thank you for your support and for helping me continue to hike and ski to this day. I treasure my time with you.

Junior Bounous

Junior Bounous

Table of Contents

Forewords

In the summer of 1971, I was hired by Ted Johnson, the founder and visionary of Snowbird Ski Resort, to help build this new resort. It was a far-reaching vision with an aerial tramway and tall concrete buildings replicating some of Europe's most renowned ski areas.

Junior and Sal Raio wearing the Snowbird ski school uniforms in the early 1970s. Like many of Junior's instructors who took on their own leadership roles, Sal continued on to become Deer Valley's director of skier services. *Snowbird archives*

During that summer, I had the pleasure of meeting Junior Bounous, the legendary skier whom I had read and heard about through mutual friends. He was gracious and very enthusiastic about the potential to create an outstanding ski school. I was fortunate to work for him that first winter and then for the next 10 years as a ski instructor, coach, and supervisor. In those years, I learned many life skills from Junior that I have taken with me throughout my professional and personal life.

In the spring of 1981, another new Utah ski resort was in search of a ski school manger. With Junior's encouragement, I applied for the position and became the new ski school manager for Deer Valley Ski Resort. The position eventually became the director of skier services, and I was responsible for 750 staff members and millions of dollars in revenue. I owe much of my success to Junior's mentoring and positive influence. Fifty years later, he continues to be a special friend and is a person I hope to emulate throughout life because of his positive attitude, his gentle kindness toward people, and his love of life. He is always inspired by the Utah mountain environment that he knows so well.

This book is written by Ayja Bounous, Junior's granddaughter, who has grown up in a family of skiers, hikers, and nature lovers, so her perspective of the Bounous family is extensive. She has captured much of the young history of skiing in America, as well as Junior's significant role in developing the American ski technique and, consequently, the way Americans learn to ski today. Much of Junior's life—from farm boy to legendary skier and beyond—has been brought to light in this book.

Junior is one of a kind. At 96 years old, he has not lost his outstanding storytelling ability—especially when it comes to the early days at Alta and Snowbird—nor his fun-loving manner and his love of the mountains. This book highlights Junior's skills, both natural and hard-earned, and his unique characteristics, allowing readers to see this legendary person as he really is!

Sal Raio

Not long ago, a group of students studying recreation management at a local university scheduled a panel discussion to guide the development of their goals. Having spent much of my life in a leadership role in the skiing industry, I was invited to participate on the panel. One of the students asked me specifically, "What can I do to get a job and keep it, so I can then help develop people through recreation management?"

I immediately thought of my sport and life experiences with Junior Bounous. Junior inspires the powerful principle of living with a cheerful heart and bright countenance, which is just one of the many great principles of life I have learned from Junior, a powerful mentor in both sport and life.

So, to answer this student's question, I explained my method for hiring at Sundance Mountain Resort: hire for attitude and train for skill. If I were considering two individuals of similar skill, the person with the more cheerful approach and brighter countenance would get the job every time because that's what the job was—to cheerfully edify others.

By example, Junior has taught me and countless others his natural cheerful approach to living, and he has done so with a consistently bright attitude you can see in his eyes as he assists others with humor and tender compassion. Along with his dear wife, Maxine, Junior inspires us to live and work cheerfully, to be powerful examples of the way our creator would have us live in this world.

A master teacher, Junior teaches skiing in a simplified way that brings people into the experience, helps them love learning, and increases their capacity to do things they could not do before. His teaching ability was especially evident one time when Junior was standing at the top of a steep chute at Snowbird, and he noticed the worried looks on the faces of a few skiers in his group as they asked him technical questions on how to ski it. To the delight of the group, Junior began humming a rhythm until they all joined in: "tada, tada, tada, tada, tada," with each *tada* representing a turn. Then he had the whole group watch and repeat his rhythm as he masterfully skied a short distance away. Then the now-smiling group each repeated the "tada, tada, tada" rhythm for each other as they laughed and skied the chute successfully. They all learned the answers to their technical questions by just skiing it like Junior.

Junior shaking hands with Jerry Warren in the fall of 1967. Junior had just hired Jerry as a Timp Haven ski instructor, the start of a long and happy partnership and friendship.

Skiing is often driven by overly technical solutions that steal the fun and cheerful expression of learning. Junior makes learning fun through slowing down a little, simplifying, and truly seeing others, as he cheerfully makes great effort to edify others in some way. Junior's character and manner of living have been imprinted on my heart and soul, informing all aspects of my life.

Junior and Maxine have lived a glorious life of artful simplicity that has stimulated their gracious hearts. Cheerfulness increases the possibility that good things are understood more easily. Junior and Maxine's cheerfulness inspired us to live deeply effective and wonderful lives.

As you read this marvelous book, you will find their mentoring mastery coming through into your own heart and your own life, as it most definitely has mine.

Jerry Warren

"The teacher's task is to initiate the learning process and then get out of the way."

John Warren

Author's Note

"As you turn, you're going to want to bounce like you're on a trampoline," my grandpa instructed while he demonstrated, bending his knees and hips, then straightening again, his arms in front of his upper body as if he were getting ready to row a boat. His skis sank slightly into the soft snow around his feet at the motion.

"Stay loose in your joints, in your knees and hips," he continued, "and then press down into your boots as if you were trying to jump right out of them. When you bounce back up, try to pull your skis up off the ground a little bit to help."

He demonstrated again, this time with more movement. Next to me, my younger sister, Tyndall, mimicked his motions enthusiastically. Her skis lifted off the snow slightly with each bounce, and she bunny hopped a few inches forward.

"Try it out, Ayj," my father encouraged.

I bent my legs and hips, then tried to bounce, pretending the snow beneath my skis was a trampoline. But the snow didn't react like a trampoline, and it stunted my momentum instead.

"It feels weird," I said, trying again.

"It's going to make more sense when you're moving through powder snow," my grandpa replied. "It will feel like the snow's pushing back against your skis when you bounce."

The winter air around us was crisp and cold, the sky above as blue as a jewel. My grandfather's bright yellow helmet stood out against the stark white, glistening snow. The basin we stood in, shaped like a half moon with jagged peaks jutting toward the sky, was blinding in the white winter sun. A light breeze wove through the trees and caught a handful of snow from the bough of a nearby pine. Tossed into the air, the loose, light crystals fell slowly around us, shimmering as though we stood inside a snow globe filled with tiny diamonds.

We were at Snowbird Ski Resort in the Wasatch Mountain Range of Northern Utah. It was a sunny January day, and a storm had deposited a few inches of fresh snow the night before. Following my grandfather's lead, my sister, my parents, my grandma, and I had abandoned the smooth, groomed runs for something a little more adventurous. My grandpa, Junior Bounous, broke trail on a hill of untracked, powder snow, shuffling his skis back and forth to create a path. We followed, using our poles to push us along the track. We had gone skiing that day with a purpose—Tyndall and I were going to learn how to ski powder.

My dad called from behind as he brought up the rear: "Ready for some good ol' Bounousabuse fun, girls?"

My grandfather reached for his ski poles and explained, "Now, your ski tips are going to want to dive under the snow when you start moving. You'll want to lean back a little as you start, so the weight of your body brings your tips up. Don't be afraid to pick up a little speed—it will help keep your skis afloat. And bouncing into your heels is going to help lift those tips back out when they dive under during your turn as well."

He shifted his weight toward the back of his skis, and Tyndall and I mimicked the motion.

"Okay! Now for the fun stuff," my grandpa said. "Are you ready? We're going to ski through those trees right there. Just make sure not to hit any, okay? And the most important part," he said, his familiar smile stretching across his face, "is to make sure to sing!"

He pushed himself forward with his poles and began to sing.

"Ba-dump, ba-dump, ba-dump, ba-dump . . ."

The soft powder snow was tossed to each side of his skis like a wave on sand, each turn accompanied by a "ba-dump." He left a snake-like trail behind him as he picked up speed. Then, with one last turn and a puff of sparkling diamond dust, he and his yellow helmet ducked into the trees and disappeared.

It's impossible to say how many people Junior Bounous has taught to ski. After giving private and group lessons for more than 70 years, organizing "ski weeks" when hundreds of people learned to ski within a few days, and writing how-to-ski articles published in countless ski magazines over the decades, Junior's ski legacy is far reaching. His hand has shaped the American ski industry in ways that are hard to comprehend. He taught and influenced all the ski instructors who worked for him, and they in turn taught countless others, sometimes becoming ski school directors themselves. By conservative estimates, Junior likely has had a part in teaching at least 20,000 people. By more moderate estimates, that number could be over 50,000. Even so, the most important person Junior taught how to ski was himself. Without him, the American ski industry wouldn't be where it is today.

It's a bit embarrassing for me to admit, but until writing this book, I had only a vague understanding of Junior's contributions to the ski industry. Growing up, I knew he wasn't quite like my friends' grandfathers. My parents would frame newspaper clippings with headlines like "Bounous to Join Ski Hall of Fame" and place them around our living room. Sometimes a teacher at my school would pause while doing roll call when they reached my name and say, "Bounous—like Junior Bounous?" And there was, of course, the moment when he and my father carried the Olympic torch when the Winter Olympics came to Salt Lake City in 2002. When I asked why Junior was so famous, I was told that he "helped develop the modern powder skiing technique," but I had no idea what that really meant at the time. Basically, I knew he was a big deal, but I just didn't know why.

My ignorance of his contributions made this book all the more exciting to write. His place within the larger world of skiing in America—particularly powder skiing—is truly remarkable, and I treasure the experience of discovering what American ski culture was like as Junior was rising through the ranks. I initially approached this project with the intention of providing a distant, professional take on both his life and the development of the American ski industry. Once I dove deep into the writing process, however, my approach shifted. While telling Junior's story, it became clear that it would be impossible to leave myself out of it—nor did I want to, I found. As one of his direct descendants, I could offer my own stories and insight into Junior's character. Anyone could have written about the history of Junior's life, but I am proud to be able to share intimate insights from the relationship that grandfather and granddaughter share. That being said, writing from a granddaughter's perspective does have some implications, which I'd like to quickly address.

The first is that I don't shy away from being biased. You will find many words of praise and very few words of criticism. And despite writing an entire book about him, words really do fail me when trying to describe him. Junior is one of those people who seems almost too magnificent to be real, and while that might sound a bit dramatic, I'm confident that those fortunate enough to know him would agree with me. The hardest task in writing this book, at least for a granddaughter who loves her subject matter fiercely, has been trying to document that which makes someone sparkle—the way it feels when they make you laugh, how you feel their pain like a knife in your chest, how you could watch them smile all day, the way the expression in their eyes changes when they witness something beautiful. I strove to make him shimmer on paper like he shimmers in real life. I ask the readers to forgive my writing if it seems a bit starry-eyed at times—just remember that you're reading the words of a granddaughter who's obsessed with her grandfather.

I'd also like to address the fact that, while I have done plenty of my own research into the history of skiing in America, my number-one source of information was Junior. For a 90-something, he has an incredibly clear and reliable memory. However, even the best memories can be fickle. While I did my best to fact-check everything he told me, minor errors are likely, such as an incorrect date, name spelling, or a person inadvertently left out of a story. Assuming some readers will have first-hand memories of some stories, I ask in advance for forgiveness, if they remember events differently.

I'll also take a moment here to address the photos within these pages. Most were taken from Junior's personal collection. This means that giving photo credit to whoever took the photos was quite difficult, though I did my best to do so. Many of the classic skiing shots of Junior and Maxine were likely captured by their friend and one of the most important ski photographers of the era, Fred Lindholm. Because we couldn't confirm many of these, however, most photos remain uncredited.

It's been hard keeping up with a 97-year-old—especially one as lively as Junior. Even as I'd finish a chapter and set it aside for months, thinking it was finished, another story relating to that time in Junior's life would emerge while on the chairlift or at a family dinner, and I'd have to revisit the chapter and figure out how to incorporate it. Plenty of stories, events, people, and places inevitably will have been left out of this book, which is by no means a comprehensive account of Junior's life. It's simply impossible to include every aspect of such a well-lived life as Junior's has been.

Also difficult to include were the experiences Junior was having in real time as I was writing. Recently I went on a walk with him up Rock Canyon, a canyon near his house, and he pointed out a small field of a flower called "lady slippers" that he and Maxine loved visiting together—an experience that, though it doesn't seem like much, was a very special moment that happened late enough in the writing process that I didn't include it. In one chapter, I talk about how many ski days Junior had skied "at the time of this writing" (the beginning of 2022), and I kept having to go back and change the number as "over 60 days at the time of this writing" became "75 ski days," then "over 80," then "96." (For the record, he ended the 2021–22 ski season with 101 ski days!)

To kick off this biography in typical "Bounousabuse" fashion, I'd like to tell an exceptionally entertaining experience that didn't make it into the book. Junior was skiing with family friends Mark and Liane Magelssen at Alta Ski Resort in April 2022. Junior took the couple through a less-skied grove of trees between Sunnyside and Supreme lifts. There's a creek that meanders through these trees, and, depending on the time of year and snow levels, parts of the creek can be exposed. At 96 years old, Junior is quite capable of skiing fast, but can have a harder time stopping his momentum. As they skied through the trees, Junior hit an unexpected dip in the trail, and the compression caused his skis to double eject—right at the edge of a 10-foot drop into an exposed creek bed. Thankfully Junior's momentum was stunted by the soft snow. His skis had no such luck—one went flying off the trail and landed in the creek. There being "nothing else for it," according to Junior, he boot packed down through the powder, skirting around trees and navigating steep hillsides to a flat enough area where he could enter the creek.

And that's how Alta ski patrol (waved over by Liane) found Junior Bounous on that April day: his ski boots six inches deep in a partially frozen creek, wading through the water in pursuit of his missing ski. (His biggest takeaway from that experience was realizing that his rear-entry ski boots are 100 percent waterproof.)

And with that, I hope you enjoy reading this book about the vibrant and magical life of Junior Bounous as much as I enjoyed writing about it.

Introduction

Water Master

Every year, when the earth tilts back so the southern hemisphere is warmed by the sun and the northern hemisphere recedes into shadow, something magical happens in the sky above the mountains of Utah. Six-pointed crystals begin to take shape in the clouds and then fall like feathers from the sky. The snowflakes twist and tumble as they fall, changing shape, becoming larger, smaller, more intricate, each one as completely unique as they spin on the winter winds. When they come to rest on the earth in enormous volumes, they change the shape of the landscape, creating a snowpack that alters the way of life for plants, animals, and humans. Snow defines both climate and culture on this planet—regulating the temperature of the earth with its reflective properties, flushing ecosystems and reservoirs with fresh water, and providing a medium on which people can float down the side of a mountain with skis on their feet. Some might enjoy the weightless feeling of snow beneath them so much that they might even earn their livelihoods through a career dedicated to the wondrous substance.

Junior Bounous is one of those people. Since before he was born, Junior's life has been defined by snow, both directly and indirectly. Snow and water. It was access to water, both irrigation and culinary, from Wasatch snow melt that led to Junior's father, Levi Bounous, purchasing a plot of land on the bench of the Wasatch Mountains in Provo, Utah. From that moment, the Bounous family was defined by water and how water changes through the seasons.

While this biography is focused on the life of Junior Bounous, it also ventures into the ski and snowboard culture that developed around snow in the American West. From Junior's eyes, this book examines the different trends, advances, people, and places that played a role in the development of the western American ski industry. For that reason, the narrative begins by first providing a sense of what the ski culture was like when Junior entered it, around the middle of the 20th century. From there, some chapters focus on places where Junior lived, and some focus on topics that are relevant to his life. For this reason, this book will not read in a strict, chronological order; instead, the reader can expect the narrative to meander through the relevant phases of Junior's life, depending on place and subject matter, almost all of which are centered around Junior's relationship with snow and water.

Junior's knowledge about water came through experience, starting in his teenage years when he became "water master" for the nearby foothills. This meant that Junior was in charge of monitoring all the waterways—ditches, cement flumes, or springs—from Provo Canyon to Rock Canyon to ensure they were functioning correctly, bringing water to the farms below. If he found a clog or some rockfall that had broken the line, Junior would fix it, tracing the length of the flume to determine where the problem was, a shovel or rake over his shoulder. If there were more serious work to be done, like fixing the concrete, Levi would join Junior. (Having built the flume down Rock Canyon, Levi had a knack for concrete.) Ensuring others had access to water was not unlike the career Junior would choose for himself: providing others with the access and the skills to enjoy skiing, especially powder skiing.

The job of water master could be very time-consuming. Junior had to trace each ditch and flume from farm to source every week. To make the job quicker, he began running rather than walking. Wearing a pair of old work boots, he'd jog along the primitive trails that followed the water. This was one of Junior's introductions to long-distance running and a lifetime of exceptional athleticism. Running and ultra running would become lifelong passions of his, and he'd continue to run to the tips of mountains and compete in races well into his 80s, but his zeal for running took root along the paths of water he ran as a teenager. He became a water-tracer, his boots padding along the soft dirt of the Wasatch foothills as he ran up one waterway, then back down. Up another waterway, then back down. Each time he ran, he became more familiar with the landscape through which the water flowed, with the contours of the hillsides, with the brush and the rocks and the wildlife he saw along the way, with the way the path of water curved to match the landscape.

Up one waterway, and down again—just like the path of the water molecules themselves: flowing to lower elevations to evaporate in the air and then raining or snowing high up on the landscape to flow downward again. It was as though the water in Junior's body was drawn to the water in the landscape, brought together by cohesion—the seemingly magical force that pulls water molecules together. It would be a passion that would continue to draw Junior up the canyons when snow accumulated high in the mountains, and then pull him back down to follow the water as it melted down the waterways into the lakes, rivers, and oceans. The joy he has found through his deep, lifelong connection to water, whether it takes him up or down the mountain, is one he has shared with countless others along the way.

As Junior transitioned to adulthood, this love seeped into his choice of employment and determined the lifestyle he created for himself and his family. When the snow stacked up in the high reaches of the Wasatch, Junior would load his skis into the back of his car and brave the winding winter canyons to find that snow. When the weather warmed and spring thaw sent runoff into the valleys, Junior would devote his time to bringing the family farm out of dormancy. Then as the water passed farther downstream into the deserts, Junior and his family would head to southern Utah, a place where water may seem scarce until one notices that the soft red rocks are mere canvases for erosion. Water defined all four seasons for the Bounous family.

"Water master" was his official title, but a more accurate one might have been "water worshiper."

Skiing on snow was not Junior's only talent. 1970s.

Maxine and Junior at Alta in 1969.

The king of powder at Alta in the 1950s.
Fred Lindholm

Junior at the top of Hidden Peak in the 1990s.

Junior with his Olympic torch at the top of Hidden Peak. 2002.
James Kay Photography

Chapter 1

The American Skier

A family friend once told me that the essence of Junior Bounous is in his skiing. While this statement immediately rang true in the ears of a granddaughter, it took me some time to truly unpack its implications. Once I did, the phrase—spoken by Georgia Clark, one of Junior's ski instructors—has become a sort of mantra in my own life. The essence of Junior is in his skiing. To me, that meant the qualities that define Junior, which make him such an easy person to love and hold respect for, are ones often required of those who love to ski.

To enjoy the sport of skiing, one has to enjoy spending time in the mountains, and not just on a pleasant, sunny afternoon, but sometimes in the midst of a snowstorm, if one wants to ski the freshest powder. The most adept skiers are humbled by the raw intensity of the mountains and the elements. The act of skiing is, in a way, a submission to the mountains, letting the natural shape of the landscape and gravity pull you in a certain direction. To his core, Junior has a visceral respect and love for the natural world around him and a sense of adventure that's deeply intertwined with the physical terrain of the landscapes in which he lives. Learning how to ski requires perseverance and patience, qualities which create the base of Junior's solid work ethic. Becoming a proficient skier involves athleticism and passion, both of which Junior has plenty. Beautiful skiing exhibits intuition and harmony between one's body and its place in the universe, a dance that brings together body, mind, mountain, and snow. Many people have told me that Junior Bounous is the most beautiful skier they have ever seen.

Junior learned how to ski in an exciting era. Almost a century after European immigrants brought skiing to North America and a few decades after skiers had started experimenting in the snow-rich mountains of northern Utah, where Junior was born, Junior began teaching himself how to ski on rudimentary equipment—barrel staves. There were no real teachers, no teaching system, and not much infrastructure to support the relatively new sport. As Junior matured from child to adult, much of that changed dramatically. Junior, a quick learner and a natural teacher, quickly rose to become a leader as the turbulent beginnings of a ski industry became streamlined. His leadership would influence tens of thousands of people in the coming decades.

More meaningful than the number of people he taught is the era during which Junior became involved with skiing. The 1940s and 1950s saw a rapid increase of skiing in the United States, and the drastic number of enthusiasts meant that equipment was improving, ski techniques were changing, more terrain was being explored and developed, and more ski instructors were needed. It could be said that Junior was teaching and developing ski techniques during the American ski industry's most formative years. And, because Junior was one of the first American-born ski school directors in this developing industry, it might also be said that Junior Bounous is *the* American Skier.

Skiing had been around for more than 10,000 years before coming to America. The first evidence of skiing was found in the Altai region of central Asia, where the borders of Russia, Kazakhstan, Mongolia, and China meet. The Altai mountains, sometimes referred to as "Siberian Switzerland," look similar to the Swiss Alps, the Canadian Rockies, and the Southern Alps of New Zealand. The Altai mountains birthed a ski culture that is strong to this day and looks quite a bit different from the Western Europe and North American ski cultures that dominate the world's modern ski industry.

Skiing was a staple of life in the Scandinavian countries thousands of years ago, used mainly for traversing snowy landscapes and hunting. It spread south into central Europe and gained popularity in the 1800s, transforming from a utilitarian activity to a recreational activity. As a result, ski resorts began popping up across the Alps, and with the resorts came an increased demand for people who already knew how to ski and who could teach others. As the sport progressed, an early technique began developing.

As Scandinavian immigrants crossed the Atlantic Ocean to begin new lives in the United States, they brought skiing with them. The use of skis spread from the East Coast, to the Midwest, and finally to the American West as the Gold Rush drew crowds out to the mountains. Miners in the Rockies and Sierra Nevada used skis to access mines in the mountains, and mail carriers used skis to travel from town to town. While European skiing was becoming more recreational and increasingly nuanced, skiing in the United States remained confined to utilitarian purposes until the turn of the century.

Scandinavian immigrants were the ones who introduced cross-country skiing and ski jumping in the Northeast and Midwest during the late 1800s, and the activity quickly spread west. Ski jumping, especially, rapidly gained popularity in the early 1900s, though mainly as a spectator sport. There were no US ski resorts yet, so all skiing took place in the backcountry. As early as 1912, Utah had its first ski club, formed by ski enthusiasts who wanted to explore the Wasatch Mountains while hiking, mountaineering, or backcountry skiing (though in those days it was just called skiing). There were no ski instructors. The sport was of interest to those with a passion for snow, mountain landscapes, catching air, and maybe a slight death wish.

Meanwhile, in post–World War I Europe, significant advances were being made in ski teaching. In 1925, an Austrian man named Hannes Schneider founded his own ski school after teaching hundreds of Austrian soldiers to ski while fighting in the mountains of Italy during World War I. Schneider built on older skiing techniques and improved them, creating a name for himself as the father of modern skiing. He improved on a type of turn known as a stem turn, a variation on the snowplow. In order to turn with their skis in a wedge, Schneider instructed ski students to first point their outside ski in the direction they wanted to go, and then put their weight on that ski to initiate the turn.

Schneider's turning technique became known as the Arlberg technique, named after the Arlberg massif of Austria, where he built his school. It was soon the accepted standard of skiing at the time, and he joined forces with filmmaker Arnold Frank to produce movies that spread the technique. To teach the Arlberg technique to students, instructors were advised to follow certain steps designed to guide beginner skiers "up the ladder," as they called it. European ski instructors believed students should not progress to the next level until they mastered the step they were on.

A handful of ski areas opened in the United States from 1915 into the 1920s, but the real rush to open ski areas began in the latter half of 1930s. By 1936, skiing had become so popular in the United States that many enthusiasts reached out to Schneider, imploring him to cross the Atlantic for a visit. Schneider obliged, and he put on a ski exhibition during a winter sports show at the Boston Garden. When he returned to Austria, he said, "American skiing still needs lots of organizing; the wave came so suddenly that nobody could take hold of it, but a few years from now it probably will look different when the public insists on good ski schools."

This was the same decade that Junior began to ski. He was still too young to be actively watching or competing in the backcountry explorations or ski jumping rage of that era. However, eight-year-old Junior started teaching himself how to ski, and by the time he was 15 years old in 1940, he had built his own skis and was beginning to venture into the mountains. From there, Junior's mastery of the sport of skiing took off.

While Junior was entering into the real world of skiing as a young adult in the 1940s, the rest of the world was at war. The focus of most Americans was news of the war reported from overseas.

Miraculously, Junior was never in the army. He received two draft summonses—the first instructing him to work on his family's farm, the second calling him into combat. But when he went in for a physical, he was rejected. He sat for hours in a waiting room, naked, until a doctor finally came in and told him he was unfit to serve. And not just unfit to serve in physical combat, but unfit to serve in any role. The doctor told him that he had three displaced discs in his upper back that had been displaced for a long time, and there was no way that he could be allowed to join. He was given the ranking "4F" and told to go home. Junior was stumped; he was in his prime, incredibly strong and a long-distance runner, with no physical ailments that he was aware of. When Junior racked his memory to think of when he may have broken his back, the only injury he could think of was the time he fell off a roof at a young age. But he had also broken both of his arms and had to wear two casts, so the focus of his pain was on his arms rather than his back.

With the return of the remaining soldiers from Europe after the war, a new era of mass leisure and recreation for the middle class ignited, the likes of which had never been seen in American culture. The United States' economy had rebounded from the Great Depression, and young men and women were reunited, feeling mostly victorious. The focus was no longer on war; it was on pleasure. Some of the survivors were members of the US Army's 10th Mountain Division, trained in the art of combat on skis. The division had spent a good deal of time drilling at various ski resorts in the American West (and had summited Mount Rainier), and many were now passionate skiers who accepted jobs as ski instructors, ski school directors, and helped build new ski resorts. And the need for teachers hit the rapidly developing industry. The end of the 1940s and start of the 1950s marked a booming era in the American ski industry, and Junior rode that wave.

The hot spot for skiing in those early days was Sun Valley Ski Resort—America's first luxury ski resort in Ketchum, Idaho. It was also the most prominent location in the American West where the European and American ski industries collided. At the time, Sun Valley was heavily influenced by Austrian ski instructors. In fact, there were so many Austrians there that after the attack on Pearl Harbor, the FBI showed up in Sun Valley to interrogate many ski instructors to determine if any were Nazis. Some of them were, including the man who had been given the responsbility of finding the location for Sun Valley. By that time, however, most of the sympathizers had left America to fight for Adolf Hitler.

A few Austrians were falsely arrested during the FBI raid, including a man named Friedl Pfeifer, who had been appointed director of the Sun Valley Ski School. Like many of the other instructors, he was an Austrian who had been a ski instructor under Hannes Schneider, father of the Arlberg technique, for 10 years before relocating to Sun Valley. Once it was decided that Pfeifer was not a Nazi supporter, he was sent to serve in the 10th Mountain Division. He lost a lung during battle, but he returned to the United States after the war to create Aspen Ski Resort and did so at one of the locations where the 10th Mountain Division trained in Colorado. During Pfiefer's unexpected absence from the Sun Valley Ski School, a man named Otto Lang was hired to replace him. Lang was another Austrian who had also instructed under Schneider, and Lang and Pfeifer both brought the Arlberg technique to Sun Valley. Their employees, many of them still Austrian, even after the FBI raid, used this technique to teach the would-be skiers.

The creation of Sun Valley begins with a relationship between an ancient Silesian (a region in central Europe) noble family with the name Schaffgotsch and an American politician and businessman named Averell Harriman. The wealthy son of an American railroad baron, Harriman was the chairman of the Union Pacific Railroad. He would often rent a hunting cottage in Austria from the Schaffgotsch family, where he met one of the family's sons, Count Felix Schaffgotsch. Count Felix was a member of what would turn out to be one of the last generations of the Schaffgotsch family. When he was in his 20s, Count Felix came to New York to work for Harriman. Apparently, Count Felix would often reminisce about the dazzling and luxurious ski resorts of Europe, and of the ski trains that would bring the elite from the coastal cities all the way up into the Alps to ski. Sensing a business opportunity, Harriman gave Count Felix a task: find a location in the western United States for a luxury ski resort, and make sure it could be accessed by the Union Pacific Railroad.

After weeks of visiting potential sites, in January of 1936, Count Felix decided that Ketchum, Idaho, was the place. By December of that same year, the Sun Valley Lodge had been built, complete with a bowling alley, ice skating rink, and horse-drawn sleigh rides. The collaboration of Harriman and Count Felix—one an American millionaire, politician, and New York businessman, the other a dashing and charming, young count from an old, wealthy European family—brought immediate success to Sun Valley. Soon, the once sleepy and rural town of Ketchum was swarming with celebrities.

Count Felix, though apparently not a great skier, recruited ski instructors from Austria to come west to staff the new resort. It turned out that many were Nazi sympathizers, including Count Felix Schaffgotsch himself. In fact, he reportedly once said to a friend that the ski instructors at Sun Valley were "all Nazis, too." By the time of the FBI raid, however, most of the sympathizers had returned to Germany to fight for the Nazi party, including Count Felix.

While Count Felix was fighting for Hitler, his business partner, Harriman, was deeply opposed to Germany's agenda and was actively involved in getting the United States to enter World War II. Harriman was present at the meeting of Franklin Delano Roosevelt and Winston Churchill during the Atlantic Charter in 1941, and he played a powerful role in persuading the public to support America's involvement. In 1943, Harriman was appointed as US ambassador to the Soviet Union. Ironically, it would be during Harriman's ambassadorship to the Soviet Union that Count Felix's life would come to an early end on a muddy battlefield on Soviet soil. Seven short years after the Austrian count and American railroad baron collaborated to create Sun Valley, their relationship would come to a dramatic and strangely ironic end.

Until this point, the only way for skiers to ski down a hill was to either hike up the hill, or use a rope tow. Harriman recognized that this was a constraint in the ski industry that needed to be dealt with, especially if Sun Valley were going to become the lively hub he intended it to be. In a 1936 telegram to Union Pacific chief engineer, H.C. Mann, Harriman wrote that "it is essential . . . to develop a method of lifting skiers two thousand feet above the valley floor . . . with a capacity of say one hundred people an hour."

A task of engineers at the Union Pacific Headquarters in Omaha, Nebraska, was put on the case. James Curran, a Nebraska native who didn't know how to ski and never learned, invented the chairlift in the Union Pacific rail yards. Curran got the idea from the conveyor belts used to load bananas onto ships in South America, and he was inducted into the US Ski and Snowboard Hall of Fame for his revolutionary invention.

The first chairlift in the world was installed on Proctor Mountain in 1936, and the next one on Dollar Mountain. Within a few years, Sun Valley built three more on the neighboring, but much higher, Mount Baldy. The series of three chairlifts transported skiers nearly 3,400 vertical feet from valley floor to the very top of Mount Baldy. It was the first mountain-top ski feat of its kind.

Once the chairlifts went up, the pace of skiing changed. More people could get higher up onto steeper slopes and more challenging terrain. Ski instructors were met with a challenge; in order for their students to be able to ski the terrain they were being exposed to, they had to learn techniques farther up the Arlberg ladder than they were "approved" to learn. Pfeifer first, and Lang next, tweaked the traditional technique to accommodate this evolution in the sport. Pfeifer would then carry this edited Austrian technique to Aspen after the war. Lang would eventually bring a Frenchman, Emile Allais, to Sun Valley to teach, thus incorporating the French ski technique with its focus on ski racing, alongside the Arlberg technique—a radical move at the time.

After spending some time in Sun Valley, Alf Engen, one of the most iconic ski figures of the 20th century, tweaked the technique even more while he was the ski school director at Alta Ski Area in Utah in the 1940s and 1950s. Like at Sun Valley, even beginner terrain could be quite difficult at Alta. The run accessed by the rope tow, intended for the most novice beginners, was easy enough. But if a student was enthusiastic about skiing, was a quick learner, and wanted to get on the big mountain, the lift dropped them off at the top of a run called Corkscrew. Those familiar with Alta will know Corkscrew—a steep, narrow pitch (which has since been widened by the resort) and the only way to get from the top of Collins lift to the base of the mountain. One of the first things a novice would have to learn in order to get down Corkscrew was side-slipping, though they may not have mastered all the preceding steps.

What made the Alta instructors' approach to teaching a skiing technique different from the Sun Valley instructors' approach was something that didn't fit within the Arlberg technique. Pfeifer and Lang had altered the technique to fit the terrain. They did so out of necessity, but not with the intent to change the overall approach to skiing. Engen and his disciples, however, altered the technique not just to match the terrain, but to change the way novices learned how to ski. Engen encouraged less focus on the details of the Arlberg technique, or, as it was sometimes known, the European ski technique. He emphasized a teaching technique based on eagerness. Rather than keeping novices on a rigid pathway to proficiency, instructors should edit the curriculum based on the enthusiasm of the skier.

Junior was among these instructors who paved the way for Engen's new teaching technique. If the novice wanted to learn quickly and was enthusiastic about getting onto the big mountain, Junior would do what was necessary to get them there. It didn't matter if they hadn't mastered the snowplow perfectly; if they wanted to get better at skiing quickly, why should they have to remedy small imperfections first? Their ability would naturally improve with time the more they skied, as long as they were having enough fun to keep skiing. This technique was based on feeling rather than rules.

In Junior's own words:

> *Alf broke away from the military-style approach in favor of a more humanistic approach, which focused on keeping the teacher's goals in tune with the desires or goals of the student. The lesson was built around Alf's philosophy of safety, fun, and technique (in that order!). We trained our staff to be aware of the psychological implications of teaching new skills in a new and challenging environment. Skill acquisition, while important, was not the primary emphasis of a resort-based program. Resort customers were interested in having fun in a safe, controlled environment. The growth of skills was to increase the enjoyment and entertainment aspects of skiing. This differed from the utilitarian, regimented, or competitive teaching programs then in existence. From these new levels of awareness and emphasis came the basis of the American ski teaching system.*

In 1958, Junior was hired as the director of the Sugar Bowl Ski School in California, becoming one of the very first American-born ski school directors. Many of the iconic skiers and instructors of that time had immigrated from the far side of the Atlantic Ocean. While people like Alf Engen (and his brothers, Sverre and Corey), Stein Erikson, and Pepi Stiegler had significant contributions in developing an American way of skiing, they were still products of foreign countries. Born to immigrants on American soil, Junior was one of the first truly iconic American skiers, alongside a few others like Dick Durrance, the United States' first Olympic alpine skier. And from his heightened position of influence as an American ski school director, Junior had a far-reaching impact on the sport. He had shifted from teaching others how to ski to teaching others how to teach skiing.

Now Junior was in charge of creating his own team of passionate ski instructors. Qualities Junior looked for in potential teachers included kindness and a joy-driven love for the sport. They did not have to be the best skiers, as long as they were kind humans. He hired his instructors based on a belief that he shared with Alf Engen. Junior and Alf knew that they could teach someone how to be a good skier or teacher. But they couldn't teach them "what their mothers had failed to teach": they couldn't teach them how to be kind. In Junior's words, his ski instructors were "picked for personality."

By placing more value on what kind of person his instructors were, rather than their experience or capabilities, Junior created an army of instructors who taught skiing because they loved the thrills and joys of the sport. Junior understood that one bad teacher could ruin a person's experience, perhaps for the rest of their lives. His goal was to hire people who were excited about skiing and who could get others excited about skiing. He wanted to get as many people on the mountain as he could.

Starting in the 1940s, Sun Valley Ski Resort began hosting "ski weeks," which brought hordes of people by train from California to Sun Valley to learn how to ski. These publicized ski weeks were a tactic to get as many people on the mountain (and on Union Pacific railroads) as possible. After seeing their success in Sun Valley, Engen started organizing ski weeks at Alta. These weeks were, in part, responsible for how skiing spread so quickly during the middle of the century. Junior adopted this practice at Sugar Bowl with wildly successful results. According to him, nearly 100 percent of guests staying in resort lodging would participate in lessons during those weeks. Here was an opportunity to put his army of fun-loving, kind, and passionate ski instructors to work.

Junior's goal during these ski weeks was to help as many clients as possible develop a love for skiing. His efforts translated to hundreds of guests having fun on the mountain every day and not getting bogged down by the details or discouraged by instructors who wouldn't let them try new things. The momentum around the sport of skiing had been snowballing, so to speak, for the past three decades. But until the advent of ski weeks, the popularity of skiing had been confined mostly to mountain towns. Ski weeks were a prominent reason for skiing's coast-to-coast surge in popularity.

During his time at Sugar Bowl, Junior also began contributing to skiing magazines and sports magazines, including *Powder Magazine*, as a technical writer. The articles he wrote described how to make different kinds of turns in a variety of conditions, including powder snow techniques, and the articles were accompanied by photos of him skiing. He wrote and contributed to a number of books as well: *The Junior Bounous Ski School Teaching Manual*, *American Ski Technique Manual* (co-author with Willy Schaeffler, Bill Lash, and Paul Vallar), *Inner Skiing* by W. Timothy Gallwey and Bob Kriegel (contributor), and *You Can be Good at Sports!* by Laurence Korwin (contributor). Junior's realm of influence, once just confined to a few canyons in the Wasatch, was spreading nationwide.

In 1963, a man named Ezra Bowen wrote *The Book of American Skiing*. The book encapsulates the soul of mid-century skiing in America. Its pages are packed with photos of skiers, like Stein

Eriksen, flying down the mountain just in front of a photographer with a camera strapped to his chest. Flecks of snow flying around the lens depicted motion and thrill, and the resulting photos epitomized the excitement and the joy of the sport. Bowen's writing itself highlights the emphasis that many ski instructors, including Junior, preached: skiing should, above all else, be fun. One of the first chapters, which gives parents and teachers advice on teaching children how to ski, immediately addresses one of the most poignant differences between Austrian and American teaching:

> *There is really no right or wrong age for a child to start skiing. Hannes Schneider, who systemized ski instruction first in Austria and later in America, used to say that eight or nine was the earliest anyone could be taught. . . . But the best advice comes from someone infinitely less famous than the Austrian giants, though far better qualified on the subject of little children and snow. That is Glenn Springer-Miller, mother of two small objects and instructor of hundreds of others at the Sugar Bowl in California. According to Mrs. Springer-Miller, "If they can walk, they can ski." That is, they can put on warm clothes, strap some short boards to their feet, and go out and have fun.*

Junior's time spent at Sugar Bowl was unique in another way: a section of his ski school, headed by Glenn Springer-Miller, was dedicated to teaching children younger than what was considered normal at the time. Glenn and Junior's approach to teaching children was to get them out on the mountain, make sure they're warm and comfortable, help them have fun, and then let them try out ski racing if they express a desire but not force them. (My sister and I can personally attest to the success of this last one. Though we are the granddaughters of legendary skiers and the daughters of a professional ski racer, my parents never pressured either of us to race when we didn't want to. That, ultimately, may be why we still love to ski so much.)

Bowen's book then moves to the different turning techniques directed at adults. When discussing the parallel turn, it says that "there is too much emphasis these days on parallel technique. The only reason to ski is to have fun, and if fun for you is stem-swinging down someone's mountain, then enjoy it, and don't let anybody tell you that you're not skiing." The end of the section are words from Dick Durrance, an American ski champion and, ironically, the person who brought parallel skiing to America: "All this stuff about technique is bunk. . . . Look, the whole idea is to have fun. Relax.

Do what feels natural. Getting down the mountain, learning to be safe—that's all fundamental. . . . It's not supposed to be work; it's fun, for gosh sake." The final section of the book is even titled "The Fun of Skiing." The first sentence reads, "In all the heavy breathing about athletes, eligibility, and money, people sometimes forget that the only real reason for skiing is to have fun."

The last page of the book is titled "The Best" and is a list that the author has created "of who and what represent the very finest in American Skiing." Aspen is listed as the best chic resort and party town. Alta and Taos have the best snow. Alta Lodge and Big Mountain are the best lodges for folksy comfort. Sun Valley has the best ski school for beginners. The High Rustler, Baldy Chutes, and Headwall take the cake for hairiest trails. Miggs Durrance and Ann Taylor are the best dressed. Stein Eriksen is the best packed-snow skier. And Junior Bounous is the best off-trail skier.

When Junior returned to Utah in the 1960s to become the ski school director at Sundance Ski Resort and then later Snowbird Ski Resort, he kept applying his developments in the heart of the American West. Upon opening in 1971, Snowbird quickly gained national and international esteem as one of the most challenging resorts in the world. The combination of technical runs, a yearly snowfall that often topped 500 inches, snow lighter than the snowfall on the West Coast, and excellent terrain easily accessible from the nearest city made Little Cottonwood Canyon a magnetic field from which all big mountain and deep powder skiing circled. And at the heart of that magnetic pull? A dazzling combination of kindness and creativity, landscape and adventure, and innovation and passion that manifested itself so purely in one human being.

I am, of course, biased in this matter. When I remember skiing at Snowbird in my early childhood, I remember miserable days filled with stinging lips and cheeks, cramping toes in stiff boots, and an itchy helmet-head. I remember skis coming apart in cradled arms while walking across the snow bridge in a whiteout and hiking with frozen fingers to retrieve dropped mittens. I remember tears when I accidentally pole planted between my legs and did a full somersault on the Dick Bass Highway, and I remember the urgency of trying to get every single layer off my body to use the restroom at Mid Gad Restaurant.

But I also remember the mountain school's cookie races on Chickadee, where each participant was rewarded with a warm chocolate chip cookie after making it through every gate. And learning how to turn through trees under Wilbere lift, and, more often than not, straddling the tree and getting stuck when my ski tips would cross on the other side, giggling till it hurt. I remember following my dad off every little bump we passed, bunny hopping down entire runs, then working up to jumping off cat tracks. I remember my mom being horrified when my dad taught me how to pole plant by having me pretend like I was stabbing squirrels with my pole on every turn. I remember my mom taking my sister and me over to a gentle slope off of Baldy Express where she would show us how to wiggle through powder, and then cheer us on when we made it to the bottom of the hill (or hike back up to help us recover a lost ski). I remember massive mountain-wide scavenger hunts on Easter with our cousins, finding clues our parents had placed all over the mountain that led us to a stash of treasure in the trees—baskets filled with chocolate eggs and stuffed animals. And I remember following behind Junior on bluebird powder days, singing "ba-dump, ba-dump" all the way down.

When we think of skiing today, in the 21st century, we think of it as being fun. That's why we wait in long lines to get up the canyon and spend a decent chunk of our paychecks on season passes and gear. I believe the widespread love of skiing in the American West that is so common today is, in part, a result of American ski pioneers like Junior Bounous and Alf Engen, who preached the joy of skiing as a technique itself.

"I equate skiing with Junior Bounous like playing basketball with Michael Jordan. The best in the world. It's really exciting."

— Barry MacLean, family friend

". . . Junior Bounous was one of the best powder ski skiers that was ever produced."

— Stein Eriksen, ski legend

"I always regarded Junior as a teacher, rather than a boss. It might not seem like that big of a deal, but that distinction makes all the difference."

— Roger Bourke, Sugar Bowl instructor

"I was a young instructor during Snowbird's second season, 1972–73. . . . At the end of the day, Junior set me aside and told me I had a complaint from one of my students. The student complained that she had learned nothing and wanted her money back. I was devastated and hurt, as I thought I had taught a good lesson. Junior turned to me and said, in his quiet comforting voice, 'I know you are a good instructor, Nona; sometimes people like to complain so they can get a free lesson.'

I never forgot that conversation with Junior."

— Nona Weatherbee, Snowbird Mountain School employee

"Junior entertains. He will teach you through time, through enjoyment, and 90 percent of the time you don't know you're learning until you've completed the task. And it's very peaceful, very relaxing, and it's a total atmosphere that Junior teaches with it. And it's not the classic demonstration: do this, observe, and critique. It's very much just enjoyment."

— Steve Bills, Snowbird Mountain School employee

"Junior makes you feel like the best. And that's probably because his magic is as good as he is. He always makes you feel like you're almost as good as he is. He builds you up, and he makes you feel better than you really are."

— Barry MacLean, family friend

"The biggest thing I think I've learned from Junior, and I think he strived for it, is to focus on that fun element. Focus on the people. And to realize the real secret to being in these mountains is to have fun and to try to share that with people."

— Rodger Renstrom, Snowbird Mountain School employee

"He's an amazing man. He's always been my mentor, and he always will be. I still have the patch on the back of my helmet that says, 'What Would Junior Do?' And often, when I get in certain situations, maybe when I'm stressed out or when people are agitated, I still think about that. Okay, what would he do? It's calming. It helps me keep a level head."

— Ed Chauner, Snowbird Mountain School employee

Junior in the late 1950s. Keeping those legs locked tightly together was a sign of ski mastery then.

Junior while skiing for a film at Sundance in the late 1960s.

First Day on Skis

Even a ski instructor's son needs a first lesson on skis. Here we see how Sugar Bowl's Junior and Maxine Bounous introduced Barry to the joys of skiing.

A child's first day on skis should be fun, says Junior Bounous, head of California's Sugar Bowl ski school. Both Mother and Dad should be on hand to encourage that first tentative run, and sympathize with cold hands and bruised feelings. A supporting arm or ski pole should guide the tyro on little practice slides until he finds his legs. Then watch out, folks! Here comes another skier!

Photos by Fred Lindholm

After several practice slides supported by his father, Barry starts out on a solo flight, destination—mother!

Almost there — but that darned [illegible] is too fast! Barry shows a "reverse Comma" position known to every skier.

Mother comforts Barry after he learned the hard facts of gravity. Next time he made it all the way!

Maxine, Barry, and Junior from an unknown magazine clipping. 1958.

Maxine, Barry, and Junior in 1958. Taken by Fred Lindholm for the unknown magazine clipping at left.
Fred Lindholm

A parallel christie is started from a traverse with a down-motion and a set of the edges.

Combined with an up motion, weight is transferred to outside ski, turning power applied.

Inside ski of the turn gradually advances as upper body begins to twist and angulate.

The American SKI System

WITHIN THE borders of Europe's alpine countries it is possible to travel from one resort to another and continue with ski lessons, all of which are taught within the framework of the same national system. Such an arrangement assures the pupil of a minimum amount of confusion in learning to ski and is an encouragement to continue with a steady progression of increasingly more advanced classes.

The problem of establishing a unified system in the United States has always been hampered by the great geographical distances between resorts as much as by the fierce individualism of instructors.

But a unified system is now well on its way toward general acceptance by most of America's ski schools. The Professional Ski Instructors of America, a group representing the country's top teachers, has devised an approach to minimize argument which has engendered this widespread support.

The American system is a full-fledged three-way approach to the subject of teaching skiing. The first part deals with simple descriptions of the final forms of the technique; that is, of the goals, the actual turns, toward which instructors should direct themselves and students.

The second part of the system concerns itself with the method of instruction, along with the exercises used to reach the goals, or finished technical forms.

The third part, and perhaps the most involved, deals with the theory and mechanics of movement of skiing.

JUNIOR BOUNOUS, SKI SCHOOL DIRECTOR AT SUGAR BOWL, CALIFORNIA, DEMONSTRATES THE FINAL FORMS OF THE AMERICAN TECHNIQUE, THE FIRST UNIFIED SYSTEM OF SKI INSTRUCTION TO BE OFFERED TO THE U.S.A. ON A NATION-WIDE BASIS.

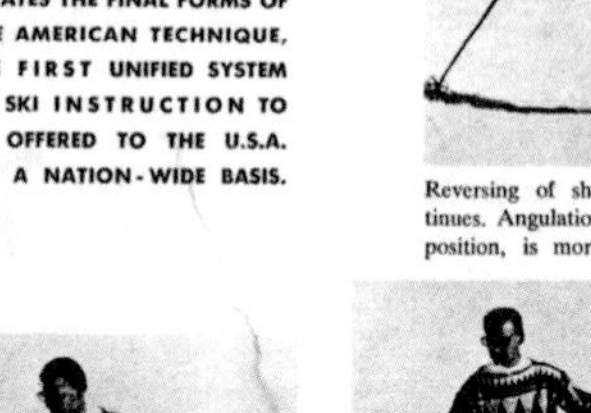

Reversing of shoulders continues. Angulation, or comma position, is more noticeable.

Traverse in new direction begins. To better set edges downhill pole may be used.

As the turn progresses, body weight is kept forward and the knees bend more deeply.

PHOTOS BY PAUL RYAN

SKIING NEWS MAGAZINE 29

An article from *Skiing News Magazine*. Around 1960.

Junior in teaching mode at Snowbird. 1990s.

First National Ski Professional Ski Instructors meeting at Alta on the run called Main Street. The resort had closed for the season by this time, but they got a lift running to cater to this event. Junior, his arms crossed and wearing a red sweater, is fifth from the right and stands next to Alf Engen, also in red. May 29, 1958.

Jerry Warren on the left mimicking Junior, who's demonstrating how to put weight on the lower leg "stem christie" turn at Timp Haven. 1960s.

Notice that Junior's lower legs and his back are almost parallel, and if you were to draw a line from Junior's head down his body, the line would end nearly in the center of his feet. That's some good technique! 1950s.

Chapter 2

House of Bounous

Junior Bounous was born with no name. On his birth certificate, where there should have been a first name fit for a young boy, there was a blank stretch of white parchment. Next to that space, the surname Bounous. Below that, the box for "boy" was checked. He was just a boy with the last name Bounous.

Imagine, for a minute, what a name is. It's the way we identify ourselves, and it's the way others identify us. It's how people address us, recognize us, remember us. Our name is tied to our identity from birth. It's one of the first words spoken to us and is what we learn to associate with ourselves, even if we decide to go by a different name later on.

In Junior's case, his parents didn't name him anything. His father, Levi James Bounous, wanted to name him, their sixth child, after himself and call him James Levi. His mother, Jennie Richard Bounous, rejected that idea. She preferred the name Henry. In the end, of course, they couldn't decide. Neither parent bowed to the will of the other, and they left the hospital with a blank birth certificate.

How he ended up being called Junior is somewhat of a mystery, and there aren't any living folks who can confirm or deny the theories. My grandfather doesn't remember; he was always just called Junior. Perhaps it was because he was the youngest child, and the name Junior just made sense in lieu of an official name. Or perhaps Levi, still wanting to name Junior after himself, used Junior as a way of pretending that his true name was Levi James Bounous Jr. My grandfather has a memory of Levi telling him that "junior" means "son" in an Italian dialect, though the true Italian translation is *figlio*.

Junior didn't realize that he hadn't been given a name until he was in his late 20s. There was no reason for him to doubt his name; he was Junior on all of his school documents, his driver's license, even his registration for the army draft. It was only when he and his wife, Maxine, went to have passports made for an upcoming trip to South America that he made the discovery. When he pulled out his birth certificate, he was surprised and amused to see that he, legally, did not have a first name. And he discovered that his family had been celebrating his birthday on the wrong day; his true date of birth was August 24, 1925, not the 23rd, as his parents had always celebrated it.

He thought, briefly, about changing his name to James—a family name and what might have even been his name, had his father gotten his way. But Junior had many friends named James who all went by Jim, like Jim McConkey and Jim Shane. The name Jim was as much a part of their identity as their skin at that point. When Junior tried the name Jim on, it felt strange. So he stuck with Junior.

As a granddaughter bearing the name Bounous, I am often asked where the surname originates from. While most try to pronounce it like *Bonus* or *Bownows*, some recognize its Mediterranean roots. "Is it French?" they ask.

The name Bounous stretches over borders. It's from Italy, and it's from France. Technically, our side of the larger Bounous gene pool immigrated from an Italian town called San Germano. It's a small mountain village where both Levi and Jennie were born, one that practically straddles the French-Italian border. While on a trip to visit distant relatives who still live in San Germano, we were told that Italians pronounce the "s," while the French leave the "ou" hanging with no such closure. *Oui*, the name is French, and *sì*, it is Italian.

Rather than saying the name Bounous is from one country or the other, I prefer to say what I feel in my heart is true: that the name Bounous comes from the mountains.

Just a few miles from San Germano lies the international border that divides France and Italy. The Cottian Alps, or Alpi Cozie, are the natural barrier between the two countries. There's no fence or river or chasm that separates the two, just a long spine of jagged rocks. The border follows a ridgeline within these mountains, carved by ancient glaciers, that winds from the Maritime Alps on the shores of the Mediterranean up into the heart of Europe.

This is no random ridgeline; it's a drainage divide. It separates the Po River watershed of Italy, which drains into the Adriatic Sea, from the Rhone River watershed of France, which drains into the Gulf of Lion. During a snowstorm in the Cottian Alps, if a snowflake falls on one side of the ridge and another falls just over the crest onto the other side, the two will become water molecules that will eventually end up on opposite sides of the Mediterranean.

The Bounous and Richard families were both from San Germano. We, their descendants, thought we were *very* Italian—*la crema del raccolto*—with relatives who still live in a beautiful yellow house set in the green, mountainous countryside. One can walk down the cobbled streets of San Germano to the war plaques outside of the church and see the names Bounous and Richard repeated again and again. Or go to the Val Chisone museum at Prali, the local ski resort, and discover that one of the most famous musical composers from the area was a Richard. Or visit the famous Fenestrelle Fort, the second-longest fortress in the world, shorter only than the Great Wall of China, and learn that a Bounous had been imprisoned there for money fraud in the late 1700s. Or hike up to a basin that still has long-range cannons and barracks from World War II and find the Bounous name carved into a rock near the ruins.

We believed we were very Italian. That is, until Junior took a DNA test. It turns out that Junior is part Basque. His ancestors lived in the Pyrenees mountains that divide Spain and France, and they moved first to France and then to the Cottian Alps sometime during the 1600s. They migrated from one mountain range to the next: from the Pyrenees, to Alpi Cozie, to the Wasatch.

The first time Junior and Maxine visited San Germano was in the 1960s. Their sons, Barry and Steve, were young, so Junior's sister Stella watched them while their parents traveled to Europe for the first time. Junior and Maxine planned to meet friends Dick and Libby Hawkins in Rome, but they arrived early to see more of Europe. They rented a VW van from friends in Amsterdam and made their way south.

Both Levi and Jennie Bounous had passed away at this point and had never made it back to Italy after emigrating to the United States. Visiting San Germano had been in the back of Junior's mind for some time, so when he and Maxine made it to Italy, Junior had his father's old address folded up in his suitcase. They drove up a canyon, lush and green in the Alpen summer. They crossed a river, driving through a town center that was barely more than a village square. The streets were narrow, lined by wooden posts that separated the cobbled road from fields of wildflowers. They parked the VW and walked through the streets, climbing higher in elevation as they searched for a house that might match the address. Eventually, they found it. It was a small building, pale in color. Carved into the retaining stone wall across the street from it was a well, a natural spring that drizzled water from the inside of the hill into a trough. Over half a century later, when my family visited San Germano, we would drink from this spring.

Junior and Maxine knocked on the door, not knowing what to expect. They did not have contact information for any of Junior's relatives who may or may not have still lived there, may or may not have even been alive. Neither Junior nor Maxine spoke any Italian, and they had not run into many English-speakers in this village. But the woman who answered the door spoke English. Her last name was Bounous. But she wasn't from San Germano, wasn't even Italian. She was from Paris. This house, the house that Levi had been born in, was her summer home. She spent the rest of the year in Paris, where she grew up, where her family was from, but she had bought this house so she could spend the summers in San Germano. She and Junior did some digging through their family trees and discovered that they were long-lost cousins.

She hosted them during the few days they stayed in San Germano. Junior and Maxine were delighted by the landscape of Val Chisone, the valley in which San Germano was nestled. It felt remarkably familiar. The Utah mountains that Levi and Jennie had chosen to settle in closely resembled the mountains that they had left in Italy. Apparently, somewhere in those Italian mountains, there are the ruins of a Bounous ghost town, as Junior calls it, marking the spot where the first Bounouses may have crossed the border from France to Italy.

The next time Junior and Maxine visited San Germano was nearly 20 years later in 1977 with Barry, who had just finished serving a two-year mission in Italy for The Church of Jesus Christ of Latter-day Saints. He was fluent in Italian and eager to meet other Bounouses. They visited Junior's cousin again, this time at her home in Paris, and met French Bounouses at a Bounous-owned pastry shop. Junior recalls his distant relatives speaking French, Italian, Spanish, and English all at once during the luncheon.

When they arrived in San Germano, Junior and Barry walked to the village square and into a drugstore. They had a name this time—the name of Levi's brother's widow, Ethel Wray Bounous. They asked the owner of the drugstore if he knew the name, and the owner responded that his own name was Bounous. But no, he did not know Ethel Wray. In a town that, as recently as 2010, had a population of just 1,800, there were enough Bounouses that sharing a last name didn't guarantee that you knew each other. Junior and Barry eventually tracked Ethel down, and Junior was able to meet his aunt for the first time.

Coincidentally, the reason the Bounouses and Richards immigrated from Italy to Utah was because of Snow—not frozen molecules, but a man named Snow. In 1850, the first Latter-day Saint missionaries arrived in Italy. According to an article published on The Church of Jesus Christ of Latter-Day Saints website, a man named Lorenzo Snow was the first to visit the region. Most towns and cities he visited were strictly Catholic and did not take too kindly to an obscure religion from America. But Snow had heard of a group of people living in the Cottian Alps who might be sympathetic to his cause, of whom he said: "I believe that the Lord has there hidden up a people amid the Alpine mountains." When Snow arrived in San Germano, he found empathy from the townsfolk.

Many residents of San Germano, including our Bounous relatives, and the larger valley of Val Chisone, are Waldensians; members of a movement within Christianity that was grounded in the Cottian Alps and started around the year 1173. By 1184, they were excommunicated by the

Pope, and in 1215, denounced as heretics. This was apparently in part because Waldensians believed that members should read and comprehend the Bible themselves, rather than relying on a priest to do it for them. This also meant that the Waldensians had a higher literacy rate than most of Europe.

In the following centuries, the Catholic Church practically declared war on the Waldensians, ordering them to be massacred. Villages were completely destroyed, and villagers slaughtered by the thousands. Near San Germano is a cave hidden in the forest where practicing Waldensians would gather in secret. The cave is also apparently a site of one of these massacres. The force the Catholic Church used on Waldensians was so violent that the movement almost didn't survive.

So, when Lorenzo Snow wandered into the Waldensian village of San Germano, just two years after the Kingdom of Piedmont-Sardinia allowed them to enjoy religious freedom again, the missionary was met with empathy when he spoke of the persecution the recently founded Church of Jesus Christ had faced in America. He was allowed to stay, and Latter-day Saint missionaries were allowed to congregate in San Germano. They spoke of a place in America similar to Val Chisone and situated at the base of the mountains, where the farming was good, the factories had jobs, and the economy was on the rise.

At the time, San Germano's economic prosperity depended almost solely upon one shoe factory. There was not much work for young men and women besides the factory, which could take on only so many employees. After Snow's visit to Val Chisone, members from 72 Waldensian families immigrated to America during the last half of the 1800s. In the following decades, letters from them confirmed that the trip to Utah was worth it. Levi Bounous watched as other young men his age left for America and made enough money that they could send money home to their family members in San Germano. Around the turn of the 20th century, as a teenager, Levi decided that he would do the same. He was the only one from his family who left Italy, so he traveled with another family he was already acquainted with: the Richards, who had a young daughter named Jennie. Neither would ever return home to the valley that raised them, though Levi would send money to his siblings back home for the rest of his life.

My family, along with my cousin Christine Bounous Pond and her husband, Steve Pond, visited San Germano in 2017, well over 100 years since Levi and Jennie had last looked upon Val Chisone. I was shocked at how much the surrounding mountains resembled the Wasatch. We went for a hike with our relatives in a basin that resembled one we know and love in Little Cottonwood Canyon. The boulders in the basin glittered in the afternoon sun like slabs of Wasatch granite lining the side of a creek. The colors of the wildflowers, though different species, were those of amber paintbrush and lilac lupine. Even the soil smelled the same, rising up around us as our boots padded down the trails and found the rock with the Bounous name carved into it.

The relatives we visited, Mauro and Wilma Bounous, came to Utah twice. Our Utah family took Mauro and Wilma all over the Wasatch mountains, showed them the plot of land that had been Levi and Jennie's fruit farm, and brought them to the peaks of the mountains we ski in the winter. They were so moved by the landscape—so similar to their own—by Junior's kindness, and by the intimate way Junior knew the mountains, that years later they would name their son James Junior Bounous. And in 2020, my cousin Christine named her own son Junior Jensen Pond.

What started as a blank space ond a piece of paper has now become a force to be reckoned with. It has become a name without borders, that stretches across oceans and plains, connecting mountains to mountains. It's a name that is shaped by everything from the arroyos of the tallest peaks to the most delicate wildflowers in the basin, to the deep powder that settles in the chutes and between trees. It's a name that came from humble beginnings, though today along the Wasatch, it's a name recognized by many. Junior didn't strive to be well-known, similar to how mountains don't intentionally grow tall; they are just lifted up, little by little, with each earthquake. Junior Bounous is as soft and gentle as a creek, yet so driving that he influences all that is downstream. What began as nameless is now a legacy.

In 2005, friends of Junior and Maxine's—Dennis and Connie Keller and Barry and Mary Ann MacLean—commissioned a film about Junior to honor his 80th birthday, titled Bounousabuse: 80 Junior Years.

The film is full of folks remembering their favorite Junior moments, many of which are quoted in the pages of this book. During one segment, the film narrator asks the interviewees what Junior's real name is. Here are some of their responses:

Jerry Warren: "Oh, Junior's name . . . what is it . . . ?"

Bob Bonar: "Oh, that's a good question. I know I've seen it; I just can't remember off the top of my head."

Dennis Keller: ". . . (silence) . . . Well, I guess I've always thought it was Junior."

Barry MacLean: "Well, I guess I don't know what Junior's real name is."

Lane Clegg: "I have no idea what Junior's real name is. Junior? It's not Junior?"

Mary Ann MacLean: "No, Junior? I have no idea. What's his real name?"

Peter Mueller, instructor: "I know him as Junior, and if he has a real name, I don't know it, and I don't know that would be something to call him by, cause he's just Junior Bounous. It just fits."

Narrator: "How fitting that the man with no name needs no introduction!"

— Excerpt from *Bounousabuse*

"What does my dad ask of me? To treat other people well and with kindness. To come over and talk whenever possible. To walk with him. To let him tell stories even if I've heard them before. To sing and play the guitar as often as I can. To take leisurely walks. And most important to plan on skiing with him often. Dad is fun, compassionate, forgiving, and kind. He just wants me to be the same. You've set the bar pretty high, old man."

— Barry Bounous, son

"One time I said to my sister-in-law, Sue, 'Junior is my lifeline.' She said, 'I know. I feel the same way.'"

— Debra Bounous, daughter-in-law

". . . he's the character of Snowbird and of the mountain. . . . He's taught me to experience . . . the white of the snow, and the blue of the sky, and the wind, and everything the mountain environment has to offer."

— George Kolbenschlag, Snowbird Mountain School employee

"The things that I've learned from Junior go way beyond skiing. It's how to treat people. It's how to be a friend to people regardless of the circumstances—not a fair-weather friend, but a friend for life."

— Jerry Warren, Snowbird Mountain School assistant director

"He's expanded all of our lives; he's made us better people. He's brought us to a point in our lives where we have been able to achieve things that we would never be able to achieve on our own. He's educated us and showed us the beauty of these mountains and how much they mean to him . . . How lucky are we to have shared time and adventures with Junior and Maxine?"

— Nancy Kronthauler, Snowbird Mountain School employee

"It is people like Junior—observing the changes, working to educate others on our individual and collective impacts, recognizing the beauty and resiliency of a bog orchid blooming in a drainage channel along the Summer Road in Alta, year over year. Small, but with a powerful scent, that flower, once recognized, leads the way to a better life."

— Margaret Bourke, family friend

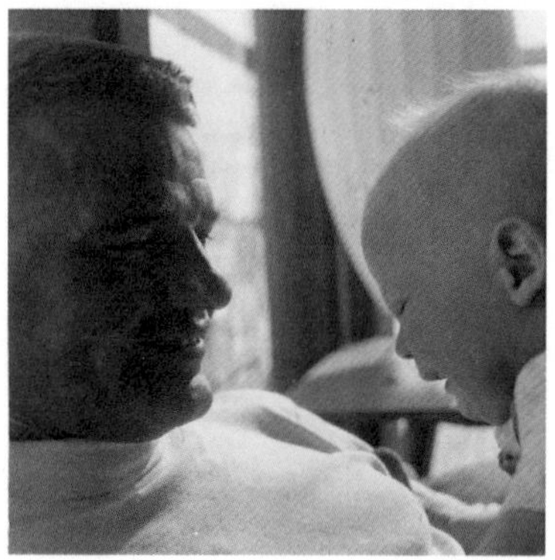

Junior and baby Steve at their home at Alta. 1959.

Junior and Steve. 1959.

Junior teaching Barry how to stand back up after you fall. Sugar Bowl in the late 1950s.

Junior, Barry, Maxine, and Steve at Alta during a photo shoot in 1972.

Junior and granddaughter Christine at Snowbird. 1988.

Bounous family ski day! Steve, Sue, Junior, EvaLynn, Ayja, Debra, Maxine, Barry, Tyndall, Christine, and James at the top of Hidden Peak. Around 1999.

Junior and Maxine teaching Barry how to ski in 1958.
Fred Lindholm

Junior and granddaughter Tyndall at Snowbird in celebration of Junior's 90th birthday. 2015.

Junior and his great-grandson and namesake, Junior Jensen Pond. May 2020.

Junior and Maxine teaching great grand-daugter Eleanor "Ellie" Bolen (daughter of EvaLynn Bounous Bolen and Mitch Bolen) how to ski. November 2017, which was nearly 60 years after the top left photo was taken, where Barry, Ellie's grandfather, is learning to ski.

Steve, Junior, and Barry at Junior's house on Father's Day. 2015.

Chapter 3

Life on the Farm

Along the spine of the Wasatch, south of Provo Canyon, and just a hair north of Rock Canyon, is a natural bench. Historically, this bench sat near the shoreline of Lake Bonneville, a massive lake that covered most of northern Utah. Now the canyons have skiers instead of glaciers, and the bench butts up against the foothills, where coyotes and deer wander from the canyons to the valley, and patches of scrub oak mix with sagebrush. It's dry and airy, lifted up slightly from the valley floor, exposed to the sky. Because of natural drainage from the mountains to the bench to the valley floor, the bench simultaneously becomes flushed with nutrients and minerals from the mountains without becoming too heavy with alkali. The natural flow of water and material keeps this area replenished and drained. It was on this bench that Levi and Jennie Bounous made a home for themselves.

By the time Levi and Jennie's family, the Richards, arrived in Utah Valley in 1901, the city of Provo was growing, the farming industry was in full swing, and homesteading was declining. Since the enactment of the Homestead Act in 1862, homesteading had been one of the most common ways to settle in the American West, embracing a lifestyle of self-sufficiency. However, many of the original homesteads created in the late 1800s lost steam after the turn of the century. City living was gaining popularity, and homesteads were being turned into industrial farms that could provide the owners better income, rather than just the means for self-sufficiency. Homesteads still dotted the Provo Bench, but they began going up for sale as their original owners passed away or their descendants eventually decided they wanted a less demanding lifestyle.

It was in this time of transition that Levi and Jennie made a farm home and raised their family. Junior was the youngest of six—five of whom lived to adulthood—and he would eventually be the one to take full responsibility of the family farm. Though he would relocate his family during the winter months to different mountain locations, like Alta and Sugar Bowl, he would never permanently move from the land his parents had cultivated in the early 1900s.

Levi James Giacomo Bounous

With barely a penny to his name, Levi settled in America as a young, ambitious 17-year-old and the only person from his family to emigrate from Italy. He was disappointed when he couldn't find work immediately upon arrival, and within a year he had moved from Utah to northern California. He worked as a logger for one or two years until a horse fell on him and damaged his leg so terribly that he was in the hospital for an entire year. For years, Levi hobbled around on a leg that hadn't healed correctly, didn't function well, and caused him great pain. The injury didn't hinder his work ethic, however, nor did it stop him from becoming a great farmer. Eventually Levi had the leg removed entirely, which gave him great relief. For the rest of his life, he walked around his farm on a wooden leg.

When he made his way back to Utah, Levi found work on an assortment of well-paying projects—all related to water. He camped in a tent for an entire summer at what is now Brighton Ski Resort while he helped build the dams that would create the Twin Lakes and Lake Mary Reservoirs. Levi also helped build the culinary water pipe that pulled water from Bridal Veil Falls in Provo Canyon and redirected the water south to the city. Perhaps because of this work, water accessibility was always on the forefront of Levi's mind.

Once Levi had saved up enough money, he began scoping out places to live in Utah Valley. He had a few requirements. The Richards had chosen to purchase a plot of land closer to Provo—land that is now part of Brigham Young University (BYU) campus—but Levi desired distance from the city limits. Even a town of just 10,000 felt too populous for Levi. And because Utah Valley is naturally dry and arid, Levi knew that he would need access to a good source of water, both irrigation and culinary, in order to grow crops successfully. He wanted to avoid overly windy regions and areas subject to hard frosts, if possible. He sought rich, loamy soil free of rocks.

As it happened, when Levi began searching the Provo Bench for property that fit these requirements, a three-acre homestead came on the market in 1908. The parcel was three miles outside Provo City limits, far enough so neighbors were few and far apart, but close enough for an easy horse and buggy ride into town. The three acres he purchased eventually became 23 acres as Levi, realizing the property had great potential, purchased neighboring homesteads. The soil was soft, loamy, and free of boulders, setting it apart from many of the other farms in the area. It was far enough south of Provo Canyon that it wasn't affected by the winds rushing out of the canyon mouth each evening as the air cooled. This meant that the property wasn't subject to snowdrifts caused by winter winds. And most importantly, the land had access to not one, but three water sources.

From the north, the Provo River flows vivaciously out of Provo Canyon before cutting due south toward Provo City. The Provo River collects its runoff from a large watershed encompassing parts of the Wasatch Mountain Range and the Uinta Mountains. It's a year-round dependable water source fed by the thick snowpack that accumulates in these mountains. A gravity-fed canal called the Timpanogos Canal had been constructed prior to Levi and Jennie's arrival to the valley, designed to deliver water from the Provo River to homesteads in the area. The canal cut through the east side of Levi's land, running the entire north-to-south length of the property and providing ample access to water for crop irrigation. Because cold air tends to sink and frost develops in more humid conditions, the areas lower in the valley around the Provo River were subject to harsh "killing" frosts that could damage crops and cause other trouble for a working farm. The higher elevation of the Provo Bench protected Levi's property from experiencing the hard frosts of the valley just downhill.

Levi's second water source originated from Rock Canyon and came within almost a stone's throw of the Bounous farm. The creek was not a reliable source of water, coming from a much smaller watershed, and it typically dried up around August. Still, the residents near Rock Canyon had built a ditch (not quite as significant as a canal) called Hardscrabble that directed water north from the creek to the farms on the bench. Having developed a knack for working with cement while constructing the dams and the culinary line, Levi was instrumental in building a cement flume that brought water from Hardscrabble down to the farm. Because it was cement, the flume didn't lose moisture to seepage like dirt ditches did. Levi used the water from the flume to water two alfalfa harvests for hay. The land became pasture for the rest of the year once the creek dried up and the alfalfa harvests were over.

The third water source was the culinary water line that Levi had helped build. At the time, Provo City received most, if not all, of its culinary water from Bridal Veil Falls. The waterway was gravity driven and happened to pass right by the Bounous farm. Levi reaped the benefits of his own hard work; he and his growing family had year-round, easy access to drinking water. It was cold, fresh drinking water as well, as opposed to water that may have been sitting in a pipe being heated by the sun on its way to Provo City. Junior estimates that the water may have taken only a day to travel from Bridal Veil Falls to their farm and remembers that his father kept water running to the horse trough year-round.

The combination of these various factors, as well as Levi's driven work ethic and smart business mindset, made the Bounous farm quite successful in the following decades. The farm's initial crops were alfalfa and grains, and when the Utah Valley farming community developed a reputation for fruit farming, Levi began planting berry crops, like strawberries and raspberries, along with other types of fruit. Sensing a desire for berries in Southern Utah, Levi began taking orders from communities south of Provo, then packing up carts of berries and sending them south on Greyhound buses. Eventually, he transitioned most of the farm to fruit trees, which became the Bounouses' most significant income. Cherries were planted to the east, pears to the west, apples in the center, grapes on the hillside. He staggered the plantings and had great crop diversity and a long harvest season.

The first crops to make an appearance were the cherry trees. Sweet cherries, Bing and Lambert, were the first to bloom in the spring and were harvested in July. White Maraschino and pie cherries followed and were sent to a local canning facility in Pleasant Grove. Apricots were next, and the Chinese variety had almond-like sweet pits they would dry out and eat for the rest of the year. The next crops were early peaches, followed by Bartlett pears and Concord grapes. Then came Italian prunes, and after those, toward the end of September when the leaves began to change color and the days grew shorter, were apples: Jonathan and Roam Beauty and Red Delicious. Their harvest ended with bushels of Anjou pears.

In addition to commercial crops they would sell, the farm provided a myriad of resources for the Bounouses. The family kept a large vegetable garden to harvest for their own use and to share with friends and neighbors. They had areas dedicated to horse pastures, and even after switching their crops to fruit trees, they continued to grow alfalfa and grains to feed the horses. They kept chickens and two milk cows, and they sold milk and butter in the early years. Levi terraced one of the hills on the property to put in grapevines he and the Richards had brought over from Italy. After the harvest, the specialty wine grapes were made into wine in the basement of the main farmhouse. Multiple barns and farmhouses scattered the property—some built by Levi, some left by the previous homestead owners. Most of these became storage sheds, but the brick house with electricity running to it became the Bounous family's home. The farm was so successful that even through the Great Depression, the family never struggled to keep a living.

Through the decades, Levi became one of the most active members of the farming community, eventually considered an "old-time farmer." As of this writing, Barry, Junior's eldest son, still lives on a parcel of the old farm in Provo. He is often greeted by people in the community who recognize him as a Bounous—not a skiing Bounous, but a farmer Bounous. It's been more than 100 years since Levi cultivated the farm, and people along the Provo Bench still associate the last name with Levi, a local giant in the farming community.

Levi had remarkable business intuition, and once he had the money to do so, he invested in early farming equipment and technology. Levi was one of the first farmers in Utah County to purchase a tractor—equipment that greatly changed the way farmers could till and manage their land. According to Junior, their tractor was one of only two tractors in Utah County. To this day, the now rusted orange tractor sits just up the street from Junior's house, tucked into vegetation. It probably belongs in a farming museum, and one of Junior's neighbors has taken on the project to get it back up and running.

Levi also invested very early on in an orchard sprayer. Junior thinks he may have been one of the first to purchase one in the entire state of Utah. Rather than distributing pesticides through a hand pump, a labor-intensive endeavor, the new orchard sprayer was gas powered. Junior credits this purchase to how the family did so well through the Great Depression. Levi seemingly emptied his savings to purchase the sprayer. Not long after, all of the banks closed. Levi was extremely fortunate. Rather than losing his money, he had put it toward innovative technology that would not only benefit the Bounouses' crops, but also provide a secondary source of income through spraying other orchards in the surrounding area. One of their largest clients was BYU, which had a large apple orchard at the time. Junior remembers being paid 10 cents a day to drive the team of horses that pulled the orchard sprayer. Levi and Jennie were able to pay for Junior's older brother Chester, the only Bounous who went to college, to earn an agricultural degree at BYU with the money they made from the orchard sprayer.

The Bounouses didn't share the sprayer only for profit. The Italian community in Provo was tight-knit. A great deal of them were Waldensians from the Val Chisone region of northern Italy. Many had even traveled over together. While some chose to go into the mining and timber industries, many became fruit farmers in Utah Valley. According to my own, albeit biased research, the Italian fruit farmers were a keystone community within the Utah Valley fruit farming industry. Much of the work Junior did while growing up was taking the horse-drawn orchard sprayer or the tractor over to neighboring properties.

As my uncle Barry once said while talking about the community, "The rain that fell on one of them would fall on all of them." If a hard frost hit one farm hard, others who hadn't been hit as hard would head over to help. If there was a crop that needed to be harvested as soon as possible, neighbors would come from all around to help, knowing that the favor would be returned. One person's success spread from farm to farm.

A charming example of this was the exchange of homemade alcohol within the community. The wine grapes planted on the hillside were sour and dry, so Levi started mixing them with a variety of Muscat grapes, which was sweeter. They'd mash them up in big washtubs in the basement of the farmhouse and then pour the juice into 60-gallon barrels to ferment. Levi put dried grass on the inside of the spout to strain the seeds and pulp, so he could try the wine as it fermented. Levi would also let his children try the wine as it turned. Junior thought it tasted terrible, but others enjoyed it, and once the wine was done, Levi would distribute it to their friends. Many of them produced their own beer, so they would make exchanges.

When the production and consumption of alcohol became illegal during Prohibition, Levi's wine-making went underground. Technically it was always underground, since the fermenting barrels were in the basement, but once Prohibition became law in 1920, Levi created a secret compartment underneath the hay in the barn, and the operation went truly underground. He would roll the barrels of wine up to the barn, through the manger and a pair of sliding doors, and then into a hidden cavern under the haystack. He'd leave a few gallons of wine in his basement for when the police inevitably came to search the farm for alcohol. They knew that Levi grew grapes for wine, so Levi would trick them into thinking that the few gallons in the basement were all he kept. The police would bring the gallons upstairs and make him dump the wine out, though they would always take one or two gallons for "evidence," or so they'd claim. Once he was in the clear, Levi would continue delivering gallons of wine to his friends.

Junior had the utmost respect for Levi as a father. Levi was an example of the kind of hard worker that Junior became, and he used to tell Junior that "if you're getting paid a dollar, you'd better do a dollar's amount of work." Levi was sharp of mind, spoke five different languages, and sat on the board for the Rock Canyon Water Company. He was generous and caring, and he taught Junior an appreciation for soil and water that Junior would carry with him after Levi passed away in 1959. Starting at a young age, Junior learned how to tend to orchard trees, vegetable gardens, grapevines, and horses. This farm would then become a home for Junior and Maxine to raise their own family. From Levi, Junior inherited both the land itself and a physical intimacy with the land.

Junior also inherited his lighthearted sense of humor and prank-pulling from Levi. Every so often, mountain lions would come down from the canyons and into the farmland. Once they were spotted, the word would spread around town, and everyone would be on guard. On one occasion when a mountain lion had been spotted on the bench, Levi hiked up above one of his neighbor's farms in the middle of the night. Thinking it would be a good prank, he started howling like a mountain lion. Levi howled a few times, until his neighbor fired off a couple shotgun rounds in his direction. Levi thought it was hilarious and loved recounting the incident.

Levi's biggest hindrance in life was the chronic pain he still experienced in his broken leg, which he had to drag around even decades after the accident. When Junior was about five years old, Levi had the leg amputated. Finally, freedom. The doctor gave Levi his leg to take home after the surgery, and Levi's eldest son, Chester, buried it by the chicken coop. That area is now under the Timpview High School baseball diamond. Our family gets a kick (pun intended) out of imagining that Levi's bones from the leg are still out there somewhere, and we await the day when some baseball player might trip over them in the outfield and think something very dark and dreadful must've occurred for just one, amputated leg to be lying around without the rest of a body: Levi's final prank.

Jennie Pauline Richard

Jennie was about 12 years old when her family, including a brother, sisters, parents, and an uncle, migrated to the United States. They picked a piece of property near Provo and started a small orchard. Her uncle bought a herd of sheep and became a shepherd, driving the sheep up into Rock Canyon during the summers. Jennie struggled learning English, which made school challenging for her. When Jennie was 15, her mother, Clementine, gave birth to Jennie's youngest sister, Emma. Emma was healthy, but the birth left Clementine paralyzed on one side of her body, and much of Emma's raising and the care for her mother fell to Jennie.

Jennie had a warm and gentle personality. It is she from whom Junior inherited his true nature. As a young woman, she was beautiful, with a round face like Junior's and a lovely smile. She was also quite tiny, standing at only 4'11", though she was known for her vivacious personality and, as Junior's sister Norma once put it, being "more fun than a barrel of monkeys." She loved the mountains and used to run barefoot while on hikes as a young woman. While she probably didn't run barefoot as she grew older, she much preferred hiking through wildflowers, tending to her rose garden, and reading romance novels rather than doing such menial tasks as ironing.

When Levi returned from California, the 12-year-old girl he had crossed the Atlantic with was now a beautiful young woman. After saving money for a few years, he proposed to her with a ruby engagement ring. The two were married in 1909 and Jennie moved into Levi's new farmhouse. They started raising their family as they built a successful farm around them, and they quickly had five children in tow. Though Junior wasn't alive yet, photos of the family from those days show a happy family, picnicking or sledding on the farm, the girls often with wildflowers in their hair.

Then tragedy struck. Levi and Jennie's two-year-old daughter, Thelma, drowned in the Timpanogos Canal that ran close to the farmhouse. Wildflowers grew along the stretch of the canal, and they thought she had been picking flowers on the bank when she slipped and fell in. After running through the Bounous farm, the canal continues its path south toward the city of Provo, about two or three miles downstream. The

Richards had settled on a plot of land closer to the city, with a smaller orchard and pastureland. Louis Richard, Jennie's father, was at the canal to pull irrigation water for his own crops when he saw a small figure floating in the water and thought it might be a doll. When he pulled it out, he saw that it was his own granddaughter.

The loss of a child hit the Bounous family hard and put a strain on Levi and Jennie's relationship, and they eventually divorced around the time Junior was five or six years old. Jennie was given about a third of the farm, and she moved out of the main farmhouse to a smaller home her brother built for her on the opposite side of the farm. Today, a Latter-day Saint church stands there. Even though they were no longer under the same roof, Levi routinely checked in on Jennie, bringing her food and supplies. Junior remembers he and his older sister, Stella, both of whom stayed living in the main house with Levi, would always visit Jennie at this house.

Even after the death of a child, Jennie remained compassionate and patient. Junior remembers her showering him with hugs and kisses and telling him how much she loved him. She became known for her homemade vanilla ice cream, and she would bring it on the picnics Levi and Jennie treated their berry pickers to at the end of berry-picking season. They'd load up the workers, picnic and fishing supplies, and Jennie's ice cream onto Levi's truck and drive up to Cascade Springs on the eastern side of the Mount Timpanogos area. There, they'd lay out sandwiches and blankets along the bright green moss and fish in the cascading creek while enjoying Jennie's ice cream.

Junior has only one memory of Jennie becoming angry enough at him that she tried to spank him. He was about three years old, and they were picking strawberries in the berry patch with about 10 of the farm's hired help. Junior was picking in a row in front of his mother. Jennie had told Junior to stand up each time he had to move, but instead, Junior was scooting down the row, smashing strawberries underneath him as he did so. Jennie warned him a couple of times, but Junior kept doing it. Finally, Jennie got so mad that she said, "I'm going to give you a good lickin'." So Junior jumped up and started running. Jennie chased Junior through the berry patch while the other berry pickers chanted, "Run, Junior, run!"

Junior ran past the farmhouse, Jennie trailing behind him, and then ducked underneath the gate to the barnyard. Jennie had to stop and open the gate, so Junior got a head start running up a long, steep hill that took them to the hayfield. Despite his young age, Junior stayed ahead of Jennie on the hill and as they ran the length of the hayfield. Then he ducked under another fence that Jennie had to open, and he cut back down the hill between grapevines. Jennie finally caught him where Junior and Maxine's current house sits today, but when she caught him she was so out of breath that she didn't have the energy to lift her hand to give him a spanking. Instead, she took him by the hand and marched him back up to the farmhouse. All in all, Junior estimates that the chase lasted about 15 minutes. That was perhaps the first sign of the type of athlete he would become—and the first instance of "Bounousabuse."

A few years later, Jennie was diagnosed with tuberculosis. During her illness, Levi had her move back into the main house. Levi went through a transformation during that time, shedding anger that had plagued him since the death of Thelma. Jennie battled for two years before succumbing to the disease in July of 1937, when Junior was only 11 years old. Though Jennie left much too soon, she had a lasting impact on Junior's life. Besides giving him his gentle and patient personality, Jennie also gave Junior something else: his first pair of skis. And years later, when Junior wanted to take lessons from Alf Engen, a decision that would steer him into the ski industry for good, he was able to use some of the money Jennie left him to pay for the lessons. The ski industry can thank Jennie Richard for giving us Junior Bounous.

Chester Charles Bounous

Chester was the eldest of the Bounous children. He graduated from high school during the Great Depression and struggled with finding work, traveling out to California and Montana in his search. He had graduated from BYU after studying agriculture, but the agricultural work in Utah Valley was lacking in jobs. He wound up working for an uncle who owned a cattle ranch in Montana and was able to save up some money. Wanting to settle down in Provo, Chester returned in hopes of finding some work, but he was still unsuccessful.

He returned to Montana and started driving a truck for a prominent beet factory in Hardin, a small town near Billings. The owner of the factory had invented the beet topper, a device that cut the greens off the top of the beet—a task that previously had to be done by hand. The man had a daughter with whom Chester fell in love, and the two married and had two sons together. Still wanting to live in Provo, Chester moved his new family back to Utah. Levi gave him three acres of the farm to help him get on his feet, and Chester began working for a local power company. On those acres, Chester built a small house where his younger brother, Barney would live, where Junior and Maxine would get married, and where Barry and his family would live for many years.

Chester eventually realized that he would never make as much money as he could working for the beet factory, so the family moved back to Montana. He became the factory manager and lived there for the rest of his life, cross-country skiing and raising sheep on land that Junior recalls being quite beautiful.

Norma Alice Bounous

Junior's sister Norma moved up to Alpine, Utah, after marrying a man named Emmett Moyle, whom she met on a blind date. They began raising chickens there, and then Emmett had the idea of raising animals for their pelts. Junior remembers that they may have started with foxes and switched to mink. They started having more and more success with selling mink pelts, and they eventually left the chicken business altogether. But the pungent smell of the mink farm was too much for the neighborhood of Alpine, so they relocated their business and family to a small town in southern Idaho called Burley.

Emmett unfortunately died young when he flipped his convertible on the way home one night, dying instantly. Following the tragedy, Norma and her family remained in Burley and continued operation of the family farm. After some time riding out the fur industry, which had its ups and downs as interest in animal pelts declined, the family shifted their business to tanning.

Junior remained close to Norma's descendants through the years. One of Norma's sons, Jay, ended up purchasing a Model T car from Junior. Junior had acquired it from relatives on his mother's side who lived in Price, Utah, when he was 16 or 17 years old. Junior drove the car for a while, but it eventually ended up just sitting in his garage. When Jay visited his uncle Junior one time, he saw the car. He bought it from Junior, and then sold it to his younger brother, Lee, who restored it and still owns it to this day.

Burley has a local ski area called Pomerelle Mountain Resort. Norma's grandson Ryan Moyle started ski racing at the resort as a boy. One Saturday in March of 2020, I had the pleasure of meeting him. He still operates the family business in Burley, but he buys a season pass to Snowbird and drives down to Salt Lake City every weekend during the winter to ski. My sister and I skied alongside Ryan, with Junior taking the lead. Of all the distant family members I know are out there somewhere, there was something special about meeting Ryan while doing the thing that ties us all together. That ski day happened just in the nick of time. Exactly a week later, all the ski resorts shut down operations due to Covid-19.

Lawrence "Barney" John Bounous

Barney (Lawrence on his birth certificate) was perhaps the sibling with whom Junior remained closest in adulthood. When Junior was a child, Barney gave him coins whenever there was a circus or a fair, so Junior could play the games. Barney was a joyful spirit, but like Chester, he had difficulty finding work during the Great Depression. He went out to Nevada for some time to work for a cousin who owned a bakery, and then worked as a blacksmith there for a few years before returning to Provo.

A few years later he married the love of his life, Veola Booth, whose father helped build the deck on the Bounous farmhouse. The couple moved into the house Chester had built. Barney worked as a milkman, picking up the milk from a dairy farm in Orem and delivering it to stores from Springville to Eureka. He then got a good job at Geneva Steel, which is where he worked for the rest of his life. He and Veola had three daughters, one of whom happens to live just down the street from me in Millcreek.

Barney was the only one of Junior's siblings who learned how to downhill ski, but he didn't learn until he was in his 60s. Junior was the one to teach him, and while Barney could never quite keep up with his younger brother, he did master the "flying wedge." All of Barney's daughters were good skiers, as well as Chester's sons and a few members of Norma's and Stella's families.

Stella Margaret Bounous

Stella was the closest sibling in age to Junior. She and Junior spent the most time together when they were children, though the four-year age difference meant that Stella had graduated from high school by the time Junior started. The first job she had after high school was at a cafe up Provo Canyon called Wicks.

She moved to Alpine to be closer to her sister Norma, and there, Stella met her future husband, a man named Ray Whitby. Ray had been in World War II and had an incredible story he used to tell Junior. He was in a bomber plane over enemy territory in Italy, and his plane was shot down. All the men jumped, deploying their parachutes and surviving the crash, but they were trapped in the rugged terrain of northern Italy behind enemy lines. They spent upward of two weeks stealthily moving through the Italian countryside, traveling at night and stealing food from farms. Miraculously they all managed to get through the front safely and return to American troops. Upon moving back to Utah after the war, he became a contractor for Geneva Steel.

Stella had one daughter from a previous marriage, and Ray had two daughters and a son. Ray started working for Norma and Emmett's mink farm, and he enjoyed the work so much that the family would split their time between Burley, Idaho, and Alpine, Utah.

There were a few instances when the Bounous farm received workers that were sent by the US government. The two most notable times were during World War II, when they received as workers Japanese men and women from internment camps and German prisoners of war.

Between 1942 and 1945, the United States rounded up an estimated 120,000 Japanese Americans and incarcerated them in 10 internment camps across the country. One of these camps was the Topaz War Relocation Center in Delta, Utah. Internees were put to work both inside and outside the camp. Those lucky enough to work outside the camp were typically sent to work in the agricultural sector at places like the Bounous farm. Junior recalls these people, unjustly ripped from their lives in what's considered "one of the most atrocious violations of American civil rights in the 20th century," according to an article published on History channel's website, as hard workers and surprisingly happy given their circumstances—thankful to be out in the world rather than behind the barbed wire fences of the camps.

The German POWs who were sent to work on the farm were accompanied by armed military personnel. Soldiers with large guns would stand guard in the orchard as the Germans would climb up the ladders to harvest the fruit. Junior recalls one instance when he was taking a lunch break with one German soldier who spoke English fairly well. The German asked the American soldier watching guard over him what would happen if he were to run and try to make a break for the foothills. The American lifted his gun and said, "We'd see if you could outrun my bullets."

Over the decades, the Bounous farm slowly decreased in size—sometimes by force, other times willingly. In the 1970s, the city of Provo took the majority of the orchard land from Junior and Maxine with the justification of eminent domain, so the city could build the Timpview High School baseball diamond and a park there. They paid Junior and Maxine a fraction of what they could have made from selling the property themselves, which Junior had planned to do eventually for his and Maxine's retirement money. Once the deal was done, the city ordered all the fruit trees to be removed.

One day, Junior and Maxine heard the sound of chainsaws and looked out their window to see a massacre. The city ripped the trees' roots out of soil that Levi and Junior had tended to for so long. The barren field collected dust and weeds for years before they finally built the school and the park. When I ask my dad for memories of the farm, he often recounts riding his horse through this field of tumbleweeds, not thriving orchards.

Nutrient-rich soil that had been responsible for feeding a community was now covered with concrete and grass. The natural slope of the orchard, the slope where Junior taught himself how to ski, wouldn't work for a baseball diamond and track field, so the city leveled it and sent the Timpanogos Canal underground. Junior and his siblings planted pine trees toward the southern end of the property, as a donation to the park that replaced their farm. These pine trees still tower over the rest of the park and surrounding neighborhood. You can see them clearly from Junior's window. The irony is that now one of them has begun intruding on their otherwise perfect view of Mount Timpanogos.

Patches of the farm remain. Junior lives on one section. Their property has an Italian prune tree in the backyard and a Bartlett pear in the front, reminders of what was once a productive farm. When I was growing up, a field of cherry trees separated Junior's house from his brother Chester's house, which my Uncle Barry moved into and raised my cousins. We used to run back and forth between our grandpa's house and their house and play on a swing that hung from the branches of a massive cottonwood tree. Barry and his family moved out of Chester's house when they were expecting their fourth child and needed more living space. The tiny house was demolished, the Cottonwood tree torn down, and the cherry trees ripped up and replaced with two massive, and, in my opinion, terribly ugly houses. Sometimes when I look up the street, my eye still tries to find Chester's old, humble house under the giant Cottonwood.

Just a stone's throw up the road is another remaining area of the farm where Barry now lives with his wife, Debbie, and their daughter Jennie (named after her great-grandmother). The horse corral and barn were in that location originally, and Barry jokes that his lawn still has some uneven fertilizing properties to it due to lingering horse manure in the soil. I remember peering into that old, eerie barn as a child. The wood had begun to rot and decay, so we were never allowed inside, but that just made our imaginations run even more wild. The Timpanogos Canal cuts directly in front of that house. But the canal, the same that was responsible for the irrigation and overall success of the farm, and the one that took the life of a two-year-old girl, has been pushed underneath the pavement of the cul-de-sac and runs mostly underground these days.

A few years ago, Junior hiked up that same hill his mother had chased him across during his "wild Junior chase." At 90 years old, he had finally sold the last plot of land from his family's farm (except for the lots on which his and Barry's houses sit).

This lot had been the prime lot, on the hill above the rest of the farm, spacious, and with a view of the valley. Junior's plan had been to build a house on this property for him and Maxine, but he never quite got around to it. So, he sold it. After he did, Junior hiked up that hill and sat there for an hour, reminiscing about memories that were nearly a century old. He thought of his kind-hearted mother—gone for 79 years now—chasing him up and down that hill, and he broke down in tears.

That plot of land had been an alfalfa field meant for providing hay for the horses, and it was irrigated by the intermittent water supply from Rock Canyon. But the pitch of the slope down to the farm was so steep that it proved difficult to transport the stacks of hay to the horses. Always the problem-solver, Levi built large cement pilings on the top lot and at the base of the hill. He acquired 16 long and thin, but strong wires, which ran from one piling to the other, slicing through the air above the canyon, 20 feet above the ground in some places. Levi could place a haystack on top of the wires and push it, and it would zoom down to the bottom of the hill on the cables. Always the daredevil, Junior would don thick gloves and durable jeans, sit on a layer of hay for extra protection, and then zoom down the wires himself.

Junior took me to that upper lot once, so I could see the vista. Junior had sold the piece of property to a man named Dennis Flint, who was charmed by Junior's stories of life on the farm. He allows Junior to come up and visit anytime he likes. He designed the new house and yard to not erase the natural features of the landscape. The land now hosts a large vegetable patch, flower garden, a beautiful patio overlooking the valley and canyon, and fruit trees that are lovely shadows of the orchard that was once there. And perched at the very edge of the precipice is a large cement piling that once had wires running all the way down to the valley floor. Levi's cement piling (he did have a knack for cement, after all) is still standing, spotted with tangerine and burgundy lichen. Junior and I stood between the towers of the piling and looked down, picturing the wires swooping through the air like a suspension bridge, imagining how much of a thrill it would've been for a teenage Junior Bounous to ride them down.

Junior knew the farm was not a business that he would be able to pass to his children; times had changed enough that family farms were no longer supportive as they once were. But even as the farm began to shrink in size, Junior continued to hold on to pieces of it. The land and trees had more value than what could be counted in a bushel of fruit at a market—decades of memories that twisted through the grapevines and threaded through the knobs of gnarled peach trees. It has been a multi-generational place for our family over the past 120 years.

There, Levi and Jennie carefully cultivated a myriad of crops. Their children—Chester, Norma, Barney, Thelma, Stella, and Junior—sledded on the hillsides and ice skated in the fields and slept beneath the stars in the orchard on those sweltering summer nights. Barry and Steve and their cousins rode horses from the corral up into the mountains. My sister, Tyndall, and I and our cousins—EvaLynn, Christine, James, and Jennie—darted between cherry trees and swung from the giant Cottonwood. And now, my cousins' children—Ellie, Henry, Aurora, and J.J. (which stands for Junior Jensen)—will grow up playing in a perch that Junior and his grandsons-in-law created in the spring of 2020, a dugout fortress made of branches, tucked into a ravine in the hillside above Barry's house, a secret place they're calling "Grandpa's Hideaway." We all have made memories and are still creating memories on this storied landscape, five generations since Levi turned over the soil for the first time on this bench at the foot of the mountains.

When folks think of Junior, they think of him in the mountains. That landscape is certainly where he made a name for himself. But it was actually this landscape, these rows of orchard trees in the foothills of the Wasatch, that shaped so much of his life. Even as his ski career took off, he remained rooted in his family farm, living up at Alta or relocating his family to Sugar Bowl during the winters, but always returning to the farm in the summers. I've heard some folks wonder why Junior didn't move to someplace closer to the mouth of Little Cottonwood Canyon once he started working for Snowbird in the 1970s. He sacrificed almost three hours each day to drive from Provo to Snowbird and back. But the farm was his home.

To know Junior is to witness a deep connection to land; the physical realm we live in, travel to, and survive on. This devoted sense of place started amidst berry patches and cherry trees, developed under the guidance of his parents, and expanded as Junior stretched his wings and ventured farther into the mountains, down to the desert, and across oceans. To know Junior is to witness a level of intimacy with the birds and the beasts and the wildflowers and the thickets that also inhabit these places. Much of the qualities we associate with Junior—his kindness, his work ethic, his athleticism, and even his skiing—all started on the Bounous farm.

"He's an incredible individual. I like to think that I grew up under Junior. Three years after I met him, my father died. And I pretty much used him as a surrogate father."

— Craig Spooner, Snowbird Mountain School employee

"My brothers and I grew up as Junior's neighbors during the early '60s, and our house was next to his field and horse pasture and kitty-corner from his cherry orchard. I was about 12 at the time of this story. There were four of us in the cherry trees, picking away, and all at once, we see a jeep come tearing up the gravel road, stirring up a cloud of dust! It was Junior and he was yelling something like "I see you in my trees and you're in trouble!" He'd stopped the jeep, but then he started laughing! He pointed to a tree and said that he had a good crop except for that tree. So, if we wanted any cherries, take them out of that tree, since it wasn't a big producer. So we nodded our heads and said thanks . . . with great relief! The next summer we picked cherries for him at 4 cents a pound. When he actually let us work for him, we didn't put his income in a higher tax bracket—I think we ate half of his profits! (And it affected my digestive system, too.) I would pick 100 pounds and get roughly $4 a day. I thought that was pretty good, but this high school boy in a tree next to us would do 1,000 pounds a day! That's $40 a day in the '60s! We envied him but definitely didn't work like him. Looking back, it was great of Junior to hire us, and we did learn about some responsibility of showing up and spending some hours working. And by the way, the other cherry orchards in the area were only paying 3.5 cents a pound, so at 4 cents a pound, Junior paid a high dollar—and he put up with us!"

— Dave Dunn, neighborhood rascal

"Dad has bailed me and my family out of trouble and hardship more times than I can count. From my high school days to the present, he has unfailingly looked for cars, homes, jobs, performing opportunities, and financial traps. He has fixed every car and appliance we've owned. And if I didn't stop him, he'd be mowing my lawn at age 96. He will still sneak up here with a Weed Wacker, if I'm not vigilant. He helps me prune and spray the trees and tells me how to water the plants and shrubs—even gives me advice for my roses."

— Barry Bounous, son

"I feel so honored to have been able to spend quality time with Junior. It feels like any time spent in his presence should be held deeply sacred. A man with such rich life experiences and a sharp wit that any time spent with him feels like endless entertainment. He's the grandfather to those of us whose grandfathers passed too soon."

— Courtney Sanford, family friend

"Dad stayed out of my social life except to say that if the gal couldn't handle a little hike in the hills, then I should maybe rethink the relationship. And he told me that no matter how I was tempted, to never ever EVER try to teach a girlfriend how to ski. "Give her to mom." Best advice ever."

— Barry Bounous, son

Junior's parents, Jennie and Levi Bounous, before they were married in 1909.

Jennie and Levi after they were married. Likely around 1910.

Jennie began sporting the latest fashions once the family farm became financially successful. Likely early 1920s.

Junior's father, Levi, in front of the original farmhouse. Likely between 1915 and 1920.

Norma, Jennie, Stella, Levi, Barney, and Chester, prior to Junior's birth.

Jennie and Junior, when Junior was around 5 or 6 years old.

View from the orchard, looking east to the Wasatch. The flume from Rock Canyon that Levi built can be seen cutting in a vertical line through the lower hillside. Likely around 1935.

Norma, Stella, Levi, Jennie, Junior, and Jennie's father, Louis Richard. Likely taken around 1930.

Norma, Junior, Levi, Stella, Chester, and Barney. Taken in the early 1940s, when Junior was still in high school.

Junior's siblings Chester, Norma, Barney, Stella, and Junior at a celebratory lunch in Midway, Utah. 1970s.

Junior with his old Model T at a family reunion in Burley, Idaho. July 2021. The car is still in the family!

The cement pilings that Levi built on the top lot to get hay bales down to the lower lot still stand today. Some of the original wire can still be seen wrapped around the lower bar on the right hand side. Taken in October 2020.

A photo of the farm and the road leading to the farmhouse from the top lot looking west toward Utah Lake. Around the time Junior was born in the mid-1920s.

Junior on what used to be the family farm, with the landmark honoring the Bounous family. Junior's home is to the right, just out of sight. May 2022.

The view of the farm from the top lot. July 1967. The white house bordering the farm in the left photo (the southern end of the farm) was Barney's house. The brown roof of Junior and Maxine's one-story house is barely visible to the right of Barney's house, with a grove of cherry trees between the houses. In the right photo (the north end of the farm), the tall trees shade the road and the main farmhouse, while the chicken coop is in the sun.

A (poorly) stitched together shot of Timp-Kiwanis Bounous Park in 2020. The roof of Junior's current house is still just barely visible over the vegetation, behind some blueish pine trees. The location of the outfield and the far side of the running track is where the family farmhouse, road, and chicken coop used to be.

Chapter 4

Praise for the Pioneers

While Junior's contributions to the ski industry and powder ski technique made him one of the leaders within American skiing, he was not the first Utah skier, nor even in the first generation of Utah skiers. By the time Junior started skiing, the sport had already gained a few decades of momentum. This is not to discredit Junior's early contributions to the rise of skiing, but rather to acknowledge and celebrate all of those who were already breaking trail.

These ski pioneers, who were skiing in the days prior to ski areas and resorts, faced no shortage of obstacles, ranging from technique to gear. And while the use of the word *pioneer* can sometimes be problematic, often (whether intentionally or unintentionally) erasing others' history from landscapes, the use of *pioneer* in this case simply means "to develop or be the first to apply a new method, area of knowledge, or activity." The American skiers did not invent the sport of skiing, but since they were physically separated from the European ski culture by an ocean, American skiing, especially in the Mountain West, had a separate and unique trajectory in the 20th century, one that starts with the Gold Rush and a mass immigration into the rugged terrain of the American West.

Many of the original uses for skis in the Rocky Mountains, Sierra Nevada, and Cascades were practical; miners and mail carriers used skis to travel across mountain landscapes during winter months in the mid to late 1800s. In Utah, mining communities like Alta, Brighton, and Park City began dotting the Wasatch and Oquirrh Mountains, where minerals were found. Silver, zinc, and copper brought quick prosperity to the Mountain West. Some of the earliest mine surveyors were part of the Third Regiment California Volunteer Infantry, who were volunteer militia who hailed from the Sierra Nevada during the Gold Rush. Upon arriving at Fort Douglas, which is now incorporated into the University of Utah's campus, they scoured the surrounding mountains and foothills in search of mineral deposits. Once the deposits were located, the mines drew young, strong men from the East Coast, many of them European immigrants including some Scandinavians who brought skiing with them. Their knowledge of skiing as a means of transportation opened much of the Rockies and the Wasatch to winter travel and therefore operation. Navigating the snowy landscapes on skis was much more efficient than snowshoeing. The long pieces of wood could cut smooth tracks into a hill or across a field, which made breaking trail through snow easier and allowed for other skiers to follow behind. The downhill travel became much faster as well; though they couldn't really turn yet, gliding straight down a hill was much easier than snowshoeing down the same hill.

Less than a century later, those same mining towns would become some of the world's most renowned ski resorts. Many resorts still have ski runs, lifts, and hotels named after famous mines: Silver King at Park City, Evergreen at Brighton and Solitude, and Big Emma at Snowbird. During the gap between prospering as a mining town and prospering as a ski town, some towns were considered ghost towns. But this doesn't mean that skiing had disappeared from the mountains; it just hadn't quite reached the economic threshold where goods and services are exchanged within an industry. In fact, skiing rapidly gained momentum during those decades.

Those same Scandinavian immigrants who introduced skiing for practical use also introduced skiing as a recreational activity. A group of Norwegians created one of the first ski clubs in Utah: the Norwegian Young Folks Society, established in 1915. It would later change its name to the Utah Ski Club. They focused on ski jumping and began hosting competitions. Ski-jumping hills—like Dry Canyon in the foothills above what is now the University of Utah, Becker Hill in Ogden Canyon, and Ecker Hill at Parleys Summit—began to pop up along the Wasatch.

The first competitions began in 1915, and spectators flocked to the hills to watch as competitors soared through the air on wooden sticks. Ski jumping rapidly gained popularity as a spectator sport. Not many people were willing to risk their necks soaring through the air, but they were willing to ski or hike up to these hills to watch the jumpers. Two decades later, spectators would become skiers. As Alan Engen wrote in *First Tracks: A Century of Skiing in Utah*, "By the end of the 1930s, skiing had started to change from a spectator sport to a participation sport."

Another prominent group, the Wasatch Mountain Club, was founded in 1912. Originally more focused on summer activities like hiking and climbing, the group quickly expanded to include all types of mountain recreation, including winter activities like snowshoeing and skiing, as well as rock climbing and mountaineering. The Pfeifferhorn, the Wasatch Mountains' fifth tallest mountain, was named after one of the club's climbing leaders, Chuck Pfieffer. This group emphasized a backcountry approach to winter recreation. One of the group's most popular activities, for those who were hardy enough for it, was a rugged ski tour of the Wasatch Mountains, starting in Park City and ending at Brighton or Alta. Three decades after the Wasatch Mountain Club was founded, Junior would win a race hosted by the club at Brighton in 1945—his first steps into the limelight of Utah skiing. By the time Junior began skiing around 1933, there was already a significant skiing community along the Wasatch.

Junior began skiing at a typical age for a child today to start skiing, around seven years old. Unlike children today, however, Junior didn't have a teacher or even a mentor to help him learn. His path to skiing began with ice skating. Each winter when the canal would freeze over, Junior and his siblings would go ice skating. Sometimes, Levi would flood one of the fields with water and let it freeze over, creating a large area for his children and their friends to skate. Junior was accustomed to using ice skates as a way of getting around the farm in the winter. When the snow packed down enough on the farm road, Junior could ice skate to the plowed county road where the school bus picked him up.

But ice skates had their limitations. If the snow was too soft and deep, the skates were useless. Or if the snow was compacted and crusty, like it was in the orchard during the winter, ice skates broke through the crust. Also, the orchard had a slight incline to it, making navigating on ice skates tricky. The gradual slope was ideal for an orchard because it promoted natural drainage, both in the soil and in the air. Fruit trees are susceptible to cold frosts, especially during the spring, when a hard, ill-timed killing frost can damage developing blossoms and even decimate an entire crop for the year. A slope encourages cold night air to continue sinking lower, a phenomenon called cold-air drainage that helps orchards stave off killing frosts. The gradual slope unexpectedly served another purpose—a place where Junior could learn how to ski.

One winter, when Junior was seven years old, he came up with an idea for a better way to get around the farm by repurposing the wooden staves that form the sides of barrels. Compared to skates, the staves were longer, flatter, and had more surface area. Levi helped Junior cut the barrel staves and create leather straps. Junior strapped them to his boots and, for the first time in his life, skied between the peach trees in the sloping orchard.

Humans have strapped objects onto their feet to help them move across the snow for well over 10,000 years. To find out why, all you have to do is try postholing through a field of powder snow wearing only boots. The effort is exhausting. Strapping something onto the base of a foot was an evolution of sorts—a way of adapting to the environment. Light wooden blocks, leather, and ropes tied around wooden branches were some of the first solutions to moving through snow. These gave way to early forms of snowshoes, which mimicked the paws of animals like the snowshoe hare and lynx by spreading weight over a larger area.

Skis were an upgrade from snowshoes, which required picking one foot up, moving it forward, then placing it down again. Humans began realizing that the longer and thinner the object underfoot, the smoother the motion could be. Skis allowed humans to glide across the top of the snow, a much easier task than walking through it, or even walking on top of it.

When Junior asked his dad to help him strap two barrel staves to the bottom of his feet, he was jumping over many evolutionary stages of the ski. Even more significant is that although he wanted to move across the snow more efficiently, the thing that he desired most was to travel downhill. That inclination was deep within him and would ultimately change his life from farmer to skier.

Junior and his siblings were no strangers to thrilling winter activities. Besides ice skating, they also tied sleighs to their horses and had them trot on the snowy roads on the farm, snowballs kicking up from the horse's hooves and spraying the kids in their faces. Sometimes, they'd take the sleighs up past the barn, open the gate, and get a running start before hopping in for a ride down the hill and onto the road. As they grew older and bolder, they took the sleighs to the top of the much steeper hill, at the base of which sits Barry's house. Being familiar with the hill, I can confirm that it would have been quite the wild sleigh ride.

I once asked Junior if he or his siblings ever hit any trees while sledding. His response: "Probably did." I asked because I did hit a tree one Christmas when my family was staying at The Lodge at Snowbird. I had asked my cousin to push me as I lay on the sled headfirst. You can guess what happened next. I still have a dimple on my right cheek where my face hit the tree. In the blinding pain that followed the impact, I questioned why I would have wanted to go headfirst and why I felt the need to ask my cousin to push me, when the consequences were so painful. It was that same inclination to move downhill in a more exciting way, to carry more speed, to feel that rush of air on your face and the thrill of gravity pulling you closer to the world that my grandpa felt when he began pushing himself between peach trees on pieces of wood. It's the same thrill that drives hundreds of thousands of skiers and snowboarders to pack up their cars and drive into the mountains on a winter's day.

Barrel staves were Junior's first pair of makeshift skis—a combination of ice skates and the wooden sleighs. They were about 16 inches long, 2.5 inches thick, and just wide enough for his boot to fit. A simple, leather strap held the boots to the skis. When Levi would shovel snow out of the yard, he would dump it into big piles, about four or five feet high. Junior would carry his barrel staves to the top of the piles and then coast to the bottom.

His second pair of skis was a pair his mother bought from the Gessford sporting goods store in Provo when he was 10. They were heavy and wooden and about four or five feet long. Barrel staves had been rudimentary, not a true pair of skis but a toe in the door. Junior's second pair were the foot that cracked open the door to skiing.

The skis from his mother lasted longer than she did. Even after she was gone, the gift's impact on him was lasting, and the skis continued to carry him across the farm for quite a few years. Being young still, he didn't venture too far from home when he did take his skis out adventuring, but the farm had plenty of acres to test his developing skills on. Since the county didn't plow the farm roads, post-snowstorm roads developed a layer of packed snow that created the perfect medium for a horse-drawn sleigh or a pair of skis. Junior often convinced his father to pull him behind the horses on those skis.

Low angle hills, like the orchard, were the best landscapes for Junior to practice his newfound skills on, and he quickly graduated to the steeper hills he and his siblings would sled down. He could ski down these hills in a straight line and coast to a stop at the bottom. Before the advent of the "hockey stop," coasting was the only graceful way to stop. If a more abrupt stop were required because of a tree or bush in his path, Junior would have to jump out of the skis or jump over whatever low object was in his way. He credits this early pair of skis with the beginnings of learning how to ski jump at an early age.

During his skiing excursions, Junior tested and developed the stabilizing muscles around the ankles, knees, through the groin, and into the core. If he flexed his ankles this way, what would happen? What if he leaned his upper body to one side at the same time? Where should the bulk of his body weight be? Toward the back of the skis or the front? On the right ski or the left? Maybe Junior wasn't consciously thinking of these things quite yet, but his body was navigating these motions, learning how to react to changes in speed and terrain.

As Junior grew into his teenage years, he made improvements on the skis his mother bought him, which had just a toe strap. He experimented with two separate ways of holding the feet on the skis. The first was rubber from an inner tube to hold the toe, the other a leather strap that went around the heel. But heels would slide out from behind the inner tube toe strap, and this method didn't allow the skier to twist the foot or use it to guide the skis at all. The addition of the leather heel strap, however, allowed for more controlled heel movement. With this design, skiers could walk while strapped in, allowing for uphill travel and more maneuverability. It was then that Junior began to learn how to turn.

Junior's favorite story about turning includes a manure pile near the barn that housed the family's horses at the bottom of one of the hills Junior carried his skis up. Once the snow had compressed, becoming firmer and faster, Junior could carry some speed down the hill. Unfortunately, this speed would take him all the way to the side of the barn where Levi often shoveled the horses' manure. The pile was a strong motivation for Junior to learn how to turn.

With no guidance other than his natural instincts, he began using his ankles to maneuver his right ski so the angle of the ski on the surface of the snow pointed away from the manure pile. With the tips of the skis together and the tails of the skis wide, he created a wedge-like formation. He put most of his weight on that outside, right ski, and then turned his shoulders away from the manure pile. The skis followed his upper body, directing his motion away from the pile to effectively outmaneuver the manure. It was more of a lean than a turn, but it got the job done.

Junior made his next pair of skis in a woodworking class in high school when he was 15 or 16 years old. They didn't have bindings, just a toe strap that allowed him to ski straight and jump out of the skis easily, if necessary. These homemade skis broke fairly quickly, but the creation of them—cutting the wood, sanding it, shaping it—guided Junior's developing mind toward the how of skiing. How would the skis move if they were longer in the tail? Would they react differently if the tips were shaped differently? How thick should they be? It helped Junior turn a critical eye to the design and functionality of skis, and it laid a foundation that would become critical in developing both skis and skiing techniques later in life.

Toward the end of high school, Junior was able to purchase a pair of army surplus skis and poles from a sporting goods store in Provo. They had been painted white in order to camouflage with the snow—good for when you don't want to be spotted by potential enemies, but bad for when you lose a ski in the snow. Junior sanded the white paint off to reveal their wooden base. He covered them with flower decals and revarnished them. The poles he kept white. Because the skis had real bindings on them, with a leather heel strap and a buckle, they kept the heel and toe within the same functioning system. This key design shift would be critical in allowing skiers to guide the ski, and it was on these skis that Junior would truly learn how to turn.

Junior put some serious miles on these skis the next few years. Junior and a high school friend named Sammy George, who also owned a pair of skis, would drive part way up Provo Canyon to a place named Vivian Park. It quickly became a favorite spot for Junior and Sammy and others as well. Junior remembers it being a hot spot for learning how to ski, a place where people interested in skiing could meet with others. They'd sidestep the hill on their skis to pack it down, and then hike to the top. Not many people knew how to turn, and there were no ski instructors at that time to teach them. But the lack of knowledge didn't deter them. Skiing and winter recreation had caught fire in the Wasatch Mountains. The increasing population was documented in newspaper articles including one published in the *Deseret News* in 1937 that quoted Wasatch National Forest ranger W. E. Tangren:

> *Winter outdoor recreation is in full swing in Salt Lake Valley. Thousands of fresh-air folk are crowding skating ponds, toboggan slides and ski runs throughout the valley and into the foothills. It seems that all of the sudden, we are becoming aware of the possible fascinating thrills in the combination of human enthusiasm, skis, toboggans and mountains of clean snow.*

Junior and Sammy were two of those "fresh-air folk." But an unfortunate broken leg, caused by catching a tip on a log while skiing one time with Junior on a logging road at Vivian Park, turned Sammy off from skiing. Junior then began skiing with a young man named Frank Hirst, who would become Junior's partner in crime. Frank would be by Junior's side as they ventured into the backcountry, contributed to the early development of Timp Haven Ski Area, and even when they got caught in an avalanche for the first time. Frank would also witness the early days of Junior and Maxine's courtship, be Junior's best man at their wedding, and remain a loyal friend for the rest of his life.

By the time Junior neared the end of his adolescence, he had become a proficient and talented young man in the mountains. He was familiar with much of the mountainous terrain around Utah Valley. He was a capable runner and hunter, and he spent significant time skiing during the winters and then hiking, fishing, and horseback riding during the summers. It would be this athletic ability coupled with his curiosity of and love for the mountains, as well as relationships with a few key people, that would springboard Junior into his role as an early ski pioneer.

One of those key people was a young man named Reed Biddulph. The Biddulph family had a few children, almost all of whom worked for Levi as fruit pickers on the Bounous farm, including Reed. He was 11 years older than Junior was, owned a photography studio, and was a more advanced skier than Junior when they began skiing together. Reed enjoyed embarking on longer and more advanced excursions than Vivian Park provided. The Biddulphs owned a cabin near Aspen Grove, and Junior would often accompany Reed to the cabin. Reed, though not involved with the budding Timp Haven, was interested in seeking areas for potential ski area development. At the time, there were a few different rope tows scattered around the outskirts of Utah Valley, but not many enthusiasts were willing to put in the effort to develop these simple tows into true ski areas. Reed began scouring the nearby mountains in search of a spot. When he saw how much Junior enjoyed skiing and how strong of a skier Junior was, Reed began inviting both Junior and Frank on tours with him.

So, a few times a season for two or three years, Junior and Frank would follow Reed into the mountains. Their excursions ended up being quite adventurous. One of the first ski tours took them above Stewart Falls into Big Provo Cirque, below Mount Timpanogos. It was the first time, but not even close to the last time, that Junior would ski on Mount Timpanogos. Their next ski tour was in the South Fork of Provo Canyon. It was during this excursion that Frank and Junior were caught in an avalanche, both miraculously emerging on top of the snow and uninjured. Another outing took them onto the east side of Provo Peak, far above the Bounous farm. They were starting into a back bowl, hiking with skins on their skis, when the snow they were skinning up settled on itself with a crunching sound—an avalanche warning sign. They quickly retreated and were safe. And on their fourth excursion with Reed, near the top of Maple Mountain, about 7 miles and almost 4,000 vertical feet from the valley floor, Junior made a turn and broke one of his army surplus skis. Time spent following behind Reed jostled Junior's sense of adventure and risk-taking.

Ray Stewart, who founded Timp Haven, was another key person in Junior's life. Their relationship is discussed in more detail in a later chapter, but it's worth noting here that it was Ray's ad in the local paper for a ski rescue group that would be Junior's first, more serious involvement with a group tied to skiing. Their relationship also led to the creation of the Timpanogos Mountain Club around 1947, which assisted Ray in the early stages of developing Timp Haven resort by helping to build and maintain the first few rope tows and ski runs.

Another notable figure in the early days of Junior's ski career was Earl Miller, a Provo man who opened a ski shop in Provo. (This Earl Miller is not to be confused with the Professional Ski Instructors of America examiner Earl Miller who is associated with Snowbasin and is another local ski legend.) Earl was born in Manti, Utah, and grew up skiing at a local rope tow, where he would take Junior many times over the next decade.

Earl was a tinkerer and an inventor and saw much room for improvement with ski gear. He became one of the most significant ski technicians in history, creating gadgets that we still use. His most significant contributions to skiing were designing the ski brake, Twincam bindings—step-in bindings that could release in multiple directions—and the Miller Soft, one of the first true powder skis. Earl was also the first to classify ski injuries, connecting different types of falls with different types of bone breaks and injuries. His invention of a binding that released when a skier fell reduced certain types of injuries common at the time, so Earl began hosting falling competitions at Alta. And he would lead the charge in these competitions—crashing spectacularly at high speeds on the side of High Rustler and emerging (mostly) unscathed, or at least with fewer injuries than if he had been wearing the non-release ski bindings more common at the time, which were responsible for many a broken leg.

Earl was an accomplished ski instructor (he was the first ski school director at Timp Haven), and he was an athlete. In 1943 he won Utah's four-way ski competition, which combined cross-country, ski jumping, slalom, and downhill. Earl was in the know about local ski events and icons, and he told Junior about a cross-country race happening at Brighton in 1945, hosted by the Wasatch Mountain Club. Earl convinced both Junior and Frank that they should race in it with him, and though neither of the young men had even considered ski racing at that point, they decided to try it.

On race day, the three of them, along with Junior's father, Levi, and Junior's relatively new girlfriend, Maxine, loaded up into a car and drove to Brighton. Junior remembers it being a beautiful day with skies the deep, jeweled blue that feels unique to the Wasatch. Junior started off the race with no expectations. He had no concept of how talented a cross-country skier he was, having never raced or even been trained. It didn't take long, however, for him to realize that he was one of the best skiers there—not because of his technique, but because of his athleticism. At one point, Junior started seeing small specks of blood in the snow, coughed up by the racer in front of him—the only racer in front of him, in fact—caused by lungs overworked in cold air, and he realized that he was going to win. Junior, a no-name son of a farmer from Provo whom they would nickname "prune-picker," surprised everyone and won the race. By Junior's memory, Earl got third place, and Frank ended up in sixth or seventh. The Utah County boys had made an impression on Wasatch skiing.

This race was a catalyst for another important relationship in Junior's life. The Wasatch Mountain Club hosted an award ceremony and social gathering after the event. A young couple, a few years older than Junior and Maxine, approached Junior and congratulated him. Jim and Elfriede Shane were friendly and outgoing, and the two couples hit it off right away. The Shanes would become a local power couple up the Cottonwood Canyons after building the Goldminer's Daughter Lodge at Alta. Jim, who would one day become a ski patrolman and the president of the Intermountain Ski Association, had also competed in the race that day and was impressed with Junior's athletic ability. Jim and Elfriede invited Junior and Maxine to ski and stay at the Wasatch Mountain Club's rope tow and lodge at Brighton. They accepted the invitation, and it was the start of a friendship that would continue all the way until December 3, 2020, when Elfriede passed away at the age of 97.

In the aftermath of his unexpected win, Junior decided he wanted to take ski lessons. He had muscled his way through the race, but he didn't know how to run or glide correctly on skis. Earl had told Junior about a man named Alf Engen, who had already become a living legend by the 1940s. He was known as a world champion jumper and had been recruited by the US Forest Service to help develop ski areas including Alta, Brighton, and Snowbasin. Junior had seen a ski movie starring Alf and his two brothers,

Sverre and Corey, filmed at Alta and titled *Ski Aces*. Made in 1945, this iconic promotional film features the three brothers skiing through powder snow. It was one of the first Technicolor films produced by 20th Century-Fox. If Junior wanted to learn how to ski from the best, then Alf was it.

Around the same time Junior was considering ski lessons, Alf was relocating back to the Wasatch after a 10-year hiatus spent in Idaho. At the direction of the US Forest Service, he had been working at Sun Valley as a promoter, run developer, and jumping competitor. Sun Valley had gained a national reputation as America's first luxury ski resort, complete with multiple locations to take lessons from European-born ski instructors, ride rope tows, fly off ski jumps, and ride the country's first chairlifts. It was well organized and well developed. Alf returned to Utah at the end of the 1940s, at the height of a growing public desire to ski but without the infrastructure to support it. Though Alta, Brighton, Snowbasin, and Timp Haven were operational, the ski areas weren't reaching their full potential, as recorded by Alf's son, Alan Engen, in his (and Gregory Coyne Thompson's) book *First Tracks: A Century of Skiing in Utah*:

> *What Alf found [upon returning to the Wasatch] was a growing interest in alpine recreational skiing by the public at large, but it was still far from what was required to create a viable market that could provide a reasonable means of making a living at the sport. Alf knew that in order to help make the sport grow, some way had to be found to get local Salt Lake people of all age groups on skis at a very low cost and provide them with appropriate instruction to the point where they were able to navigate properly.*

Alf's neighbor in Salt Lake City was a man named Wilby Durham, who was the assistant general manager of the *Deseret News*. Durham was looking at ways to promote the paper, and Alf was brainstorming ways to get more people into ski programs along the Wasatch. The two decided to create a partnership, and one of Utah's first ski schools was born in 1947: the Deseret News Ski School. Around the same time, Alf was taking control of the Engen Ski School at Alta, which his brother Sverre had been running for a few years. With Sverre's help, the Deseret News and Engen Ski Schools formed a partnership. The Deseret News Ski School would hold free classes at Alta, and the Engen Ski School would provide the ski instructors, headed by US Olympian Jack Reddish.

On the opening day of the ski school in December 1948, a massive storm rolled in and closed the canyons. Unable to hold the lessons at Alta, Alf and Durham relocated them to the Salt Lake Bonneville Golf Course at the last minute. They expected only a handful of participants to show up;

instead, more than 1,000 people arrived at the golf course to learn how to ski. According to Alan Engen in *First Tracks*, Alf said, "Ya, by golly, I never saw anything like it, skiers everywhere, all over the golf course! I yust [sic] knew we had started something big."

The program, which helped feed the ardor of Wasatch skiing in its earliest stages, continues to this day, charging folks only $30 or $40 for three ski lessons—chump change in the ski industry today. Alan wrote this about the program in *First Tracks*:

> *As an outreach ski program, the Deseret News Ski School is the largest, longest running ski school of its type in America. Its impact on the ski industry in Utah is significant. While no official records were ever kept of the exact number of individuals who first got their start in skiing through this particular program, the best estimates are in the tens of thousands.*

With the creation of these learn-to-ski programs, ski instructing and learning along the Wasatch was set in motion. The interest in skiing now had a channel to travel through. Junior entered into this churning and growing system right as it gained momentum. After unexpectedly winning the race at Brighton, Junior reached out to Alf about taking private cross-country lessons. It could be said that the decision was the beginning of the rest of Junior's life. Junior worked part time as a gas station attendant for extra cash, and he had inherited $600 or so from his mother after she had passed away—a significant chunk of change for a young farmer in those days. Junior used some of that inheritance money to pay for lessons with Alf. Though Jennie was no longer alive, her influence once again helped guide Junior to a skiing career.

Alf taught Junior better techniques for jumping, as well as cross-country, downhill, and mogul skiing. But Junior's interest in skiing quickly shifted from competitor to teacher. He had already been teaching the BYU ski class informally for a couple of years, and with Timp Haven gaining momentum, Junior was starting to teach ski lessons there as well. Alf, sensing a natural teacher in Junior's kind nature and passion, took Junior under his wing. Alf instructed him on how to teach beginners strapping boots to skis for the first time. Then how to foster improvement for someone who already has a grasp on how to get down a hill. Then how to help an intermediate student in this type of situation on that type of terrain, and so forth.

Unlike the stringent Austrian ski instructors of the time, Alf didn't use a regimented technique, even though he had recently moved from Sun Valley, where the rigorous Arlberg technique was primarily taught. Alf taught Junior a more intuitive approach to teaching, one based on personal experience that could be adapted to how the student was reacting to the movements and the terrain. Junior remembers loving the way that Alf taught him. He took his recently learned instructing skills and used them on Maxine, who was still learning how to ski.

I once asked Junior how well that went. In my personal experience, having a significant other teach you how to do something doesn't always go so well. Egos, annoyance, miscommunication, frustration, and sometimes tears can lead to failed lessons and even discourage the student from ever trying the activity again. But, Junior said that Maxine loved their ski lessons. He remembers fondly that time together and speaks almost reverently about the passing of knowledge from Alf to him to Maxine, as if it were a sacred thing. And in many ways, it was.

What Junior first experienced when taking lessons from Alf was something like peering through a cracked door into a world of possibilities—a narrow opening that revealed what his future might, and, in fact, did become. After training with Alf, Junior pursued competitive skiing to a certain extent. The Timpanogos Mountain Club hosted a fundraising banquet to send Junior to Minneapolis so he could compete in the Nordic Combined National Championships, a competition dominated by Norwegians. According to Junior's memory, he finished as one of the top five American competitors, and Junior would become one of the most impressive gelande (terrain) jumpers at Alta for decades to come. But his true calling was always teaching, that sacred passing of knowledge that Junior experienced as he learned from Alf and taught Maxine.

There are some who might hold things close to them, who learn skills that they don't want to share, who want to keep knowledge for themselves. We, who love skiing, should be thankful that our local ski legends were not those types of people. Imagine if Alf and others at Alta hadn't shared the knowledge of powder skiing with others. If they had seen the terrain and the snow and thought that it was better to keep it to themselves, to not promote it, to not teach others how to ski it. Imagine if all the skiers of that time decided they would rather have the mountains and the snow all to themselves. Skiing would not have disappeared, by any means, and people would have continued to teach themselves how to get down a hill for the sheer pleasure of it. But without teachers, each generation would have had to reinvent the wheel. And skiing would certainly not have progressed to where it is today.

I would like to end this chapter with a word of thanks. To the daredevils who built the early jumps on Ecker Hill, and others who constructed rope tows to get people higher on the mountains. To those explorers who invited friends on ski tours with them into the deep backcountry. To the tinkerers who saw a need for improvement in gear and did something about it. To the teachers who organized ski schools and invited the masses to come and learn. To the innovators who developed ways of skiing in powder snow and spread the word. Thank you. It has been more than 100 years since the Wasatch Mountain Club was formed, since skiing started catching fire in the Wasatch, and those of us skiing today are reaping the benefits of the early pioneers' hard work.

"As you take a look at the name Junior Bounous, he's in the category of not just a good skier, not just a good ski teacher, but you have to put him in the realm of a remarkable man who is a true ski pioneer."

— Alan Engen, Alta skier and historian

"The one thing I think about Junior is that he's so congruent. He's always Junior; I've never seen him not be. What's so special is that I've never seen him not be Junior.

— Maggie Loring, Snowbird Mountain School director

"Junior would go to all lengths to get powder turns. I'd get off the tram with him, and I'm ready to jump down and just take whatever was below, and he'd go, 'No, no, Jerry, we must go this way.' And we would start trudging across underneath Mount Baldy, or we'd be heading across over toward Gad 2, skirting the edges of White Pine and whatever, and I'm going, 'Junior, look it's good, right there it's good.' 'No, no, no, we have to keep going over here.' And we would hike for hours to get three or four turns. But my goodness were those turns unbelievable. Unbelievable."

— Jerry Warren, Snowbird Mountain School assistant director

"Junior's always there on the great powder days—he has a nose for it."

— Bob Bonar, Snowbird president and general manager

Junior as a young buck in 1945, taken by his friend Reed Biddulph.

A very serious looking Junior with his cross-country ski trophies. Taken by Reed Biddulph in the late 1940s.

Junior and his trophy after winning the Wasatch Mountain Club's cross-country race at Brighton in the spring of 1946. Junior still has this trophy in his living room.
Special Collections, J. Willard Marriott Library, The University of Utah.

Some of the competitors and sponsors from the Wasatch Mountain Club's race at Brighton in 1946, which Junior won. Earl Miller is on the far left, with Frank Hirst in bib 27 to his right. Junior is in the middle wearing a white shirt and bib 19. Jim Shane is third from the right, bib 39.

Junior all smiles in his Alta ski school uniform in 1954.

Stein Eriksen, Junior, and Alf Engen on Snowbird's official opening day in January 1972. Junior would become the first to ski the Pipeline chute with Jim McConkey on this same day.

Early skiers in Utah had to learn how to ski powder on heavy and stiff wooden skis, and they made it look easy. Here Junior is on his old HEAD skis at Timp Haven. 1960s.

Junior on his way to becoming a solar eclipse. Sundance, 1960s.

Chapter 5

Fast Max

There is, of course, no way to tell Junior's story without also telling Maxine's story. After 67 years of marriage, Junior and "Fast Max" were as intertwined as a couple could be. And besides being Junior's first student, Maxine came into her own ski notoriety over the course of her life, becoming one of Utah's most iconic female ski instructors. She, like Junior, was rooted in the soil and snow of the Wasatch Mountains, toes dipped in mountain lakes and reservoirs, lungs full of pine and oak, skin speckled with shadows of flickering aspen leaves, eyelashes made of wildflowers.

Maxine was born on September 18, 1925, in Provo, Utah. She was put up for adoption immediately after birth, so we will likely never know who her biological parents were, or what their reasons for adoption were. Maxine's true parents—the couple who adopted her—were Urban and Ada Overlade. Urban was born in 1886 in Ephraim, Utah, and was one of nine children. (Coincidentally, one of Urban's younger brothers, Linford, would also marry an Ada. The couple then named their daughter Ada, so Maxine had three Ada Overlades in her family: her mother, aunt, and cousin.) Urban moved to Provo, where he started working for the Provo Brick Company. Ada Safford was born in Provo in 1885, and the two were married in 1908.

Urban would go on to start his own sand and gravel company. He dug his mine at the base of Slate Canyon, the remnants of which can still be seen today. Levi Bounous would hire Urban to bring sand and gravel to the Bounous farm, which he'd use in his cement work. Junior remembers Urban being a very strong man, loading gravel and sand into a wagon by himself and then unloading it—no easy task. He had two enormous draft horses, Rocky and Rowdy, that would pull the wagon from the mine to its destination. As a child, years before Junior ever met Maxine, Junior remembers seeing the draft horses compete in and win a pulling contest in the state fair.

Growing up, Maxine was passionate about dance and music. Her parents put her in dance classes starting at a young age, and she immediately took to all kinds of dance. She had a ballroom dance partner throughout junior high and high school, and she began singing in her school's choir. One of her biological parents must have been a talented musician because she was born with nearly perfect pitch, a trait she passed onto both of her sons. Her passion for music and dance followed her through her entire life, and she continued dancing in shows while studying at BYU. She and Junior would go dancing on many of their dates (despite Junior insisting that he was club-footed) and would take dance lessons together. Maxine went on to perform in musical shows well into her later years and was part of the chorus for productions such as *Kismet* and *The Pajama Game* at a theater in Orem in the 1960s. Junior reckons that if she could have, she would have loved to become a professional dancer.

As she grew older, Maxine also became diligent and talented in her academics. She was a straight-A student in high school and college, being especially interested in sociology, English, and Spanish. She became an excellent typist and began competing in typing and short-hand competitions in high school, going on to win awards while studying at BYU. She graduated from high school in 1943 (she and Junior, both graduates with the class of '43, never received yearbooks due to workforce and material shortages as a result of the United States' involvement in World War II), and then she graduated from BYU in 1948.

She had a somewhat short-lived but very successful career as a secretary. She was the first female employee at the Columbia Steel Corporation in Ironton, the secretary for the president of BYU, and then secretary for a high executive at Geneva Steel. When she and Junior got married, she quit her job at Geneva Steel to move up Little Cottonwood Canyon and work as an instructor at Alta, ending her stint as a secretary. Junior looks back on that decision somewhat regretfully; though they would have to live at Alta because of Junior's job as Alf's assistant, Maxine had been making $300-400 a month, a good wage at the time and much more than she'd make as a ski instructor. But the pull of the mountains for the newlywed Bounouses was too great.

Probably because she grew up around Rocky and Rowdy, Maxine developed an affinity for horses at a young age. When her childhood friend, Lorraine Lindey, got a riding horse, Maxine was inspired to save up money to get her own. She began babysitting while in high school and used the money to purchase a retired racing horse named Dixie, and Urban saved up more money to buy her a riding saddle. Dixie was three-fourths thoroughbred and so fast that Maxine would often race along the railroad tracks and outpace the train. When she sold Dixie, needing the money to help pay for college, the new owner, seeing how fast the horse still was, started Dixie racing again.

Junior remembers that Dixie was a very tall horse with long legs. When it came to height, Maxine never broke the 5-foot threshold and was perhaps even shorter when she got Dixie. In order to ride Dixie, Maxine would have to get her foot into a stirrup that was almost shoulder-height for her. She couldn't reach the saddle horn, so she'd have to grab onto the tie straps attached to the saddle, meant for strapping on random items. She could then pull herself high enough to grab the back of the saddle or use one hand to grab the saddle horn and pull herself the rest of the way up. As Junior recalls, "It was something to watch, her getting on that big horse."

It would be this love for horses that would lead Maxine to meet Junior one fall afternoon in 1944. She and Lorraine were riding their horses up Rock Canyon when a rainstorm rolled in and showered them with what I assume might have been refreshingly cool drops on a hot and dusty fall day. The downpour didn't last too long, and soon the young women found a place to start a fire and dry themselves off. I like to imagine the grove of maple and oak they settled in smelling of rich, earthy soil after the rain, the bark of the trees dark with moisture, the persimmon and crimson leaves of the surrounding vegetation vibrant in the golden afternoon sun.

Junior had been working on the farm that day, but the rainstorm had caused his work to halt. Once the skies had cleared, the afternoon was too beautiful to spend waiting for the farm to dry. So he saddled up his own horse, Neg, and rode up Rock Canyon, one of the family dogs loping alongside.

What happened next might be best told through Junior and Maxine's own conversation about the incident in the film made for Junior's 80th birthday titled *Bounousabuse: 80 Junior Years.*

> *Maxine: Well, that was a strange meeting. I was riding my horse with a girlfriend who was riding her horse. And we went up Rock Canyon to cook some hamburgers and it poured rain on us. So of course we were smart—we had wood under the saddles, so when it finally stopped we built a fire and were proceeding to try to dry off. In other words, we were trying to dry off our jeans that were soaking wet. And along came a dog trotting up the trail. It came over to us and we knew that behind that dog was gonna be a person. And it was. Junior was riding his horse. So that was how we met; he showed up, and that was how we met.*
>
> *Junior: She's leaving out a few things.*
>
> *Maxine: No, I'm not.*
>
> *Junior: I don't know whether I should add to that or not.*

Maxine: No, *don't—*

Junior: Cause she had her pants off and was holding them up by the fire to dry—

Maxine: No, *we were pulling them up, both of us, trying to jump into wet jeans.*

Junior: They were slow at getting their pants pulled up.

Despite the somewhat unfortunate meeting (depending on whose perspective you look at it from), Junior, Maxine, and Lorraine ended up chatting for a while and rode out of the canyon together.

Maxine and Junior wouldn't see each other again for a few months. It wouldn't be until that December when both of them, by chance, responded to Ray Stewart's ad in the paper for a Civilian Defense Ski Corps for Mountain Rescue. Junior and his friend Frank Hirst arrived, and Junior recognized Maxine and Lorraine. His interest was piqued. He had now crossed these two ladies doing two things he loved: horseback riding and adventuring in the mountains. He and Frank finished off the first Defense Ski Corps meeting by inviting the two out on a double date. I once asked how it was decided that Junior and Maxine would be a couple and Frank and Lorraine would be another. Junior replied that he and Maxine both had darker hair, while Frank and Lorraine both had lighter hair. It was (apparently) that simple.

Their first date was ice skating on a pond at Vivian Park, up Provo Canyon. Junior and Frank were good skaters, having grown up using figure skates on local ponds. It turned out that Maxine and Lorraine were also good skaters, often dancing as they skated. They encouraged the boys to not just skate beside them but to dance across the ice with them, spinning them around and around.

It solidified what Junior had sensed about Maxine: that she loved being outside and active. That winter, Maxine, Lorraine, Junior, and Frank would spend a decent amount of time together at Ray Stewart's house as they learned about mountain rescue and first aid. They became friends with Ray and his wife, Ava, during this time as well, and Ray began inviting them to visit his homestead up North Fork Canyon. Junior and Frank asked Maxine and Lorraine on a second date, and the four of them hiked up to the cabin of Hank Stewart, Ray's brother, near the rope tow. Hank had chosen a beautiful forest glade to build his homestead, surrounded by pines. It was quite the romantic place for what would be a very special date for Junior and Maxine.

Junior and Frank had brought Maxine and Lorraine here with the intention of teaching them how to ski. There was just enough of a pitch in the clearing to gather speed and coast for 30 or 40 feet without being in danger of hitting a tree. Since Maxine didn't have her own pair of skis yet, Junior had brought his. Maxine didn't have the right size of boots to strap into his bindings, however, so Junior took off his boots and let her wear them. Junior then taught her the basics of skiing, walking around the snowy clearing in his socks and then taking her hand to pull her back to the top of the small hill.

It would be some time before the four of them would go skiing again. But by then, Maxine and Lorraine had caught the ski bug, both being very athletic and adventurous. They didn't need the boys' encouragement. They went out together and bought full ski outfits, complete with skis, bindings, boots, and poles. Soon, the two couples (Junior remembers those early dating days as being mostly double dates with Frank and Lorraine) were frequenting Ray's rope tow quite often, hiking the mile up to the tow with their skis on their backs, doing a couple of laps on the tow, and coasting that same gentle mile back to the car.

When winter shifted to spring and then to summer, Junior and Maxine shared their love for riding horses. They'd go on long rides up Rock Canyon and across the Wasatch, or down to Cedar Breaks National Monument or Capitol Reef to camp in sleeping bags under the stars. They once drove up to Yellowstone in Junior's convertible and rented a small cabin there. They'd drive north to ride Utah's first roller coaster at Lagoon, or to see the Saltair, which had a big dance band and dance floor. Being the dancers they were, Maxine and Lorraine loved dancing the night away with their beaus, and the couples saw Nat King Cole and other famous musicians at the Rainbow Randevu in downtown Salt Lake City. According to Junior, "Maxine and Lorraine were great dancers. Frank and I were great stumblers."

During one of their more adventurous dates, the four decided that they would try to raise some money for the Timpanogos Mountain Club to build a lodge at Timp Haven, similar to the Wasatch Mountain Club's lodge at Brighton. They made a plan to sell hot cocoa, not in the city, nor at Vivian Park, nor at the base of Timp Haven, but at Emerald Lake, a glacier lake underneath Mount Timpanogos' highest peak. And they were going to do it early in the morning. They packed up a horse with a camping stove, gas, and the makings for hot cocoa, and started the five-mile hike at 10 p.m. Carrying flashlights, Junior and Frank slowly led the horse up the trail, gaining almost 3,500 feet in elevation. Maxine and Lorraine, who had never even been on Timpanogos before, were tied to the horse with a long rope, partly to make sure they stayed on the trail and didn't fall behind or get lost, and partly so the horse could help pull them up if they needed it.

The group got to Emerald Lake before the sun had risen—about four o'clock in the morning. It was freezing. They hadn't thought to bring a tent or any extra layers, and they had no protection from the gusty, frigid wind at 10,397 feet. Once it got light enough, Junior asked someone who had spent the night camped at the lake if Maxine could lay on one corner of the outside of their tent, so she could get some sort of protection from the wind. When daylight hit, they set up their hot cocoa shop, heating lake water over their camp stove. As Junior remembers, "My gosh, we didn't sell two dollars' worth of hot chocolate. We drank more than what we sold." Miraculously, Maxine and Lorraine didn't dump Junior and Frank right then and there. Junior admits it may have not been the easiest fundraising tactic, or the most romantic way for the two women to hike up Timp for the first time. In his own words, "You'd think that would've been enough to turn Maxine and Lorraine against both Frank and me." (Besides when Junior led his mother on a wild goose chase through the strawberry patches on the farm, this might be the first known and confirmed case of "Bounousabuse.")

In the winter of 1946, Junior, Frank, Maxine, Lorraine, Levi, and Earl Miller drove up to Brighton to watch Junior, Earl, and Frank compete in a cross-country race. With Junior's surprise win, his life's trajectory changed, steering him toward Alf Engen and a career in ski instruction. It had been easy to spend lots of quality time with Maxine during the winters he helped at Timp Haven. But once Junior starting working at Alta and moved into the employee dormitory up in late 1948, the time he spent with Maxine became sparse. He was working at Alta six days a week and working one day at Timp Haven, without even a single day off during the average week.

Meanwhile, Maxine had been a college student on and off during their first few years dating. While she had received a scholarship to BYU for her first year, she had had to take quarters off to work and earn money to finish her degree. She graduated from BYU in 1948, and she started to think more seriously about her life, her career, and where she wanted to live. Always driven and carrying the desire to see other parts of the world, Provo wasn't quite cutting it anymore.

In 1948 Maxine decided she needed a change of pace, and she and a friend hatched a plan to move to California. They packed up their lives and drove south to Los Angeles. Junior and Maxine continued to write letters to each other frequently, and Junior drove to Los Angeles once to visit her. His car didn't have air conditioning, and he remembers being miserable the entire drive.

Meanwhile, the distance had caused Junior to realize what he truly wanted in life. He had a friend who worked at a local drug store and had a mile walk back to her house after her late-night shift. Junior would often drive her home, and during the ride she'd ask about Maxine and their relationship. Through these conversations with her, Junior realized that Maxine was the most important person to him. Junior knew that she had started dating other men in Los Angeles, but he realized that Maxine was worth fighting for. Over time, tempting her with ideas of living in the mountains and proclaiming his love for her, he convinced her to move back to Utah in 1952.

They were an unlikely couple in many ways; he was a fruit farmer turned ski instructor, and she was a straight-A college student with her sights set on being a secretary or working in the academic world. But their shared love for the Wasatch, skiing, horseback riding, hiking, and camping did the trick. By the end of 1952, the two of them were married. On December 7, 1952, they had a small ceremony in Junior's brother Barney's house on the farm, with Frank and Lorraine as best man and maid of honor.

They had a brief honeymoon in Las Vegas, and then it was time for the ski season. Junior convinced Maxine to become a certified ski instructor, and she received the best score out of the 30 people in her class. Alf hired her on, she quit her job at Geneva Steel, and Junior and Maxine moved into the Alta Lodge together, starting what would become lifelong careers as ski instructors.

Their first few years of marriage and beginning their family had ups and downs, which were usually tied to a difficult living situation in which Maxine was learning to be a mother. There were certain hardships the young couple had to endure right after marriage, including a failed pregnancy in 1954, Maxine's father passing away almost immediately after she gave birth to Barry in 1956, her mother passing not long after that, and Junior's father passing in 1959, just two months shy of Steve's birth. Despite all of the wonders their lives together presented them, the stacked tragedies within their first few years of creating a life together did take its toll. Maxine bore much of the brunt of these hardships while being tied down taking care of young children in tough living conditions. But as their children got older, Maxine had more freedom, and life became much easier, especially once the family moved back to Provo full time.

While working at Alta and Sugar Bowl, the little family spent the summers living in Maxine's mother's house in Provo. This was very convenient for them financially, though it never quite felt like their own space. They kept living there during the summers after Ada passed away, though it still wasn't the permanent home they desired. They spent a few summers renting apartments on BYU's campus when the children got a bit older, but they needed more space. Junior had been sitting on property from his family's farm for some time with the intention of building on it, and with a flood of inheritance from the passing of his father in 1959 and making more money as a ski school director, the family finally had the financial means to build their own home. Junior took out a farm loan, and construction began in 1964 while they were still at Sugar Bowl, finishing right before the summer of 1965, just in time for the family to permanently relocate from California to Utah. Maxine and Junior were finally able to start creating a home that was truly their own, rather than a rented apartment that they would move out of every season. The family began to have a sense of true stability and rootedness.

As Junior started teaching at Timp Haven once more, Maxine did as well. They started Junior Bounous Ski Incorporated together, and Maxine worked both weekdays and weekends, teaching group classes and private lessons and leading Timp Haven's "Ladies Day." She was also Steve's and Barry's primary teacher during this time, since Junior was working full time on weekends, running the ski school and ski shop and county program, as well as getting the Timp Haven Ski Team up and running, which both Barry and Steve participated on. Junior credits Maxine with being the organizational wizard behind the county programs, which brought, on average, about 1,600 students to Timp Haven from a variety of Utah County schools over the course of a weekend. Officially, she was both secretary and treasurer for Junior Bounous Ski Incorporated.

Barry and Steve grew into stronger skiers while at Timp Haven, both racing for the Timp Haven Ski Team (which Robert Redford later renamed the Sundance Ski Team). They were naturals, with an instinctual feel for the snow and taking a line around a gate, and they were fearless fliers as two of the youngest to participate in gelande jumps. When Steve started carrying a shovel around while skiing to build jumps around Timp Haven, Barry began shying away from the competition aspect of skiing and started taking more of an interest in teaching.

Junior recalls that, starting when Barry was about 12 or so, Barry began accompanying Junior in his teaching clinics, mimicking his father as Junior taught his instructors how to teach beginner students. Barry could do all of the demonstrations perfectly, in front of a group of professional ski instructors, no less. It's no wonder to anyone that Barry went on to become a ski instructor at Snowbird and then at Sundance, where he still teaches today. You could say it was in his blood.

Maxine loved to socialize and loved to dance just as much as she did when they first started dating. Looking for a way to become more integrated with their non-skiing community, she convinced Junior that they should join the local country club shortly after moving back to Provo. They began attending dances almost every Friday and Saturday, as well as the parties the club would throw for special occasions. Already a good golfer and avid tennis player, Maxine started taking lessons and was part of a women's group for both. She even began competing in tennis and golf tournaments with Elfriede Shane.

Just a few weeks after joining the club, Maxine took Barry and Steve to go swimming. Steve, only about six or seven years old, wandered away from the pool at one point, always looking for an adventure. Waddling around in his flippers, he caught sight of one of the golf carts parked outside of the clubhouse.

Perfect, he thought.

Thinking it'd be jolly fun to pretend as though he were driving the cart, he hopped in the front seat, flippers and all, and started playing with the wheel as though he were racing in an arcade game. Then he pressed the pedal—or, flipper—to the medal. The cart had not been left in park, but in reverse, kept motionless by the slightly downhill slope of the sidewalk. The cart shot backward and straight through the floor-to-ceiling picture windows of the club house, immediately shattering them.

I imagine the poor soul working the golf shop must have had a heart attack. The shop was covered in shattered glass, a golf cart was somehow among the clothing racks, and what had moments ago been beautiful picture windows was now a jagged and dangerous gaping hole to the outside world. And right in the middle of it all was a little boy in flippers, white with shock, but luckily uninjured.

It solidified what Maxine and Junior had been starting to guess about their young son: he was a walking hazard, likely to sniff out trouble wherever possible. You couldn't take him anywhere.

Maxine's golf and tennis swing were unfortunately affected by an injury she had while skiing: a torn rotator cuff from a collision with another skier while she was teaching. Maxine was prone to accidents and injuries, though as Junior aptly puts it: "Poor gal, she didn't do it to herself much." Despite being just under five feet tall and very petite (barely taking up any space on the ski hill) and despite being someone who always skied to her ability level and in control, Maxine somehow became target practice for out-of-control skiers and snowboarders on numerous occasions. A few times the collisions happened while she was teaching students. Why those individuals who hit her felt the need to be carrying that much speed around a ski lesson we'll never know, but I've never known someone to get hit by so many other people while skiing. Because Maxine was always about half the size of the person hitting her, she typically sustained significant injuries from these unfortunate encounters, including a broken neck from a hit-and-run. Luckily her ailments never kept her off the mountain for too long.

Many lovingly know Maxine as "Fast Max," so nicknamed because of her skiing talent, her hiking speed, and her proficiency in water skiing and wake surfing. She was very athletic and very talented in almost any sport she tried. But her level of confidence could wane at times, though not because she was incapable of doing the activity. Steve created the nickname "Fast Max" for her because she would often be saying that she couldn't do a certain activity, even as she was actively doing that activity she claimed she couldn't do. She'd say she couldn't make it up a certain pitch of a hike as she was cruising up it, leaving others to breathe in her dust, or claim that she wouldn't be able to ski a certain slope even as she was navigating her way down it.

Georgia Clark, a longtime ski instructor at Snowbird, used to hike with Maxine often. On one occasion, the two of them were hiking up American Fork Canyon on a trail that was a bit primitive. Maxine had hiked it before, but the entire hike she kept saying that she hoped they were on the right trail and was fretting that she wasn't certain she knew the way, even as she was correctly leading them. As Georgia recalls, "Oh, she knew the way."

Maxine was a guiding light to many in the Wasatch. I've heard countless stories from folks who tell me that it was Maxine and Junior who first led them on this hike or showed them the way down this run. While Junior did these activities with such a casual and humble sense of confidence that it could almost be unnerving, Maxine would vocalize a lack of confidence while showing others how to find their way in the Wasatch. She helped others gain their own confidence. She was a leader who didn't think of herself as a leader, but who nevertheless would lead others just by doing the things she loved doing in the places she loved.

Maxine had many endearing traits, though they could get her into trouble occasionally. Despite having thorough knowledge of the landscapes she frequented and loved, she could often get lost if she were navigating alone. Even though she knew her way, she'd often second guess herself so much that she could lead herself in the exact opposite direction she was supposed to be going. Or she could be so careful and intentional about something that she could accidentally neglect something else.

Once, she was driving up North Fork Canyon to Sundance in a brand new car. Being the lover of sweets that she always was, she had bought a delectably warm, gooey cinnamon bun. The cinnamon bun started dripping onto the seat, and Maxine reached over to try to prevent it from ruining the brand new upholstery. In the split second she took her eyes off the road, the car went off the shoulder and into the ravine. Maxine was thankfully okay. The brand new car, on the other hand . . .

Perhaps the situation wasn't ideal at the time it happened, but looking back on it now, our family can laugh at the fact that Maxine could care so much about the new car seat that she crashed the car. That trait of hers—that she cared so much—was one of the things that made her such a warm and wonderful person. Georgia Clark once asked her partner what struck him about Junior and Maxine, and he said that when you're talking to them, they give you their full attention. They really listen to what you have to say because they truly care.

Another endearing trait of hers, which had a major role to play in the car story, was how much she *loved* sweets, specifically chocolate. Junior also loves chocolate, but Maxine had a love for it that went even further than Junior's. Ski school instructors recall how the two of them would always have some form of chocolate on them while they were skiing, usually a Snickers bar in their pockets. My family would always laugh when we were at dinner and our server would ask who wanted dessert. Maxine would politely say, "No, thank you," perhaps even saying that she shouldn't or couldn't because she was so full, while Junior would order the most chocolatey thing on the menu. Without fail, Maxine would then reach over and pick apart Junior's dessert until there wasn't a smudge of chocolate left. Even as she grew older and started eating less, she could always be counted on to take a bite of whatever sweet treat, preferably chocolatey, was put in front of her.

It's no wonder that every single person in our family has a severe chocolate addiction.

"I'd describe [Maxine and Junior] as two very different people fundamentally in their backgrounds . . . but who have both managed to find wonderful commonalities. . . . They both have a way of trying to get the best from people . . . My mom [encourages] you to do your best and not give up, and my dad is the kind of person who just sees the best in you. He just assumes that you're a good person."

— Barry Bounous, son

"Junior and Maxine have always encouraged Barry and me in our singing and performing. They attended every performance possible and continued attending as our children began performing as well. Their faces were beaming and often teary eyed as they hugged and complimented us after performing. While Junior loved listening to our music, Maxine had a lovely voice and enjoyed singing along and harmonizing when our family sang together.

I cannot adequately express what it means to have had the support of Junior and Maxine. It is very difficult to make a living in the arts, and it has been as much a challenge as a joy to follow our dreams of performing and teaching in the arts. From living in Junior and Maxine's basement for a year, to them helping with student loans, to building a house on his property that we live in today. They truly are heroes for supporting us in the arts!"

— Debra Bounous, daughter-in-law

"One of the key things I see in their relationship is they really enjoy doing things together, whether it's hiking or skiing or traveling. And they spend a lot of time together. They don't spend time apart; it's not like my dad's off doing one thing and my mom's doing something else. They're always concerned that they're doing things together and have the same goals."

— Steve Bounous, son

"Fast Max—she is an amazing little skier. She'll come down a hill [and] . . . she'll say, 'I'm not sure I skied that so well.' And you look at her and you go, 'That was amazing! That was amazing—how can I ski that way?' She's always saying, 'Oh, I need a lesson, I need a lesson.' I have to laugh because Maxine never needs a lesson."

— Judy Fuller, ski legend

". . . Maxine, Nancy Kronthaler, and I were skiing down from the tram. It was really lovely powder. We would ski and then stop and talk for a little bit, and then keep skiing and then stop again and talk. And here I am skiing behind Maxine and Nancy down Chip's Face, and I realize they're talking and still having their conversation while they're skiing down this steep hill in deep powder. I don't know how many people could actually do that.

My nickname for Maxine always was "The Powder Queen" because she didn't always seem super confident, but give her two feet of snow, and she was queen. And her skiing was so beautiful and majestic. She'll always be the powder queen to me."

— Georgia Clark, Snowbird ski instructor

"I can always remember Maxine as a skier that just seems to float over the snow in such an easy manner. She didn't seem to have made any effort to do it—even today. I skied with her up at Mike Wiegele's a few years ago, and she skis the same way with no effort. She can ski through any kind of snow; she's effortless. She's a superb skier."

— Jim McConkey, ski legend

Maxine's father, Urban Overlade, with his award-winning draft horses, Rocky and Rowdy. Likely taken around 1940.

Maxine hiking in the Tetons in her favorite shirt. 1950s.

Maxine at the Rustler Lodge. Mid-1950s.

Maxine as a young woman in the 1940s.

Maxine and Junior on their wedding day, December 12, 1952. The ceremony and the reception were held at Junior's brother Barney's house.

Junior and Maxine snuggling at the Rustler Lodge in 1953 with their little dog, Chico. They picked up Chico while at a service station in Heber. They had been admiring the little dog, which the gas attendant guessed may have been abandoned or accidentally left behind at the station. When the attendant asked if they wanted to take the dog home, Maxine said yes!

Maxine in the old Snowbird orange. Early 1970s.

Maxine, a total babe, is the tiny dancer with perfect posture on the far right. She was part of the chorus for the production of *Kismet* at a theater in Orem in the late 1960s.

Maxine looking pretty in blue. 1990s.

Maxine, a woman of many talents, practicing her swing at the Riverside Country Club. 1970s.

Maxine and a Maxine-sized philodendron leaf in Tahiti. Around the year 2000.

Maxine in her iconic yellow one-piece ski suit while skiing with Mike Wiegele Helicopter Skiing in Canada in the 2000s at almost 80 years old. This photo was used in a *High Country News* Instagram post about vintage ski fashion in the Utah Ski and Snowboard Archives in April 2022.

Maxine and Junior for their 50th wedding anniversary party at Snowbird in 2002. The party was a surprise for Maxine, and it was planned by the newly appointed Snowbird Ski School director Maggie Loring.

Chapter 6

Timp Haven

In 1943, around the time Junior dabbled in teaching, he saw an ad in the *Daily Herald* for the Utah County Division of the Civilian Defense Ski Corps for Mountain Rescue. Junior and his friend Frank Hirst attended the first meeting, along with 20 other young adult women and men.

It turned out to be a pivotal moment in Junior's life. He met Ray Stewart, the founder of Timp Haven, who was in the midst of building a rope tow on his family's property up Provo Canyon. Junior also met fellow Wasatch enthusiasts who became lifelong friends, and he began embarking on more serious journeys through the Wasatch with the mountain rescue group. And most importantly, it was at this meeting that he reconnected with Maxine Overlade.

A few years prior, while living in Salt Lake City, Ray joined the Utah Civilian Defense Ski and Mountain Corps in Salt Lake City and was made chief of the Salt Lake division. When he relocated to Provo, Utah, he was asked to create a Utah County division. He did so and began teaching the division first aid, signaling, map reading, and survival skills—skills that are taught today in wilderness first response courses.

The corps' formation occurred during World War II, and though there were no attacks happening on US soil (besides Pearl Harbor a few years prior), many military planes were moving back and forth across the country and the Mountain West. The group's main focus was to learn how to respond to a plane crash in the mountains, which would require either hiking or skiing to get to the site, depending on the time of year. Ray Stewart's students didn't face any real tests during their time together, but they embarked on long treks through the mountains on skis to practice their skills, gaining knowledge of the Wasatch and backcountry skiing.

Ray Stewart's civilian defense corps never had to make a rescue during the war years, but a few members did respond to a plane crash about 10 years later. Junior was working and living up at Alta at the time and was called south to respond to a plane that had disappeared over Mount Timpanogos during a heavy storm. It was an army plane, a B-25 bomber destined for California. When the storm moved in, the plane was supposed to land in Heber, but the occupants decided that they would shoot for Salt Lake City instead. They were trusting their communication radio to direct them through the storm and over the mountains. They began circling, trying to gain enough altitude to get them over the range. But their flight path took them too close to the broad shoulders of the mighty mountain. Their plane crashed into the side of Timpanogos, 50 to 100 feet below the summit.

Junior was among a group of Alta patrol personnel sent to respond to the crash. By then, he had much more athletic experience in the mountains than when he joined Ray's rescue group, and he was much more prepared to respond to an emergency of this sort. But the storm was of such intensity that the group couldn't even start trekking into the mountains to look for the plane. Mount Timpanogos is vast, and they had no idea where exactly on the mountain it was, nor should they risk their own lives in such avalanche-prone and dangerous conditions. So they waited on standby for two or three days until the storm broke apart enough for another plane to do a flyby and locate the remains of the fallen plane. It had snowed so much that only the tail could be seen, and there was no sign of life. Correctly assuming that no one could survive a crash and storm of that intensity, the group brought body bags.

They started from the Aspen Grove trailhead, their skis cutting through snow so deep that every movement was a challenge, even with skins on the bottom of their skis meant for uphill travel. Those who have done this well-traveled hike in the summer will have some idea of the level of athleticism required to get up to the crash site. Even in fair summer weather, the eight-mile trek and almost 4,000 vertical feet of elevation gain up to about 11,000 feet above sea level are already a feat. Add in freezing temperatures, avalanche danger, a hardy snowpack, plus a few feet of new snow, and the journey becomes formidable. But all four men in the group were seasoned skiers in the Wasatch Mountains. Within a few days they found remnants of the plane, as well as the remains of four of the five passengers on board. All had been killed immediately on impact; the force was such that the pilot had been shoved into the gears and the fifth body had been ejected from the plane entirely. It was not until the end of May, about two and half months after they located the first four bodies, that they were able to return again on skis and recover the fifth body.

Though most of the bomber plane has been stripped away by other hikers, parts of the plane still remain on the side of Mount Timpanogos, under the fateful summit that's been aptly named "Bomber Peak."

Utah Civilian Defense Ski and Mountain Corps headquarters were at Ray's family cabin, up the North Fork tributary canyon of Provo Canyon and near the base of Mount Timpanogos. This location, steeped in its own history, would later become the site of an early rope tow, cable tow, T-bar, and eventually chairlifts that would become Timp Haven and then Sundance Ski Resort.

Ray and his eight siblings were grandchildren and great-grandchildren of Andrew Jackson Stewart Jr. and Andrew Jackson Stewart Sr., who were two prominent surveyors in Utah during the late 1800s. A. J. Stewart Sr. was one of the original surveyors of Provo City and moved his family there in 1851. And A. J. Stewart Jr. continued his father's legacy by making the first sectional and topographical survey of Utah County and creating his own surveying business, which he called Stewart and Sons. In 1899, he and his two sons, Scott (Ray's father) and John, surveyed the area just east of Timpanogos, now known as North Fork Canyon.

Scott and John Stewart saw promise and beauty in North Fork, and they decided to homestead at the base of the mighty Mount Timpanogos and convinced many extended family members to join in homesteading. At that time, the Homestead Act allowed each person 160 acres. By the time the family was able to combine all the acreage by selling it to what the brothers deemed the "North Fork Investment Company," the family had accumulated more than 2,600 acres of land on the east side of Mount Timpanogos, a large portion of which would later become Sundance Ski Resort.

During the summers, the families would make the 16-mile trek from Provo to the homestead in horse-drawn wagons. Scott and John built a handful of small cabins that became their mountain homes at locations known to avid Sundance-enthusiasts today, like Aspen Grove and Stewart Flat. The family would also stay for a few nights over Christmas, and in 1932, Ray and his brother Hank decided that they would spend an entire winter at Aspen Grove. By that time, they both owned store-bought skis and had developed a deep familiarity with the area. If the moon was bright, the brothers would go on ski tours at night, their long shadows gliding across the silver snow, the looming ridges of Mount Timpanogos glistening against the sky. In March, they toured to the top of the Timpanogos glacier, skiing down in big, long traverses. It was likely one of the first, if not the first, descents of that side of Mount Timpanogos on skis.

By the mid 1940s, a few rope tows had been built in the Wasatch that could pull skiers up a small hill. One of those tows, built by a man named J. W. Daniel, had been relocated from its original location in Hobble Creek Canyon, where it hadn't had much success, to North Fork Canyon in the fall of 1944. Those involved didn't manage to clear the area of trees and shrubs and have the tow ready by the time the ski season was going, and the tow suffered another unsuccessful winter. In the spring of 1945, Ray Stewart purchased the rope tow from Daniel for a combined price of $186: $125 for the Chevrolet and the engine responsible for powering the tow, and $61 for 1,200 feet of rope. Sensing a blooming opportunity, Ray was determined to give the device a makeover and get it up and running for the next season.

Junior and his friend Frank Hirst became very involved with Ray in this process, and they helped him deconstruct and reconstruct the tow that summer. The engine had been moved out of the hood to sit on the bed of the deconstructed truck, which still had wheels on it even as it pulled skiers up the hill. A system of V-belt pulleys, connected to those truck wheels, pulled 500 feet of rope up the hill while the other 500 feet of rope was tugged back down the hill. The speed of the tow was determined by the gears of the truck's transmission and how far the throttle was pulled. The team fixed the tow successfully, and, though far from being an official ski resort, the first inkling of Ray's ski business opened once the snow started falling in 1945.

The original owner had built the rope tow almost a mile from the nearest road, which ended at Stewart Flat. Since an area had already been cleared out for the tow and a ski run, Ray kept it there for the first year. This meant that all the required supplies, like the battery for the truck engine, gas, and oil, had to be carried in. Junior and Frank were often tasked with bringing supplies, and they brought gas and oil each time they drove up North Fork. This was more than just a kind gesture like bringing wine to a friend's house. This was during World War II, when gas was hard to come by casually. Because of Ray's involvement with the defense corps, he was given gas rations that they could collect on his behalf. Levi, too, had secured gas rations for the farm and his equipment, and they typically had some surplus they could share with neighbors or give Junior to take up to the rope tow. The batteries for the engine couldn't hold their charge if left for too long in the cold, so every day the rope tow was operating, Junior and Frank helped carry the batteries up to the tow and back down to the parking area, leaky battery acid staining their ski jackets. Junior fondly remembers those days of he and Frank being "packhorses" for Ray.

Besides manual labor and supplies, Junior brought to the tow another asset even more valuable: skiers. Because he could borrow his father's farm truck, which always had a supply of gas and chains for the tires, Junior could bring friends up to ski who would not have had reliable access to the canyon otherwise. This was what Ray needed most—skiers who would continue to return as customers, which would help him get the local reputation and revenue he needed to turn a single rope tow into a ski resort.

These early folks who enjoyed Ray's rope tow didn't have to earn their turns, in the backcountry sense, but they still had to hike to get to the tow because of the distance from the parking lot—that is, if they could even get to Stewart Flat. Provo City did not regularly plow from the Provo Canyon turn off, so Ray's team often had to manually push the snow off the road, and the skiers would have to hike even farther to get to the hill. Or skiers could rely on trucks, like Junior's, that had chains. But these difficulties didn't deter early enthusiasts, and Ray's tow gained popularity during that first season. He charged a dollar for a day pass and waived the fee for anyone who helped maintain the tow.

Those early Timp Haven skiers weren't daunted by the two-mile round-trip hike required to get to the ski hill, but Ray recognized that having the rope tow so far away would discourage other potential clients, in addition to making supply transportation difficult. So, in the summer of 1946, he and Junior and Frank worked to clear a new ski hill. The spot they chose now sits at the base of Sundance Ski Resort. They hired a man named Stanley Roberts to bulldoze the trees, creating a clearing that stretched up the hill about 600 feet for the tow.

Ray worked for Geneva Steel at the time and found a capstan in the scrap pile one day at work. With permission from his boss, Ray took the capstan and attached an engine to it, and it became the new piece of machinery to move the rope and skiers up the hill. Ray then purchased two small cabins to set up the base of the ski hill. One housed the capstan and the towing machinery, the other became a lunch stand for Ray's wife, Ava, to make hamburgers, chili, coffee, and hot cocoa on a two-burner propane gas stove. Timp Haven was beginning to take shape.

When the first rope tow opened, Ray and his team ran it on Saturdays and Sundays. After a second larger rope tow was installed in 1946, Ray, along with Junior's friend Reed Biddulph and a woman named Jessie Schofield, made a request to the city of Provo to install lights on the ski hill to allow for night skiing—the first of its kind in Utah. The request was approved, and folks were able to ski under the lights on Monday, Wednesday, and Friday nights.

Jessie Schofield was the Provo City Recreation Supervisor, and once she saw the growing interest in skiing, she began organizing a bus program to take Utah County residents up to what would soon be known as Timp Haven. She played an integral part in making the rope tow more accessible to the public by facilitating transportation to and eventually relocation of the rope tow. This meant that many people who were unfamiliar with skiing could easily get up to the ski hill to try it out. And if they didn't have any gear of their own, Earl Miller, who owned the local ski shop, Miller Ski Shop, could help them get equipment. Ray may have been the one to purchase the original tow to get it up and running, but the overall success of Timp Haven's early days was a result of local community support.

Involvement from Jessie Schofield and Leona Holbrook, BYU's women's athletic director who hired Junior early on as a teacher for BYU students, led to the creation of Timp Haven's first ski school. Schofield arranged an eight-week program that skiers could purchase for a fee, which included transportation, rope tow rides, and lessons. Holbrook arranged for BYU buses to bring students up in the afternoon after they finished classes. According to a 1947 article from an unknown publication, more than 260 BYU students participated in ski classes during the winter of 1946–47.

This influx of beginner skiers was not unique to Timp Haven. All over the Wasatch, a need for ski instructors was growing. Because the skiing was on Forest Service land, the USDA Forest Service created a certification process that would become a precursor to today's Professional Ski Instructors of America and the American Association of Snowboard Instructors (PSIA-AASI). The Forest Service wanted designated ski instructors teaching on Forest Service land, but it didn't want to actually oversee the certification process. So, in late December of 1946, Felix Koziol, the Forest Service supervisor of the Wasatch-Cache National Forest, designated Sverre and Alf Engen, Art Johansen, and Walter Prager as examiners and gave them the ability to certify those whom they deemed worthy of being ski instructors. Among the first round of ski instructors, and the only one in Utah County, was Earl Miller, the owner of the ski shop. Though Junior had not yet become a certified instructor by Forest Service standards, he, too, assisted in early ski lessons at Timp Haven while he continued to help Ray with the area development.

In late 1946, the ski area gained attention from the local newspapers. On November 10, 1946, *The Salt Lake Tribune* printed a photo of North Fork Creek—Mount Timpanogos standing tall in the background—with this caption: "Who wouldn't be more than willing to be snow-bound in a scenic setting like this?" Another newspaper announced the new ski classes that would be available starting on December 7, 1946, under the direction of Jessie Schofield, and that buses to the mountain would leave the city county building every Saturday morning at 9 a.m. and would cost $0.50 a ride. An article published on November 12, 1946, in the *Daily Herald* highlighted a winter sports show—"the first of its kind in Provo"—that would showcase "the latest in winter sportswear, and a demonstration of ski and skating equipment will feature the show. Ski movies are also scheduled." It was at this show that the name of Timp Haven was announced after Ray had held a competition, calling on the local community to submit potential resort names. Ruth Biddulph won with the iconic name of Timp Haven and was rewarded a season pass as her prize.

Ray knew that in order to keep taking advantage of the growing interest in skiing, he'd have to keep expanding the facilities. So, in the summer of 1947, he decided to bulldoze a larger section of the ski hill they had been on and replaced the rope tow with a cable tow that stretched to the top of the hill. This increased the amount of "inbound skiing" on the designated ski hill and allowed access to what could have been considered "side country skiing" at that time. The cable-tow moved up the pitch of the hill at waist level, and skiers were given small metal hooks with a rope and a small wooden plank to latch onto the cable.

The method proved to be fairly efficient. It did not wear out the clients' gloves like the rope tow did, but it did have its own limitations. Rather than being able to let go of the rope on their own, the skier was hooked into the system and was more responsible for getting off safely. At the base of the cable, the skier was given a metal hook that was attached to a wooden plank by a rope. They would hook the metal part to the cable wire and then hold onto the wooden paddle to get pulled up. The skiers were then responsible for releasing the hook, and they would take the hook and paddle with them back down the hill, wrapping the rope around their waist and knotting it.

The next improvement was a T-bar, which was installed in the fall of 1948. It was built so the cable was suspended about 10 feet in the air, with ropes that hung down with metal upside-down T's that skiers could put in between their legs to get pulled up. There was a slightly traumatic moment when Maxine's pants got stuck in the "T." Unable to get free when she'd normally disembark the T-bar, Maxine was pulled by the machinery around the pulley and back down the hill on the flat of her back. Eventually the guys running the machine at the bottom realized what was happening and stopped the machinery.

Right around the time the T-bar was installed, Junior started working at Alta. He had met Alf Engen in 1947 and began taking lessons from him—not just ski lessons, but lessons on teaching others how to ski. In 1948 he passed the Forest Service's instructor examination and became a certified ski instructor. Alf hired him immediately, and that winter Junior lived in the Alta Lodge's employee housing. This move didn't stop Junior's participation at Timp Haven, however. He taught at Alta from Sunday through Friday, and then on Saturdays, his one day off during the week, he would drive down to Timp Haven to teach there.

Ray then decided that he wanted to build a chairlift. After seeing Alta build its first chairlift using old mining equipment, Ray had been keeping a lookout for old mining equipment up for sale. He and Junior hiked into Mary Ellen Gulch once to check out a line of cable system that had been left there by a mining company. The mining company was now looking to sell it, but whoever purchased it would be responsible for removing it from the remote location. The cable system was still suspended in the air and stretched for miles from Mary Ellen Gulch to Tibble Fork Canyon up American Fork Canyon. Ray and Junior decided the cable would be too much of a project.

Then in 1953, Ray found a single chairlift that had been stationed near Kimball Junction and was listed for sale for $3,500. Junior, along with Ray's brother Paul, decided that they would contribute their own money to help pay for the ski lift, and a partnership was formed between the three of them. They dismantled the lift, relocated it to Timp Haven, and installed it adjacent to the T-bar. Patrons who rode on the new lift enjoyed 600 feet in elevation gain.

In 1958, Junior was hired as the ski school director at Sugar Bowl Resort. He relocated his young family to the Sierra Nevada during the winters for the next 10 years. While he was gone, Ray and Paul began arguing about how to run Timp Haven. Paul, who had always had more money than Ray and technically owned the land that Timp Haven sat on, built a new restaurant and started making upgrades on facilities. Paul wanted a higher return for his monetary involvement, which was something that Ray couldn't provide. Ray, who worked full time at Geneva Steel, had been running the resort with almost no capital or compensation. After a few years of disagreements, Ray finally decided in 1960 that he had to sell the resort to his brother.

After that, it was just Paul and Junior in business together. It was only another year or two before they also got into a disagreement. Paul, who was a devout Latter-day Saint, wanted the ski lifts and all of the area operations to close on Sundays. Junior, who recognized that their clientele wasn't limited to members of The Church of Jesus Christ of Latter-day Saints, thought that the lifts should remain running to accommodate those folks who want to ski on Sundays. This brought about the end of their partnership, and Paul bought out Junior in 1964. And of course, as anyone working in the ski industry today knows, operating only one day during the weekend did not cut it financially. Within a few years, Timp Haven had to resume operation on Sundays.

That did not end Junior's involvement in Timp Haven, however. When Paul decided it was time to install a second chairlift, he hired Junior to work during the summers and clear the hillsides. Junior moved from

California back to Utah in 1967 and began getting involved in Timp Haven once more. Paul let Junior have control of both the ski shop, which offered rentals and repairs, and the ski school.

Junior quickly realized that the real money maker was not just the normal ski school, but the learn-to-ski programs that Leonna Holbrook and Jessie Schofield had started during the early days of Timp Haven. Junior immediately expanded the programs, organizing city buses to bring folks from the cities of Orem and Provo first, and then Payson and Lehi. And now with two children old enough to fend for themselves, Maxine was able to participate more in ski instructing than she had since giving birth to Barry in 1956. She helped develop a ski program geared toward kids in the fifth and sixth grades. These youth programs, which were staggered to accommodate thousands of kids, are still relevant in Utah today. Maxine and Junior understood that if you could interest children in skiing at a young age, they could encourage siblings and parents to get into skiing as well. And they might become lifelong, passionate patrons for decades to come.

While at Sugar Bowl, Junior had become more involved in gear development. He was hired as an advisor to the HEAD ski company and was also a Rosemount boot technician. He started selling HEAD skis and Rosemount boots at the Timp Haven ski shop and earned commission from the sales. He was so valuable to HEAD that they even gave him and Maxine a Chevrolet for their personal use.

During this time, the resort kept expanding to include more lifts and T-bars, as well as a lodge—the foundation of which is still underneath the general store and Grill Room. Paul Stewart had decided to subdivide his property in Stewart Flat and sell plots of land for housing development, and Junior and Maxine began looking at the lots, thinking they would purchase one. Sadly for us, their descendants, they never did make a purchase.

Robert Redford purchased one of those lots from Paul in 1969 and began building a house there. That same year, Junior and Maxine happened to hire the same contractor to build a house in Provo—the home that Junior still lives in today. Junior, Maxine, and Redford would spend time visiting each other's houses to see how the building was coming along. Redford, a rising star within Hollywood, had married a woman from Provo in the 1950s and had fallen in love with the Utah mountains. He purchased the Stewart Flat property without knowing that he would soon after buy the entire resort. He had recently finished filming *Butch Cassidy and the Sundance Kid* when Paul expressed interest in selling Timp Haven.

Junior had been interested in purchasing the ski area as well, but he didn't have the means for the nearly $1 million price tag. Redford, not quite a wealthy celebrity yet, didn't have the financial means either. But Redford did have connections, and he reached out to a few of his financially successful friends on the East Coast to see if they'd be willing to help him purchase the area. In 1969, the same year that *Butch Cassidy and the Sundance Kid* was released, Timp Haven changed ownership, and Redford changed the name to Sundance as a nod to his character in the film.

Redford kept Junior on to assist with area development and to remain in charge of the ski school and ski shop. By this time, Junior supervised more than 100 ski instructors. He was content with remaining at Sundance for the foreseeable future; it was the closest ski area to his home, and he had managed to build a small empire of a ski school within just a few short years—a school formed under Junior Bounous Ski Incorporated.

Right around the same time Redford purchased Timp Haven, another person set their sights on developing a new ski resort in the Wasatch. Ted Johnson, a passionate Alta skier, had quietly been purchasing mining claims down the canyon from Alta for years. Finally, he had accumulated enough to make known his intentions of building a new ski resort there. Ted reached out to Junior, and during the early spring of that year, Junior began designing runs and clearing hillsides to develop Snowbird Ski Resort. Junior had initially been hired for run design, and he had no intention of being the ski school director. But in the fall of 1971, on the cusp of the resort opening, Ted still didn't have a ski school director. Disappointed with his options, Ted reached out to Junior, though he hadn't applied for the job.

It was an excellent opportunity, and Junior, a powder hound from his days at Alta, could not pass the job up despite the far distance and despite his relationship with Robert Redford. Sundance is much lower in elevation than Snowbird and experiences completely different weather patterns at times. A storm that rolls through the Wasatch can dump 10 inches at Snowbird while the base of Sundance gets only rain or even has blue skies. Junior had had that taste of true Wasatch powder, and he knew the Snowbird terrain from skiing backcountry there for years while working at Alta. He accepted the job.

Sundance still holds a special valley within Junior's mountainous heart. It represents his earliest entry into skiing as a career. Those years at Timp Haven were full of hard work. But they were also filled with thrills and excitement. Junior, Frank Hirst, Ray Stewart, and all of the others involved were trailblazing in many ways—in how to build and operate skiing machinery, how to manage public accessibility to the mountains, how skiers interacted with mountain landscapes and how to design runs, in public engagement, how to build a ski school from the ground up, and how to run a skiing business.

"My mom took lessons at Sundance from Junior . . . There was this one time when my mom was with a few other women, and they were taking a lesson with Junior, and at the end of the lesson Junior said, "Well, ladies, your lesson is over, and I have to go meet my private lesson." And they said, "Well, we want to see your private lesson—we want to know who it is." And he said, "Okay, line up and I'll tell you who it is, and if you race to the bottom, you'll be able to see him."

So they all lined up, and my mom sat there looking at them thinking that by the time all the ladies would get down there, he'd be on the chairlift. She decided to just sit there and wait to see them at the top of the lift. And then Junior said it was Robert Redford and skied away. So my mom sat there on the ground at the top and waited for Junior to get off the chairlift with Robert, and Robert fell on his butt because it was before he knew how to ski. Junior was teaching him so Robert could look like he knew what he was doing when he starred in the film Downhill Racer.

I skied with Junior once at Sundance when I was just skiing around by myself and bumped into him. He asked if I wanted to take a run. The next thing I know, I'm following behind him trying to keep up, and I wound up flying through the air. You always end up in the air when following behind Junior because he always jumps off something unexpectedly that you didn't even know was there because he knows the terrain so well."

— Joan Berrett, family friend

Ray Stewart (far left) and the Utah Civilian Defense Ski and Mountain Corps in 1943. Junior is third from the right. Note Junior's dirty white pants; he was hard at work at Timp Haven prior to this photo being taken.

Fast Max teaching a group of students at Timp Haven in the 1950s, when Junior and Maxine would teach six days a week at Alta and one day a week at Timp Haven.

Junior passing out awards at Timp Haven. 1960s.

Junior teaching Robert Redford's then-wife, Lola Redford, how to ski. Photo taken around 1966, prior to Redford's purchase of Timp Haven.

Junior airborne at Timp Haven in 1967. Mount Timpanogos is in the background.

Barry headed into a tuck at Timp Haven in the late 1960s.

Junior and Maxine on a wildflower hike with a friend on Mount Timpanogos in 1979.

Chapter 7

Like an Eagle

When Junior was 75 years old or so, he had an experience that not many 20- or 30-year-olds would have been able to accomplish. He was skiing at Snowbird late one afternoon with Doug Pfeiffer, one of the founding members of PSIA who later became the editor in chief for *Ski Magazine*. They had been cruising around with a conservancy group led by Alan Engen. Somehow Junior and Doug, perhaps thinking they'd take a classic Bounous shortcut, became separated from the group. Junior led Doug over to the cliffs that are skier's right of Anderson's Hill, just around the corner and out of sight from where the Peruvian lift now traverses. Junior was planning on taking a more mellow route to the bottom, but Doug, seeing what he thought was fresh powder just underneath a rope line, ducked the rope, despite Junior calling for him to stop. Junior, knowing what was beneath that rope line and the situation Doug had just gotten himself into, had no choice but to follow.

The two of them, both in their 70s, were "cliffed out." A band of cliffs wraps around the entire slope, and there's no way down but to jump or to hike out. Pfeiffer had skied all the way down to the edge of the cliff, and Junior told Pfeiffer they'd have to hike out of there. Thinking it'd be easier than trying to sidestep his way back up to Junior, Pfeiffer took off both skis. One immediately fell out of his grasp and tumbled off the cliff. So Junior skied down to Pfeiffer to break trail for him so he could hike up. But it was deep, deep powder that day, and Junior realized their efforts were in vain. They were going to have to jump.

After some testing, Junior and Pfeiffer determined that Pfeiffer's boots could fit Junior's skis. Pfeiffer was a strong skier, but Junior was the stronger jumper. Junior would be the one to send it off the cliff on just one ski.

By this time, the resort was closed for the day. Ski patrol, knowing the two of them were up there, were waiting at the bottom of the cliff.

Pfeiffer went first, disappearing into what was luckily a deep, soft landing. Then it was Junior's turn.

I was with Junior once when he was telling this story to a group of people. At this point, one person, who has some experience jumping off cliffs, asked, "Did you bail sideways?"

Junior replied, "No."

The person followed up and asked, "You tried to land it with just one ski in your 70s?"

Junior responded confidently, "I did land it. I don't bail." And then everyone around the table heckled the questioning person. Junior Bounous doesn't bail.

Junior's notoriety as a jumper began prior to his notoriety as an American ski instructor. While he helped Ray Stewart clear areas for ski runs, he also helped build the area's first ski jump. It was a Nordic jump, and skiers brave enough to jump it would fly over 100 feet. The problem with the jump was that the creek was close to the bottom of the hill (the creek has since been redirected to its current location), and a skier who had just successfully landed the jump would then have to jump over the creek to avoid ending up in the bank or in the water. Then they'd have to jump over the road before they could try to turn their skis to slow down.

After Junior won the cross-country race at Alta, he began taking lessons from Alf Engen. Nordic combined—a competition that combined the scores of a cross-country race and a ski jump—was very popular back then. Junior took a few jumping lessons from Alf, but it was when he started working for Alf as a ski instructor that his jumping technique would really progress. It was at Alta that Junior started more seriously experimenting with what would soon be known as "gelande" jumping.

While gelande jumping had been around for more than 100 years in Scandinavia, it was the skiers at Alta in the 1940s, '50s, and '60s who caused it to garner significant national and international attention. The word *gelande* comes from the German word *geländesprung*, *gelände* meaning "terrain," and *sprung* meaning "to leap or jump." Terrain jumping differed from Nordic jumping, where the jump was more man-made and often had a ramp to assist the skier in catching air. As Nordic jumping progressed, jumpers started to have their heels loose from the skis, allowing the skiers more freedom while in the air. Gelande jumping was the act of sending it, heels locked in, off whatever the terrain presented—be it a rock, a cliff, a snowbank, a rooftop, or a cornice.

Gelande jumping at Alta would become a famous ski jumping event in the 1960s, but in those early days it was mostly instructors and local personalities jumping off anything and everything. Alongside other air-happy folks like Alf Engen and Jim McConkey, Junior began jumping off cliffs, cornices, and whatever else he could physically get his skis to catch air. He once sailed so far off a rock on the Baldy shoulder, not anticipating the way the steep slope would fall far, far away as he flew through the air, that it's named Bounous Rock. In one classic photo captured by notable ski photographer Fred Lindholm and featured on the cover of this book, Junior is jumping off the roof of the Bounous' house near Grizzly Gulch—Maxine with Barry as a babe-in-arms watching from their porch, Mount Superior in the background.

One memorable gelande jumping experience occurred while Junior was skinning up Mount Timpanogos with a group of people including Jim Shane. They had made it up to Provo Cirque, which they used to call Stewart Cirque, and most of the group turned around to ski down. Junior and Shane saw a cornice that they wanted to get to the top of, so they continued climbing to its base. The crest of the cornice loomed 20 or 30 feet above them. Without considering the fact that the cornice could break, the two of them took off their skis and stuck the tails of them into the cornice, creating a makeshift ladder with their four skis they could step on to get to the top.

They enjoyed the view for a while, but then it was time to get off the cornice. Shane asked if they should make another ladder to get back down. In response, Junior stepped back into his skis, backed up a bit, and flew off of the cornice. He stopped after landing so he could make sure Shane got down all right. Shane was petrified. He was not the fearless jumper that Junior was, and he was stuck on top of the cornice by himself. Junior hiked back up to the base of it, and Shane decided he'd rather jump off without skis than with them. So, with Junior standing beneath him to try and catch the skis if they landed and started sliding, Shane threw his skis down. They both stuck straight up in the snow. Then Shane slid as far down on the cornice as he could before jumping off, landing on his butt in the powder 20 feet below. It was an experience neither of them would soon forget.

In 1953, Junior had the chance to participate in a truly unique event. A man named Art Theobold, who ran the Utah State Fairgrounds in Salt Lake City, contacted Alf and Sverre Engen. He wanted to build a ski jump at the fairgrounds and host a ski jumping tournament that would take place at the fairgrounds, not during the winter, but in September. He contacted the Engens in hopes that they would lead the charge and generate public interest in the event. They agreed, and in the summer of 1953, a 110-foot-tall Nordic ski jump was built. According to *First Tracks: A Century of Skiing in Utah*, 90 tons of steel scaffolding and 60,000 pounds of lumber were used to construct the jump.

Once the structure itself had been built, the next challenge was creating snow during Utah's hottest season. A local facility cranked out ice as quickly as it could, which was then crushed on site and blown onto the hill. Hay and haystacks cushioned the finishing arena to create resistance to help the skiers stop and to cushion them if they couldn't stop on their own.

Alf gathered a crew of about 12 individuals to participate in the tournament. Junior was one of them, along with the three Engen brothers and Alf's son, Alan. The contestants had to hike up the scaffolding structure to get to the top, and there is a photo of Junior and Corey Engen, skis on their shoulders, partway up the jump. A large crowd turned up to see the event. Junior recalls the unique experience, remembering how, after they landed the jump, the contestants had to sit back with their hips below their knees, so they didn't get pitched forward as they charged into a pile of straw in the flats at 50 miles per hour.

In the 1960s, gelande jumping transitioned from a casual sport to a competitive one. Alf organized the first official gelande-jumping competition in 1963, while Junior was working at Sugar Bowl. In a letter written for the sake of the judges, Alf laid out a few differences between Nordic jumping and gelande jumping. While a Nordic jumper's legs are straight and their skis are in a "V" shape, gelande jumpers typically have their knees bent "in an exaggerated tuck" with their arms and poles in a more forward and aggressive position. The first competition was held on an old mine dump at the base of High Rustler, and, according to *First Tracks: A Century of Skiing in Utah*, "after two hard landings and breaking two pairs of skis, Alan Engen ended up the winner."

Jim Gaddis, a local ski racer who had recently won the NCAA Alpine Combined title while racing for the University of Utah, became Alta's public relations director the following year. Inspired by the success of the previous year, Gaddis took the competition to a national level, and in 1965, Alta hosted the first National Gelande Championship. Gaddis moved the competition to the mine dump near the bottom of Collins Lift, where spectators could more easily gather and watch the jumpers fly. That year Keith Lange took the win, and he would later become one of the most notorious gelande jumpers of that era.

Junior competed almost every year the gelande competition was held. As he recalls, he placed between 10th and 2nd and everywhere in between until 1971, when, at 45 years old, he took first at the National Gelande Championship. When the competition returned in 1989 to honor Alta's 50th anniversary, Junior took second in the senior division. And his son Steve took third in the official competition—a surprise podium.

Though he was a professional racer and knew his way around the cliffs at Snowbird quite well, Steve hadn't competed in much jumping, if you don't count the times he and Barry jumped the Alta National Gelande Championship when they were kids. Steve even took first place in the under–12 years old division one year.

During one particularly memorable competition, a surprise guest came to the event. It was Junior's turn to jump, but as he got ready to take off, he noticed a man hiding in the trees nearby, looking as though he were about to jump as well. The man was wearing skis and nothing else. Not wanting the man to endanger both of them by trying to jump alongside him, Junior waved the man to go ahead and jump—right as the announcer declared that Junior Bounous was the next competitor. The naked man hit the jump and flew through the air, landing before a crowd who all thought the man to be Junior Bounous. Fully clothed Junior Bounous then took his turn and cleared up any confusion.

Alta ceased holding the competition in 1974. It had become so popular, even airing on ABC's *Wide World of Sports* in 1969, that the crowds had become too wild and rambunctious to handle. Most of the spectators weren't even skiers and just made the trek up the canyon to watch the event. Junior remembers there would be beer cans and food packaging littering the hillside afterward, and Alf would often take it upon himself to clean up. They eventually canceled the competition, but not until after it had made a lasting impact on the world of skiing. Besides the jumping itself, the event became one of the first places where aerial freestyle skiing made its debut. According to *First Tracks: A Century of Skiing in Utah*, some of the first front and back flips used in competition were during the National Gelande Championship.

It's easy to take gelande jumping for granted these days. Most people on the hill today are trained from a young age to leap off cat tracks or catch air off bumps along the tree line, and many feel comfortable jumping off cliffs. But in the 1940s and '50s, serious jumping was still gaining momentum. While Nordic jumping had gained popularity in the early 1900s, terrain jumping was still a relatively new form of skiing, and mid-century Alta skiers are credited with being some of the first to harness the "coolness" of gelande jumping and make it a nationally acclaimed sport. Today, of course, people don't really refer to the sport as gelande jumping. The more common phrase is *sending it*.

"Some of the things he did people would maybe . . . say, 'My gosh, look at this crazy man jumping off all these cliffs.' But Junior . . . was always cognizant of the time and the place and the conditions. And when they were right, yes—he would do many, many things that would just leave everybody's mouths wide open."

— Alan Engen, Alta skier and historian

"I was on patrol [at Snowbird] in '72, and we had the Gelande in the springtime, and I was 24 years old. A lot of us at Snowbird jumped in the Gelande at Alta. We were thinking we were pretty hot back then. It turned out that this older 47-year-old fella basically kicked our ass in the Gelande, and he won it."

— Mongo, Snowbird patrol

"Junior and Jim [McConkey] would jump off some big things. I remember going to the one rock, and I'm looking up and, you know, we're way up there—even by today's standards, you were way up there. And they were in their 30s, between 30 and 35. And my God, they went off big stuff. Huge."

— Mike Wiegele, Sugar Bowl instructor and
the owner of Mike Wiegele Helicopter Skiing

"Well, we sure enjoyed jumping and challenging each other, trying to outdo each other in a friendly way, and it was a lot of fun. And we would pick these rocks and cliffs and cornices to jump off, get the blood circulating, and we learned how to kind of stay back when you land so you keep from being pitched forward. It was a challenge between the two of us, and I say each trying to outdo each other but, you know, in a very friendly way."

— Jim McConkey, ski legend

Junior and Corey Engen at the Utah State Fair in the summer of 1953. If you look at the snow to the left of Junior, you can see the hay they used to create the landing. The ice machine, blowing crushed ice up the hill, is near Junior's right ear.
Special Collections, J. Willard Marriott Library, The University of Utah

Junior competing at the Alta's National Gelande Championship in 1971 (the year he won). Note his HEAD skis and HEAD poles and the Rosemount boots with a spring on the heel and no brakes on the skis. As a 45-year-old, Junior beat many men half his age to take the win.

Junior jumping off a cornice at Alta sometime in the early 1950s. It was likely off the Wildcat ridgeline cornice.
Fred Lindholm

Steve working on his jumping technique at Timp Haven, with Mount Timpanogos in the background. Late 1960s.

Junior in 1962 jumping off a cornice on Mount Timpanogos during a heli-skiing excursion.

Junior competing at Alta's 50th Anniversary Gelande Tournament in 1989.

Junior on the podium for Alta's 50th Anniversary Gelande Tournament in April 1989. He snagged second place in the senior division, while Gene Christiansen got first and Alan Engen took third. *Special Collections, J. Willard Marriott Library, The University of Utah*

Junior and Steve after competing together in Alta's 50th Anniversary Gelande Tournament in 1989. Junior borrowed one of Steve's racing suits for the event and both Bounouses were on the podium. (Junior took second in the senior division, Steve third in the professional division.)

Steve in flight during Alta's 50th Anniversary Gelande Tournament in 1989. Steve took third in the main event.

Chapter 8

Alta Magic

The decade that Junior worked at Alta was a critical one. It would be here that his own skiing ability would drastically improve and where he would truly fall in love with instructing, with Little Cottonwood Canyon, and with powder skiing. It was also where he and Maxine would begin their life together.

When Junior began working at Alta at the end of 1948, he and the resort shared similar trajectories. Alta was not yet the "place to be," but, like Junior when he was hired, it was on the cusp of becoming something great. And the catalyst pushing both Junior and the ski resort toward greatness was the enthusiasm of the same person—Alf Engen.

Decades prior to either Junior or Alf skiing up Little Cottonwood Canyon, Alta had been a very prominent mining town, boasting thousands of seasonal residents at times. That success was short-lived. Around the turn of the century, many of the mineral veins had nearly dried up, and by the early 1930s, Alta was a ghost town. The only person who stuck around after the final mining bust was one eccentric resident, the self-proclaimed "mayor" of Alta: George Watson.

Watson was born in Michigan in 1883 and moved to the Wasatch at the age of 19 in hopes of striking it rich as a miner. An article published in the December 1946 issue of *The Utah Magazine* describes how Watson ended up out west:

> *In 1903, [Watson] was looking for news of the new silver strikes in Utah, for he had come West as the pathfinder for a group of young Michigan miners who had agreed that the fellow among them who drew the longest straw should make the trek. George drew the straw and out he came.*

But Watson was about a generation too late; the bulk of Alta's mining boom had occurred at the end of the 1800s. As the town's financial success dwindled, most abandoned it. Hoping for another wave of mining frenzy, Watson acquired 80 "worthless" mining claims—worthless in regard to the dying mining industry, but those claims were about to become priceless in another budding industry. Watson hadn't struck silver like he had intended; he had struck something soft and white that glittered—snow.

While Watson sat on these claims, with debt gathering and without a clear path ahead, the United States was transforming. Franklin D. Roosevelt had passed the First New Deal in 1933, stimulating the US economy through a variety of public service projects. There was a Civil Conservation Corps (CCC) camp located at the base of Big Cottonwood Canyon, and it was from here that the US Forest Service drew the manpower to build trails and infrastructure in the Wasatch Mountains. The increased number of skiers frequenting the Wasatch in the 1930s had not gone unnoticed by the Forest Service, and it recognized the need for avalanche research, backcountry navigation, crowd control, and emergency response. The Forest Service began recruiting people to help them mitigate these concerns.

Two of these people were Alf Engen and his brother Sverre. Alf was hired by the US Forest Service as a recreational supervisor in 1935. That same year, the Union Pacific Railroad baron Averell Harriman sent Austrian Count Felix Schaffgotsch to the American West in search of a site the railroad company could develop into the country's first luxury ski resort. Schaffgotsch met up with Alf in Salt Lake City in November 1935, and the two of them scoured the nearby mountains in search of a potential ski area. Two of the locations were Alta and Brighton, both of which Schaffgotsch passed on. He ended up backtracking to Ketchum, Idaho, in 1936, which he deemed fit for Harriman's resort, Sun Valley. Alf, on the other hand, saw great potential in both Brighton and Alta, as well as Snowbasin.

At Alf's suggestion, the Forest Service began looking at Alta as a viable location for a ski area. It was beautiful, accessible, and already had material from the old mining camps that could be used for ski area infrastructure. But there were some concerns. Decades of intense mining and town-building had stripped the slopes of all the trees, destabilizing the yearly snowpack. The mining town had always been plagued by destructive avalanches because of this. But with FDR's signing of the New Deal and the CCC camp at the base of Big Cottonwood Canyon, where Alf worked, the Forest Service had an army of workers to reforest the canyon and to begin studying the new practice of avalanche mitigation.

Another concern was finding interested parties to rally behind and fund the project. The Wasatch Mountain Club had already utilized the land at Brighton for backcountry excursions, so its members were the ones most involved with building a lodge and a rope tow at Brighton. Ray

Stewart and the Timpanogos Mountain Club did the same for Timp Haven. But there wasn't one person or organization so involved with Alta, yet.

Here enters another key player in Alta's creation: a man by the name of S. J. (Joe) Quinney. Quinney was a Utah native, born in Logan in 1892. He graduated from Harvard with a law degree and then was elected to the Utah House of Representatives in 1921. Quinney became involved in skiing when his two children started competing in ski events. While watching his son jump, Quinney met some of the local Norwegian jumping enthusiasts, including Pete Ecker (after whom Ecker Hill was named). Together, Quinney and Ecker established the Utah Ski Club, of which Quinney was the president from 1935 to 1938. The US National Jumping Championship was held at Ecker Hill in 1937 under his direction, and the event was widely accepted to be one of the largest and most successful sporting events held in Utah at the time. Quinney was disappointed when Schaffgotsch visited Utah and passed on the state's potential ski areas, and the rejection fueled Quinney's desire to build Utah's own ski resort.

The true pinnacle of Alta's creation was a confluence of three things: George Watson's financial trouble and ownership of much of the land, the Forest Service heeding Alf Engen's advice to build a ski area up Little Cottonwood Canyon, and Joe Quinney—a man with finances and legal expertise—developing an interest in the ski industry. The following is a paragraph about Quinney, Watson, and the Forest Service's three-way deal from the winter 2008 edition of *Alta Powder News*:

> *Joe Quinney's law firm, Ray, Quinney and Nebeker, in Salt Lake City represented the American Smelting and Refining Company which held mortgages on the Alta United Mines Company, owned by a gentleman named George H. Watson. Because of tax delinquency problems concerning the Alta claims he owned, Watson was looking for a way out of his predicament. After much discussion, a plan was set in motion where-by Alta United Mines Company would arrange the conveyance of the surface rights to its claims to the U.S. Forest Service. For that, Watson would be relieved of his delinquent tax obligations and the Forest Service would make the Alta area available to the skiing public.*

Quinney helped establish the Salt Lake Winter Sports Association in conjunction with this move. The corporation would be the one to raise $10,000 to build Alta's first lift, Collins Lift, named after an old Alta prospector by the name of Charles Collins. As the corporation's secretary-treasurer from 1939 to 1958, Quinney did all legal work involved in Alta's early days. Quinney thought skiing should be accessible to everyone, not just the wealthy, and he worked diligently to make sure that Alta's prices were raised only to cover operational costs. He was perhaps one of the most important and early figures to think Alta should avoid mass commercialization and should be a slow-moving place where people could admire the beauty of the surrounding mountains.

While Quinney worked tirelessly behind the scenes at Alta, Watson became the public personality associated with the ski area. Watson had sold all his mining claims to the Forest Service for a dollar. It was a win-win for him; he was able to get rid of his debt, while becoming a local "hero" for helping to develop Alta. He was already a skier from his days commuting around Alta as a miner, and he loved the idea of it becoming a ski area. Being the colorful character that he was, he insisted in conversations that Alta be called "Romantic Alta." He continued to be very involved with and passionate about the resort for the rest of his life. He passed away peacefully in his sleep in his home at Alta in 1952. Both Quinney and Watson were inducted into the US National Ski Hall of Fame for their contributions to Alta's development.

Alf Engen and his two brothers, Sverre and Corey, were born in Norway, the sons of a talented skier who tragically died during the 1918 Spanish flu pandemic. In 1929, at the ages of 20 and 18, Alf and Sverre traveled to America, settling briefly in Chicago before moving out west. Both brothers immediately began competing in ski jumping and Nordic competitions, and they quickly made a name for themselves as some of the most prominent ski competitors in North America.

In the next half-century, Alf would go on to claim 16 US National Championship titles and more than 500 sports trophies. In 1931, just two short years after immigrating, Alf won the National Professional Jumping Championship at the age of 22. In 1940 he was awarded the American Ski Trophy by the National Ski Association. He coached the Olympic team in 1948, received the Skier of the Century Award in 1950, and in 1966, won the Utah Ski Cup.

It's easy to list athletic achievements because they are often accompanied by an award or a title. It's harder to list Alf's most impressive accomplishments in that same way. His ski area development with the Forest Service resulted in the creation of Alta, Brighton, Snowbasin, and Bogus Basin—just to name a few. He also helped clear and design runs and build Nordic jumps for countless other ski areas, including Bald Mountain and Ruud Mountain at Sun Valley. Alf also was a key player in the early success of powder skiing, and his role as a teacher would have far-reaching impacts on

American skiing. It could easily be said that Alf was one of the most noticeable and influential skiers of the 20th century.

Sverre was also a successful competitor and played an important role in ski area development. He and his wife, Lois, initially purchased a small cabin at a place called "Fish Camp" in the San Bernardino Mountains, outside of Los Angeles. They transformed the area into Snow Valley Ski Resort, and then sold it to a group of Hollywood celebrities in 1939. Upon returning to Utah, Sverre worked at Alta as America's very first Forest Service "Snow Ranger" and was awarded the Silver Merit Star by the National Ski Patrol System for saving a man's life after an avalanche at Alta in 1945. He served in the 10th Mountain Division and became Alta's seventh ski school director upon returning from the war. In 1948 Sverre handed the Engen Ski School over to Alf, so he could build and manage Alta's Rustler Lodge. Sverre would go on to become a successful ski filmmaker, and he filmed Junior on many occasions.

Corey (born Kaare) and his mother followed Alf and Sverre to America a few years after the brothers made the crossing. A very successful competitor like his brothers, Corey started ski instructing at Sun Valley, and then served as captain of the 1948 US Olympic ski team. He placed third in the jumping portion of the Olympic classic combined event, which included jumping and cross-country. He would later become the ski school director at Snowbasin Resort.

All three Engen brothers are in the National Ski Hall of Fame.

Junior started skiing at Alta a few years after it opened, when a friend from high school suggested they check out the ski area. Junior hadn't quite mastered turning by that time, and as strange as it sounds, he remembers feeling quite out of control. He wouldn't even go up Collins Lift; he would just ride Rustler, a little bucket chair later destroyed by an avalanche. (Whoever decided to build a chairlift at the base of High Rustler clearly did not have much foresight.) As Junior said in his own words, "The run was so steep, my gosh. I don't know how I ever survived without getting hurt." This would have been in the early 1940s, and Junior remembers seeing the 10th Mountain Division of the US Army on skis, training at Alta. According to Junior, none of them knew how to turn yet, either.

His novice skiing skills, of course, didn't remain novice for long. By 1945, he had won the cross-country race at Brighton. Junior then started taking lessons from Alf at Alta, while Alf's brother Sverre was the ski school director. Over the course of the next two winters, Junior first took cross-country lessons, then jumping and downhill lessons. And finally, of course, Junior began learning how to be a ski instructor.

In 1946 the Forest Service decided that it wanted a certification program to regulate who was qualified to teach skiing on Forest Service land. They hired Alf and Sverre as two of their examiners. Alf advised Junior that he should take the exam, and, in November of 1948, with Sverre and Alf as his examiners, Junior passed. He remembers his test being all of five minutes, one ski run from the top to the bottom.

It's strange to think about now, but initially, Junior didn't have much interest in working up Little Cottonwood Canyon. He had built relationships in Utah County and Timp Haven, and it was there he thought he would end up teaching the most. But destiny had a different plan. At the end of 1948, there was a convergence of three things that nudged Junior in an unexpected direction: Junior becoming a certified Forest Service ski instructor, Alf taking over the ski school at Alta, and the man whom Alf hired as his assistant breaking his leg badly right at the start of the season. Alf immediately called Junior and offered him the assistant job, even though Junior had never been an official instructor before. Alf's intuition told him Junior would handle the responsibilities just fine.

Because Little Cottonwood Canyon often closed due to heavy snowfall, Alta needed some of its employees to live at the resort to keep it running for guests staying up the canyon. Since the Bounous family farm didn't operate during the winter, Junior was free to relocate. So, a few short days after getting the call from Alf, Junior packed up a bag with his winter clothing and boots, chucked his skis in the car, drove up Little Cottonwood Canyon, and moved into an employee dormitory in the Alta Lodge.

And that's how Junior Bounous was thrown headfirst into the realm of ski teaching. Here was this novice instructor, a fruit farmer from Provo with flower stickers all over his beat-up skis, now second-in-command at what was about to become one of the most prominent ski schools in North America. But when Junior arrived, the ski school was still in its early years of development. There were only a handful of full-time instructors besides Junior, including Alf's wife, Evelyn, and Sverre's wife, Lois. Charles Graziano was another. The Alta family was small, and Junior's arrival created friendly ripples of interest through the community.

Junior recalls one of the lift operators who also lived full time at Alta, a man named Warren Balsevian and nicknamed "Baldy," being exceptionally intrigued at why this young "prune picker" had been hired as Alf's assistant. Junior remembers, "We were in the Alta Lodge basement, and Baldy said let's see what skis you're using. He looked at the skis, and the edges that I'd put on had broken sections. Here are all these jagged-looking edges, with chunks and parts missing out of them on both skis. And he looked at me and said, 'This is what you're going to ski on?' And I said, 'Oh, yeah. These are my skis.' And he kept telling everyone what a goofball I was, and that my equipment was so bad."

Baldy, nor anyone else a little skeptical about the "prune picker," would question Junior's talent for long. What Junior lacked in official experience he made up for in his athletic ability, his easy-going nature, his knack for adventure, his sense of humor, and, as Alf had predicted, his quick ability to learn and his natural instincts as a teacher.

Junior settled into life at the Alta Lodge easily. It was a completely different lifestyle from the one he had been living on his father's farm in Provo, but he was ambitious and was used to hard work. Junior taught at Alta six days a week. On Saturdays, his one day off when the weekend instructors would take the reins, he'd drive south to teach at Timp Haven. The pay Junior received from both Timp Haven and Alta wasn't much, but since room and board was covered at the resort, he wasn't spending much money.

Junior was hired at the cusp of a ski instructing wave. The interest in skiing rapidly grew, and the need for ski instructors grew as well. Within a year of hiring Junior, Alf and Sverre, along with Felix Koziol from the Forest Service, made the ski instructor certification process more official with a pin certification system for the Intermountain Ski Association. Junior had passed the earliest version of the Forest Service certification, but this new program, meant to create a unified approach to ski instruction certification, had three levels that would-be instructors could qualify for: apprentice instructor, instructor, and master instructor.

The first intermountain region instructor examination occurred on December 5, 1949, at Alta. The next one happened in December 1950, after which Koziol called a meeting. The Forest Service, seeing the rapid growth in ski instruction, knew they didn't have the manpower to continue leading the certification process. It was decided that there needed to be an official organization to run these certifications, and the Intermountain Ski Instructors Association was born.

This instigated a second wave of Alta ski school instructors. Among this wave were Chuck Rowan, Bill Lash, Jim McConkey, Manford Parker, Keith Lange, Leo Fox, Adrian Siegel, and the five Nichole brothers, who not only were great instructors but talented carpenters who built many of the lift shacks and minor structures at Alta. (The brothers were Royce, Rolan, Marn, Vern, and Wayne—who only just stopped teaching at Alta a few years ago as of this writing.) And then there was, of course, Maxine, who was hired in December 1952, immediately after she and Junior were married. She passed her instructor exam with the highest score of the 30 instructors testing at the time, and she quickly became one of the top female ski instructors. Alf's ski school, previously somewhat bare bones, was starting to fill out.

Living, working, and skiing alongside Alf was never boring. Alf cultivated adventure and innovation within his ski school that extended outside the realm of teaching. It was his intention to create a sense of camaraderie among ski instructors, lodge guests, and resort employees. One of the ways he accomplished this was by hosting Norwegian folk dances every few nights at the Alta Lodge. They'd roll the carpets back to expose the wooden floors, put on a record with traditional Norwegian folk music, and Alf would teach everyone how to dance.

Alf's dance lessons weren't confined to just the lodge. While visiting Squaw Valley, Junior and Alf picked up a type of skiing called the "mambo" from French skier Emile Allais. The mambo looks like what the name implies: a form of dancing on skis. The technique involves an extreme counter-rotation of the shoulders as the skis turn, so the upper body and ski tips face in opposite directions. To switch directions, skiers use their hips to initiate the turn, as though salsa dancing, and use their edges as little as possible. The combined, fluid motion makes it seem as though skiers are dancing the mambo down the slopes.

Alf was constantly experimenting on skis and encouraging his ski instructors to do the same. There were plenty of fun, little tricks that emerged around this time, and he reveled in the playfulness of them. He was a master of the "Royal Christie"—where the skier lifted the outside ski behind them, bringing the ski tail up toward their head as they made a big, swooping turn—and he made sure all of his instructors were pros at it too.

Add poles into the mix and the tricks became even more exciting. By using poles, skiers could unweight from their skis, put their weight on their poles, and swing their skis up in the air. There were many variations to this technique, each more complicated than the last. If a skier was moving downhill, they could use their poles to do a 180-degree turn and land skiing backward, a trick called the "tip roll." If the poles were placed slightly downhill from the skier and the skier wasn't moving, the skier could use their poles to flip themselves and land just downhill without any forward momentum. This nifty trick was aptly called the "fence jump" and was useful if someone wanted to get over a fence to a closed area. (Junior claims he never used this trick.) If the poles were a few feet away from each other, a skier could swing their skis in between the poles and simply stick the tails into the snow. Or they could flip their skis over their head in an extravagant flourish of tips and tails.

With the addition of new instructors, and with Alf's continued encouragement, came even more daring adventures, more innovations, and more friendly competition, especially among the higher-level instructors and employees. Describing this time, Junior uses the word *competitive*, and in the same breath says that it wasn't *really* competitive because it was too fun.

Junior and Jim McConkey, especially, challenged each other and themselves. McConkey moved from Canada, where he'd been a certified ski instructor, to Salt Lake City to be an insurance salesman. Alf hired him to work weekends starting in 1953. Junior and "McConk"—as they called him—would follow each other across the mountain, testing out who could ski the best terrain, or be the first to ski this chute or that chute, or who had the best-looking ski tracks.

These days, a patch of powder gets tracked out within a few hours—or even a few minutes—but back then, ski tracks would last as long as it took for another storm to come through the canyon and erase the marks on the mountains. This meant that if a skier failed to get their legs locked together, leaving an "island" of snow in between the two ski tracks instead of one solid "S," everyone who saw those tracks over the next few days could see their mistake. The same went for skiers who straightened out between their turns instead of creating a fluid snake down the slope. Since they were two of the best skiers on the mountain and always exploring the toughest terrain, it was often pretty obvious which tracks were Junior's and McConkey's.

As many Alta employees will say today, one of the perks of living at Alta is the access to the mountains during free time. This was no different when Junior started working there almost 80 years ago, and Junior and the other instructors, patrollers, and resort employees would spend much of their free time exploring on skis. Baldy, having quickly learned the kind of athlete Junior was, became one of Junior's best hiking companions. They would often go on hikes at 7 a.m. before the resort opened, using skins on the base of their skis to travel uphill and often participating in some friendly competition. If it was powdery conditions, they'd hike up Cardiff Pass. If they were looking for corn snow, they'd climb Flagstaff.

Junior didn't drink alcohol, but Baldy did occasionally have a bit too much fun at night. After one such night, Junior arrived at the lift operator's bunkhouse to meet Baldy for a morning hike. He had to shake Baldy awake. Terribly hungover but determined not to wimp out of the hike, Baldy asked Junior for advice on how best to deal with the hangover. Junior, with that devious twinkle in his eye that's so familiar to those who know him, suggested that Baldy drink some milk. Baldy, too hungover to notice that twinkle, heeded his advice, and the two set off on their hike, Junior breaking trail at break-neck speed. Junior recalls there were only about six inches of new snow, and the going was fast. About halfway up, Junior told Baldy that they were making great time and could beat their previous record if they picked up the pace. Baldy agreed eagerly, and Junior put his head down and powered up the mountain, Baldy struggling through his hangover and upset stomach in Junior's wake. Junior remembers making it to the pass in 30 some-odd minutes, a time that they never repeated. Baldy could drink heavily, but he could also rally for a high intensity grunt with a belly full of milk.

Mornings were not the only times Junior would go free skiing out-of-bounds. It was common practice among the ski instructors to end their last lessons of the day a little early—15 minutes early, to be exact.

If they could end their lessons at 3:45 p.m., the instructors could catch the last chair at 4 p.m. up to the top of Collins, which ended where the current lift has a mid-loading station. Then they, along with many of the ski patrollers and other resort employees, would kick off their skis, toss them on their shoulders, and begin the long hike to the top of High Rustler. Once Germania Lift was built, which ended where the current Collins Lift ends, they could traverse and sidestep over to their desired run. But before Germania, those "last-runners" had a good hike to the top. The payoff, Junior remembers, was brilliant. They'd get a beautiful, long run down toward Sunnyside or down the face of High Rustler. No crowds, no lines, just powder or corn that would last for days after the last storm.

It was not uncommon back then to be one of the first to ski a certain chute, gully, or cliff. Jim Shane became the first to ski many of the chutes off Mount Baldy, and it would be with Shane that Junior would ski them for the first time. McConkey would be the first to claim many of the cliffs, while Junior has a rock, "Bounous Rock," named after him after he became the first to jump off it. These men were among the first to ski quite a few runs at Alta, including Eagle's Nest, Gunsight, and the Green and Yellow Trails. They'd hike up Grizzly Gulch and ski over toward Brighton, or hike up toward Cardiff Pass and then to the top of Superior, or ski down into Big Cottonwood Canyon, where they would have shuttled a car. They'd also ski over into current-day Snowbird area, still backcountry at the time, hiking up to the Peruvian ridgeline to ski the Keyhole or Lower Chips Face. Peruvian Gully was still being used for mining purposes during those days, and in order to cross Little Cottonwood Creek at the bottom of Chips, they'd cross the old mining bridge. If they hiked over Germania Pass, they'd cross into Mineral Basin to reach Hidden Peak and then ski Regulator Johnson, or keep hiking into American Fork Canyon and reach Tibble Fork. With Alta as their home base, they roamed across the mid-Wasatch, often with students in tow.

Junior wasn't given much training for his new position; in his own words, "You got your training with experience." The same could be said for the type of skiing he and his clients were doing. There was no *real* beginner terrain at Alta. Sunnyside, Alta's beginner terrain today, was backcountry back then. The closest thing to an "easy" run wasn't even a true run—it was the little rope tow that took guests from the base of the mountain up to the Alta Lodge. This was fine for students content with lapping that rope tow, but once a student caught the urge to go faster, to be on the big mountain, to experience the thrill of a steeper slope, the next move was to get on Collins Lift.

Alf encouraged his instructors to cultivate and encourage adventure, if the clients were game. If students wanted to get on the mountain, he said, take them to the mountain. There they would learn a crucial skill: sideslipping. For once they boarded Collins Lift, the only way to the bottom (besides downloading on the lift) was to ski Corkscrew—a steep gully that used to be narrower than it is today. Junior says it was actually good for the skiers to learn how to sideslip right away; it helped them learn how to control themselves.

For most beginners, the snowplow technique didn't quite cut it on the terrain. If the student couldn't manage a turn once they had sideslipped as much as they could in one direction, Junior and the other instructors would have the student sit on the snow, and the instructor would flip their skis in the opposite direction for them. Then, maybe by the bottom of the run when it flattened out, they could get a few proper turns in before they were back on the lift. This was assuming that there was no fresh snow, and that the snow on the slope had been packed down. Because, of course, this was Alta.

Alta was, and still is, one of the most iconic places for powder snow in North America, and perhaps even in the world. Even prior to a widespread powder skiing technique, people could see there was something special at Alta. It's why "Alta magic" is such a common phrase and has been for the last half a century. In a *Salt Lake Tribune* article dated December 18, 1938, Karl Fahrner (Alta's first ski school director) described an early morning ski outing at Alta:

> *It was a crispy morning, one that made one feel he is alive. Never in all my skiing days have I experienced such snow. Let me say here that 20 years of skiing in competition have taken me to all the well-known ski resorts of Europe and this country. Two years ago, I spent four weeks in the Canadian Rockies, sometimes called the North American Alps. And never have I found conditions to exceed those of last Sunday at Alta.*

When the winter storms rolled over the Cottonwood Canyons, dropping a few inches to a few feet of fresh powder snow, the mountains changed. The skies would speak, the mountain would receive. And the skiers would, in Junior's words, fight powder.

Anyone who has been powder skiing knows the feeling of fighting the snow. Those who skied on long wooden skis knew this feeling best of all. It didn't, and still doesn't, matter if the snow is heavy or light. It takes some effort to master the art of turning in powder, even with the fat and floaty skis of the 21st century. And until you do, skiing through powder can seem more like struggling through powder. There are plenty of times when even accomplished powder skiers will feel like they're fighting powder—if their equipment isn't working as fluidly as it's supposed to, if their body is tired or injured, or if the snow or the weather is challenging.

In many other ski areas of the world, big storms and deep snow meant no skiing half a century ago. One of the reasons Count Felix passed on Alta and Brighton as ski resorts was that they received too much snow during the winter. Back then, a large snowfall meant that the mountain was closed, inaccessible to skiers both because of avalanche danger as well as inability to ski in such challenging conditions. Junior remembers those early days skiing deep snow at Alta as the blind leading the blind, with both the instructors and the students fighting powder.

It was tough skiing, and tough teaching. As Junior says, "It was difficult teaching, but we didn't know any better. I thought this was just the way that it was. A lot of water under the bridge, so to speak." But in order to ski successfully at Alta, to take advantage of the terrain and the winters fully, something had to break. The floodgates of powder skiing were being held by a lack of technique and gear that hadn't yet been designed for the specific conditions. The mountains and the snow were calling for innovations and innovators. Those calls were about to be answered.

There wasn't one occurrence that could be counted as the "start" of modern-day powder skiing. It evolved over decades and was influenced by a number of early powder pioneers. The success of powder skiing was the result of two developments that happened alongside each other: advances in technique and advances in equipment.

The biggest challenge for these early pioneers was figuring out how to get the skier's weight evenly distributed over both skis while in powder. The most common turning technique at the time was the stem christie. The skier would form a wedge with their skis and place their weight on the outside ski, while pointing it in the direction they wanted to go. This asymmetric weight distribution worked well on packed snow, but this technique did not work in powder. Placing the weight on the outside ski would cause that ski to nosedive under the surface of the snow, which then would often cause the skier to nosedive as well. The only way for the skier to get their skis to float on top of the powder was by carrying as much speed as they could without hindering their momentum by turning. In other words, the only way to float on powder was to go straight.

One of the earliest powder techniques was developed by Sverre Engen. Initially hired to work at Alta as America's first snow ranger in 1940, Sverre was tasked with making the mountain safe to ski in a wide variety of conditions. He had to learn how to navigate the terrain, and upon becoming the ski school director in 1945, he passed his powder skiing technique along to instructors and students. One of the methods he used, specifically geared toward true beginner skiers trying to ski powder, was a variation of the snowplow. He taught students first how to weight both skis evenly while in a snowplow. The next step was to bounce the skis into a parallel formation for a second to gain momentum, then separate them into a wedge again.

The more common turn in powder was known as the "dipsy doodle," a level up from the snowplow and meant for more experienced skiers. Dick Durrance is credited with being the true engineer of this style of turn, which he developed alongside Sverre when Sverre was a snow ranger and Dick was the ski school director in the 1941–42 season. After the turn's creation, others would continue to improve on it—people like Dolores LaChapelle, Alf Engen, and, of course, Junior.

Dick Durrance was born in Florida in 1914. When he was 13 years old, his family moved to Munich, Germany, and it was there that Dick learned how to ski and began competing. When he was 17, he won the 1932 German Junior Alpine Championship. A year later, he was exposed to an Austrian man named Toni Seelos while racing in Switzerland. A slalom racer, Seelos strove to create a faster turn. At that time, the most common turn was one from the Arlberg technique. The beginning of the turn always started with a stem, or wedge, which took up more space and slowed the turn. Seelos started experimenting with a new way of turning, and in 1933, he invented the exceedingly quicker parallel turn.

With the escalating rise of Hitler, the Durrance family relocated back to the United States that same year, before Dick could learn the parallel turn from Seelos. But he had seen it enough to know what it should be like, and he started developing his own version of the parallel turn, which he named the "Tempo Turn." It was the first time America would see the parallel turn. Dick went on to race for Dartmouth and completely dominated the American collegiate ski racing world for some time, and he raced in the 1936 Winter Olympics. He was recruited by the Sun Valley Press Bureau to work at Sun Valley starting in 1939, and during this time, he helped Alf Engen cut and design runs on Mount Baldy.

Perhaps because of this time spent with Alf, Dick heard of a new ski resort in the Wasatch Mountains that was struggling to get off the ground. In 1941 Dick convinced the Salt Lake Winter Sports Association (a.k.a. Joe Quinney) to allow him to take control of the Alta Lodge, apparently only half-built at the time, and the ski school. He recruited the financial backing of his friend, New Yorker poet and literary book publisher James Laughlin, and they were able to finish the Alta Lodge and get it into operation. While serving as the ski school director, Dick was also tasked with training 150 paratroopers from the 503rd Parachute Battalion (which predated the 10th Mountain Division).

He was the ski school director for only one year, the season of 1941–42. The lack of guests at both the lodge and in the ski school meant that he had a good chunk of time to free ski, and it was during this time that he was able to develop the dipsy doodle. His wife, Miggs Jennings (a fellow ski racer whom Dick had met in Sun Valley), became pregnant with their first child, and the idea of giving birth and raising a child at Alta was a daunting one. They left the Wasatch Mountains, and Dick would go on to become Aspen's third general manager.

The dipsy doodle had two variations: the single dipsy and the double dipsy. The single dipsy was a transitional method of turning in powder. The skier would start by sticking close to the fall line and carrying speed. To turn, the skier would lift one ski up and out of the snow, then point it in the direction they wished to travel. That ski would become the inside ski—the ski on the uphill side of the turn. During this moment of uneven weight distribution, the other ski, the outside ski, would begin to sink. The skier could then put their weight on their inside ski, which would initiate the turn in the direction the ski was pointing, and then lift their outside ski out of the snow and point it in the opposite direction while the other ski began to sink. They'd repeat this action over and over again to keep turning, weighting and unweighting one ski at a time. When done in quick succession, the movement looked like stepping, as though the skier were almost walking down the hill.

The double dipsy improved on the single dipsy by allowing the skier to keep their weight over both skis simultaneously and avoid lifting one ski out of the snow at a time. To perform the double dipsy, the skier first extends their legs and skis into the powder, applying pressure through their heels and into the skis while angling them in the desired direction. Then the skier retracts their legs and skis up towards their body, all the while keeping their upper body still and facing down the fall line. Momentarily weightless during this contraction, the skier can change the direction of their skis before they sink back into the snow. Then extend and contract again. In simpler terms, the skier had to bounce.

Powder snow can often seem weightless and unable to support any kind of weight—especially when one's skis are sinking into it. The shape and structure of the water crystals and the spaces of air between each crystal create a "body" within the snow that reacts when pressure is applied by skis extending. The force of that pressure—the bounce—coupled with speed generated by staying close to the fall line causes the ski to float, rather than sink. Keeping both skis locked together in one system of movement, rather than apart like in the single dipsy, creates more surface area to apply that pressure. Once a rhythm can be established, with each bounce resulting in a slight change of direction down the fall line, the snow actually aids the skier's tips in rising out from the snow and carrying them down the slope.

Once the extensions and contractions in the lower body were mastered, the innovators began focusing on the upper body. Early ski techniques prescribed that the upper body face the direction the skier wished to travel. With a powder technique focused on maintaining a close path to the fall line in order to keep momentum, it was soon realized that keeping the upper body facing down the fall line, rather than following the tips of the skis from side to side, resulted in quick and tidy turns. Maintaining a tight core was key, and the goal was to keep the upper body facing downhill, while also trying not to bounce up and down like a jack-in-the-box toy, even as the lower body went through the extensions and contractions. A talented powder skier could ski down a slope with an almost perfectly still upper body, their lower body absorbing all the motion. With this new way of skiing powder, the skiers utilized gravity, their skis, and the snow to get down the hill using as little energy as possible.

Decades after these techniques were developed, 60-year-old Junior was featured skiing in hip-deep powder on the cover of a 1988 edition of POWDER, with an accompanying cover story titled "Staying Smooth with Junior Bounous," which discusses this transition to smooth powder skiing:

> *Bounous, the ski school director of Snowbird, flows with the mountain, like water seeking the sea, ever searching for the path of least resistance and the smoothest line. There is an elegance and grace about Bounous's skiing that is rare these days. His fluid, harmonious way of moving through powder snow harkens back to an era when style, technique and accomplishment were entwined in a synergistic whole. He glides down the hill with economy of motion, his upper body silent, his feet and legs working just enough to make a perfect turn. Effortlessly smooth, his simple, efficient technique is the ultimate style.*

While some skiers worked on tweaking these powder techniques, others were tinkering with equipment. A few models of metal skis, made from a lighter aluminum, were tested in the 1940s (in part because of an excess of aluminum material left over by World War II), but ice and snow would stick to the base, and the ski was often irreparable after a bad crash. Because of this, the most common skis of the time were still long, narrow, stiff, and wooden. Most didn't even come with metal edges; skiers would have to add them after purchasing. The length and the stiffness of these skis made maneuvering in powder tricky. The ability of these skis to react quickly in powder was minimal, and the skier was forced to make long, swooping arcs across the hillside in order to complete a turn (as the Engen brothers demonstrate at one point during the film *Ski Aces*). Until the creation of the dipsy, there was no way to successfully stay in the fall line unless the skier was going straight.

One of the earliest people at Alta to start experimenting with making skis more powder-friendly was Jim Shane. Prior to building the Goldminer's Daughter Lodge in 1962, Shane worked as ski patrol in the 1940s and 1950s. He could sense the need for skis to be softer in powder and began sanding the wood down on the tips, thinking that softer tips would help the skis float. But softer tips didn't give the skis the support they needed to rise up and stay above the surface of the snow. In fact, softer tips made the front of the ski more likely to sink. After some trial and error with multiple pairs of skis over a few years, Shane realized he was sanding the wrong end of the ski. He began sanding the tail of the skis instead and discovered that a softer tail would sink in the snow and help the tips stay afloat.

Shane was also one of the first to experiment with the location of the binding on the ski. Once he knew that the tail sinking helped get the tips out of the snow, he began shifting the binding farther back on the ski, closer to the tail, with successful results. Shane had a connection with Howard Head, who had recently developed a new ski in 1950 called the HEAD Standard. One of the advances with the earlier aluminum skis was experimenting with a plasticized honeycomb material sandwiched between two aluminum sheets. It would be Howard Head, after seeing a pair of these skis in the late 1940s, who would have the idea to use the sandwiching method with wooden skis to help them be less heavy. These skis were composed of a plywood core sandwiched between two aluminum sheets, with steel edges and covered with a durable, black plastic. Shane ordered the HEAD Standard for himself and for Junior directly from Howard Head, rather than purchasing them in a ski shop. Once the skis arrived, Shane and Junior moved their bindings back, placing them about an inch and a half behind the suggested location.

The results were impressive. With the skier's weight farther back on softer tails, the tips of the skis would rise more easily out of the snow. The more speed the skier carried, the more the tips would rise. Combine this with the double dipsy—two skis together creating a larger surface area and more pressure applied to the snow on each turn—and the ability of the skier to remain closer to the fall line and carry more speed, and physics began working magic in the mountains. A certain threshold could be reached where gravity, terrain steepness, speed, surface area, and substance converged and powder skiing took shape.

Powder skiing is an activity somewhere between flying and surfing, not unlike how snow is a substance somewhere between air and liquid water. Similarly to how a sailboat harnesses the wind for energy, skiers were now able to harness powder snow to help them ski. They had not mastered the mountains, nor the snow, for no one can ever truly master those forces, but they had begun to master the equipment and their own bodies within these terrains. Energy once wasted by trying to move through powder unsuccessfully could now be converted into the thrills and joys of modern powder skiing. Those powder pioneers had done it. They were no longer fighting the powder; they were flying through it.

Now that there was a technique to be taught and skis had adapted to the conditions, there arose a need for ways of teaching powder skiing. There's only so much knowledge that can pass from teacher to student by using the verbiage I've used in the last few paragraphs. A student standing at the top of a hill of powder will not suddenly become a powder skier by hearing her teacher say, "Extend your legs and skis into the powder, applying pressure through the heels and into the skis while angling them the direction you want to go. Then retract your legs and skis up toward your body, all the while keeping your upper body still and facing down the fall line." No, there had to be a more intuitive way of passing knowledge from teacher to student.

As ski school director, Alf strove to make parallel skiing in powder accessible to everyone. He continued to develop the dipsy doodle to a level where it could be passed down as a technique. Alf was a die-hard advocate of learning by experience, and he encouraged his instructors to teach students wishing to powder ski by taking them onto the big mountain and showing them. But, in order for that method to work, Junior knew he had to set up the student for success. He couldn't just take the student to High Rustler on a deep powder day and expect them to have a successful "learning by experience" moment. Instructors had to have intuition and an understanding of the terrain in order to make choices that would allow the student to learn in an informative and gentle manner.

Junior told me once that fear is very common in skiers transitioning to powder skiing. Even for skiers who feel confident on groomed runs, powder skiing is such a different beast that sometimes it can almost feel like a different sport. When I asked Junior how he dealt with this challenge, he said that the way to overcome fear is by movement. In his words, "long traverses, gentle terrain, and going straight without turning" are ways of helping a student overcome their fears of powder skiing. According to Junior, "This is where the knowledge of the instructor and selecting the appropriate terrain to take a person on is valuable." The keys to success are having a feel for which terrain the student is capable of getting down and then setting small and attainable goals that the student can master within that terrain. This might seem obvious, but it's one of the most valuable things that a ski instructor has to offer.

After choosing appropriate terrain for the student, the next challenge for instructors was finding a way of communicating how powder skiing should feel. There needed to be a method of translating a verbal description of powder skiing into the physical action. Instructors had to have a way to express the feeling of that bouncing motion. In order to bounce down a slope successfully, a skier needed to develop a steady rhythm. Counting "one, two, three" didn't cut it, nor did repeating "left, right, left" in their head. The method needed to get the student's mind *off* of skiing, so instinct and feeling could take over. This is how Junior came up with his iconic powder teaching technique: instructing his students to sing a tune while they skied.

Those who have skied powder with Junior will know this tune well. It's the rolling rhythm associated with "The Hearse Song," otherwise known as "The Worms Crawl In." How Junior came to choose such a dark, morbid song to assist in one of the lightest, dreamiest acts is beyond me. He doesn't remember, either. But the tempo of the song matched a good rhythm for powder skiing, so Junior began teaching his students to sing "ba-dump, ba-dump, ba-dump, ba-dump" as they skied down a hill of powder, the rhythm of the ba-dumps guiding the rhythm of their turns.

As Junior's granddaughter, you can bet that "ba-dump, ba-dump" would cycle through my head like a film reel or broken tape record for years after learning it. In order to powder ski, I had to focus on that song, even sing it aloud. Eventually the rhythm clicked and became a natural pulse in my body. Today when I ski powder, I'm no longer haunted by those "ba-dumps." Now the rhythm is instinctual, something so deep within me it's like a shadow of my heart beating. But when the feeling of powder skiing was new and unfamiliar, those "ba-dumps" helped anchor my mind and body into the necessary motion required to interact with a hill of powder snow. Picking up speed while powder skiing was thrilling, terrifying, and otherworldly, and it was this rhythm that gave it some sort of structure.

There was one day, about 20 years ago, when I was skiing with my father over in Little Cloud Bowl when patrol dropped the rope to Road to Provo. It was a quiet rope drop. Almost no one was there—no hordes of people tripping across each other's skis and boards trying to move along the cat track, no wide-eyed, shoulder-shoving wiggling bodies with their hearts in their throats, doing their best to get just one run before the hillside became sliced through with the tracks of a thousand carbon fiber edges. This rope drop was a sneaky thing, the rope disappearing across the entrance to the bowl like a wisp of smoke swirling silently into thin air. Following my father, we traversed underneath the cliff bands of Twin Peaks. He stopped above a pitch. It was slightly steeper than I was used to skiing in powder, making my heart flutter slightly looking at it. It became less steep farther down the pitch, leveling out into a flat section that would lead us back to the lift.

I'd been skiing powder for years at this point, but never really felt like I had mastered it. It scared me at times; powder skiing often meant digging a ski out from under the snow after a ski tip dove too far down. It meant face planting and a sense of claustrophobia as you tried to right yourself. Powder skiing was not always enjoyable for me. And whenever I skied powder, the "ba-dumps" accompanied each turn, keeping my body and motion on track like a metronome. It was helpful, but it was not necessarily fluid or natural—yet.

"Go for it, Ayj!" my dad said, implying that I should make first tracks.

"No, you go first." I still felt like I needed a visual reminder of what powder skiing was supposed to look like.

"You sure?"

I nodded, and he pushed himself into motion, looking beautiful and effortless as he sent waves of snow into the air with each turn. He got most of the way down the pitch, near where the hill began to flatten out, then stopped, looking back up the slope to watch me.

I took a breath, held it for a moment. Then, pushing myself into motion with my poles, I exhaled. I took one turn, then another, and quickly picked up speed. As gravity pulled me into the fall line, my body fell into a rhythm that I was unaware of. For a moment I was fearful that one of my ski tips might dive beneath the surface, but instead my skis floated.

For one wild second I thought, I'm flying! And in a way, I was.

"All right, Ayj!" my dad whooped as I stopped next to him. I realized I was panting, though I hadn't felt like my body was working hard in that moment. It had just felt like gravity was pulling me down the mountain.

It was only later, sitting on the lift, that I realized I had not sung "ba-dump, ba-dump" while skiing. I had not needed to. From that moment on, the rhythm was in me.

That, perhaps, is the moment Junior always strove for his clients to reach. The moment when you're no longer reliant on a set of rules guiding you. The moment when the uncomfortable becomes comfortable, or at least familiar enough to be on its way to being comfortable, even if the act still makes one nervous. It's about getting past that crux, using movement to overcome fear.

Now with technique, equipment, and a teaching system at their fingertips, the Alta ski instructors, led by Alf and Junior, began changing the shape of skiing in the American West. A two-foot snowfall no longer meant that the conditions were too difficult to ski in. And, with the realization that momentum was a skier's friend in powder, steeper slopes became coveted on powder days. By the 1950s, instructors and students alike, using movement to overcome fear, accessed more terrain and skied longer days than their predecessors. The enthusiasm for powder skiing, still in full force today, had taken hold of the skiing community. In that same POWDER article from 1988, Junior is quoted as saying, "Both Alf Engen and I worked together in the development of what powder skiing is today. . . . At Alta we had more opportunity than any place in the world to work in powder."

Junior was not the only Bounous with a knack for teaching powder skiing. After getting married to Junior in 1952, Maxine moved up to Alta to live with Junior—first at the Alta Lodge, then at the Rustler. Despite Junior teaching her how to ski only a few years prior, she was quickly one of the strongest female skiers on the mountain, along with other women like Dolores LaChapelle, Lois and Evelyn Engen, Elfriede Shane, Suzanne Rowan, and Wilma Johnson. She and Junior continued to spend six days working at Alta and Saturdays teaching at Timp Haven, spending Friday nights at Maxine's parents' house in Provo.

The couple had a few honeymoon years working and living together at Alta. Then, in 1955, Maxine became pregnant with their first son, Barry. Not wanting to raise him in a lodge, Junior and Maxine bought from Jim Shane a parcel of land off the "Summer Road," which is east of the main resort and not accessible by car during the winter months. Junior and Maxine built a house with another couple, Janis and Bill Levitt, with the intention that the Bounouses would live in the house during the winter, and the Levitts would use it during the summer. The house, which is still there today, had a beautiful view of Greely Bowl and Superior. In addition to a nice view, the house also had a roof that served as an epic ski jump, which can be seen in action on the cover of this book.

But living at this house full time during the winter had plenty of challenges. The Summer Road does not get plowed in the winter. Any time Junior or Maxine had to leave the house, they had to hike through the snow to get to the nearest plowed road. There were six other homes in that area at the time. Baldy owned one, Chip Morton owned another, and Merrill Matzinger owned another. There had originally been talk of installing a rope tow to help folks get from the parking lot to the homes, but it was never installed. Maxine and Junior often had to rely on one of their neighbors to give them rides in their personal snowcat machines.

The house, so hard to leave and access during the winter, especially if there was a storm, began to feel like a prison to Maxine, especially, who stopped working full time so she could raise Barry. With Junior gone every day to work for Alf, she was left alone in the house with the baby. In a time with no internet, no cell phones, and a million-dollar view that flaunted the beautiful mountains and snow she couldn't appreciate, it's not hard to imagine how lonely Maxine may have felt at times. Realizing there needed to be an easier way for Maxine to leave the house, the Levitts purchased a snowcat, which she learned how to drive and which gave her significantly more freedom. But after two winters in the house, Junior and Maxine knew that they couldn't sustain another winter of this lifestyle.

In 1958, Junior received a call from a man named Alex Brogle, who had worked at Alta as a lift operator. When Brogle had expressed interest in becoming a ski instructor, Junior had helped him train for and pass his certification exam. Brogle had then gone to work at Badger Pass ski area near Yosemite, then to Sugar Bowl. Brogle told Junior that there was an opening for ski school director at Sugar Bowl and that Junior should apply. Junior told Alf about the opportunity, and Alf encouraged him to take it, saying that the chance to become a ski school director wouldn't come around often.

So, leaving Barry with Maxine's mother, Junior and Maxine drove out to California in their station wagon for Junior's interview. They spent a couple of days there and climbed Mount Lasson while they waited for the Sugar Bowl manager's decision. They offered Junior the job, and Junior, looking at a salary significantly more than the one he'd been earning at Alta for the last 10 years, accepted. The Bounouses were going to California.

"So there's this place up in Alta on Baldy shoulder. This big rock that sticks out is called Bounous Rock. Junior was the first guy to jump off it, always went out there, jumped off it. And then we all aspired to do whatever Junior could do. And he probably could still jump off it today if you told him to."

— Onno Wieringa, Alta patrol and general manager

"Mary Ellen and I . . . came to Salt Lake [in 1964] and someone said there's a place called Alta. So we went to Alta to ski, and the first guy I met was Ted Johnson. The next guy I met was Eddie Morris. And we're over by Devil's Castle and there's a helicopter flying over, and the chopper landed up on top of the Devil's Castle run. The chopper let somebody out and this guy skis down in the powder all the way down to the hard-packed there. It's a long run and it's beautiful skiing. I said, 'Who is that?' And they said, 'That's Junior Bounous. He's a hell of a good powder skier.' And I decided I want to learn to ski just like he does. Junior was my inspiration to learn how to ski powder."

— Bud Gaylord, family friend and original owner
of The Cliff Lodge at Snowbird

"Singing 'ba-dump, ba-dump' is an excellent way of teaching powder. You don't have to say anything else. You know, powder—it's such a mental thing to ski it and to teach it . . . And you'll hear a lot of the general public that has taken lessons [from us], if you're real quiet in the powder . . . they're going 'ba-dump, ba-dump.' I thank Junior for that."

— Ed Chauner, Snowbird Mountain School employee

"We'll take traverse to traverse to traverse, we'll hike back, we'll hike back, we'll hike back. Anything to get some good powder."

— Connie Keller, family friend

"It's always fun. He has the ability to push you to your absolute limit, yet you're still having fun."

— Georgia Clark, Snowbird Mountain School employee

"To get powder, he could go any length. Junior certainly knows all the spots to find powder that no one else knows on the mountain. He'll hike and he'll climb and he'll cross ridges. Even several days after a powder storm Junior will find the powder."

— Herb Lloyd, family friend

"He doesn't damage people. Bounousabuse is always tempered. He'll get the most out of you with his torture techniques."

— Mark Riley, Snowbird Mountain School employee

"A few years ago, my wife and I were on our annual spring vacation trip to Snowbird, and we were skiing alone in Powder Paradise. . . . It was early in the morning with a couple inches of new wind-blown snow on top of crusty "moonscape-like" conditions.

In my own space, skiing in the morning shadows, I took off skiing (thinking I was alone) and made my turns down to our normal stopping point . . . Junior skied up next to me, stopped briefly, and with his gentle smile said, "Now those were some beautiful turns!" He then skied away with the group of skiers he was leading . . . He did not have to stop. . . . It was just his humble nature to teach and to encourage and to share his enthusiasm for skiing, even with the general public.

In my 45+ years of teaching skiing, those were perhaps the most powerful words ever spoken to me. I will always remember the aggressive and joyful attitude I had with those specific turns, because Junior recognized them! And I will always remember that a good teacher has no ego and is always happy to share humble words of encouragement. I'm sure that there are many others out there who have similar stories about Junior teaching moments that happened behind the scenes and without recognition."

— Bob Speck, Snowbird skier

Junior at Alta in 1950. Note Junior's ski instructor sweater with his name stitched on his breast.

Junior trying on the first Alta ski school jacket. 1952.

Maxine and Junior in front of Mount Superior and the old Rustler mining dump and rope tow, from the deck of the Rustler Lodge in 1953.

Junior, Maxine, and Alf Engen at Alta. Likely around 1953.

Maxine skiing powder at Alta with Mount Superior and the Peruvian Lodge in the background in the mid-1950s.
Fred Lindholm

Junior experiencing some Alta Magic off of Wildcat chairlift in the early 1950s.
Special Collections, J. Willard Marriott Library, The University of Utah

Chico along for the ride. The dog hiked up Mount Superior, but had no chance keeping up with Junior and Maxine when they skied down. While on the summit, he'd run around and sit on the edge of a cornice, his tail hanging off the side. Unabashed by his size, Chiço was a mountain dog whose adventurous ambitions were far larger than his body. Alta in the 1950s.

Maxine, Junior, and Chico on the deck of the Rustler Lodge in 1954.

Junior scoping out his line at Alta in 1958.

Junior soaring off of Bounous Rock at Alta in the late 1940s. Junior was the first person on record to jump off this rock, and flew so far that they named it after him.
Fred Lindholm

Junior appreciating the view at Alta. 1950s.
Fred Lindholm

Chapter 9

Might of the Mountain

During the late 1800s, miners had stripped Little Cottonwood Canyon's hillsides of their trees, cutting down old growth forests for timber. It was a fatal mistake; without trees to help provide anchorage for the snowpack, massive avalanches careened down the hillsides, leading to destruction and death in the town of Alta on many occasions. Starting in the 1930s, the Civilian Conservation Corps, with some help from the Boy Scouts of America, aided in reforesting the slopes. But even as the new trees provided more snowpack stability, avalanches still posed a threat for the new ski area. The dire need for a greater understanding of avalanches up Little Cottonwood Canyon would put Alta at the forefront of avalanche research and mitigation.

It was the US Forest Service that realized the initial need for research to understand the conditions that led to varying levels of avalanche risk. A district ranger by the name of W. E. Tangren was sent to live at Alta during the 1938–39 winter season and was tasked with observing and logging all avalanches. The following year, the Forest Service hired Sverre Engen to work alongside Tangren as the Forest Service's first snow ranger. Besides observing avalanches and tracking weather conditions, Sverre was in charge of safety decisions regarding the resort and the road, including making the determination to close them when the avalanche conditions were high risk.

After World War II, more enthusiasts started visiting the Wasatch, and many were adventurous. They didn't want to stick to the small rope tows; they enjoyed putting skins on the bottoms of their skis and traversing longer distances in more rugged terrain. In an article published in *Utah Magazine* in 1946, the Forest Service supervisor for the Wasatch Mountains, Felix C. Koziol, wrote the following:

> *Winter skiers wander all over the landscape. Many are not content to stay on the practice slopes and on the ski runs close to the lifts. An increasing number are seeking ways of getting far out into the alpine hinterlands, far away from the snow bunny crowd. These enthusiasts want marked ski trails, ski huts and shelters, first aid caches and similar guarantees of safety. The wandering public that seeks to use the national forests for winter recreation is making new and growing demands upon the Forest Service.*

Koziol began pushing for the Forest Service to not simply observe and understand avalanches but to control them. When Sverre transitioned from snow ranger to ski school director, Koziol hired a man named Montgomery Atwater to become the new snow ranger. Atwater had been in the 10th Mountain Division and understood explosives. Koziol had managed to convince the Utah National Guard to give the Forest Service a howitzer cannon, previously used only for ceremonial purposes. It apparently took some additional persuading to convince the US government that a ski area should be able to continue the use of military weapons for snow safety. Kozoil and Atwater were the first to begin experimenting with using a howitzer cannon to trigger avalanches prematurely.

Atwater then recruited physicist and glaciologist Ed LaChapelle to take over the avalanche program at Alta in 1952. While Atwater's experience was strictly with explosives, LaChapelle was a scientist. He had just spent a year studying at the Swiss Federal Institute for Snow and Avalanche Research in Switzerland, and he had experience as a mountaineer as well. LaChapelle did not just shoot explosives at the mountains; he began to develop an intimate understanding of how snow crystals, snowpack development, and environmental conditions create the many dimensions of avalanche conditions. LaChapelle's son, David, recollects this:

> *I remember one bright powder morning at Alta, Utah. I watched from inside the warm living room of our cabin as my father scooped up a handful of snow crystals, examined them with his pocket magnifying lens, and then let the snow fall from his hands. It was in the time the powder snow took to fall from his fingers and reach the ground that I saw a side of my father which transcended the science that anchored his life. He was, in that moment, reverent, as if listening to a greater voice than his senses could convey. He stood for a moment and I witnessed him encounter the world as if it were sacred. He turned from that moment, came inside and began to call the lodges to tell them*

that there would need to be some avalanche control work before the ski area could open.

Ed LaChapelle, along with his wife, Dolores, quickly became iconic Alta skiers. Their love for the snow and the mountains surpassed a typical passion for skiing, passing into the realm of the spiritual. And avalanches, the mighty crux where weather, mountain, and snow collided, were at the heart of their respect. As the snow ranger, LaChapelle listened to the mountain. He didn't let the desires of the resort or of the skiers distract him from snow safety. Ron Perla, a Forest Service snow ranger who worked alongside LaChapelle at Alta, recalled this story about Ed at a banquet in 1991:

I have been asked to tell a few LaChapelle stories. This is my favorite. It happened in the late 1960s. Binx Sandahl, Will Bassett and I had just completed an active morning of control, and had opened much of the Alta Ski Area. An eager weekend ski crowd was heading toward the new powder. It was a beautiful, sunny crisp day. Excellent powder. I climbed to the Upper Guard Station to assist Ed. I found him standing in front of the large window, with its panoramic view of the Alta Ski Area. He seemed to be concerned that a chute on West Rustler, which had been shot that morning, had not slid. Ed radioed to Sandahl and Bassett to shut down half the mountain, and retarget the stubborn chute. Yes, at times Ed could be critical and demanding. But I had never seen anything like this before. Reclose half the mountain just after it was opened with skiers straining at the bit to dive in! A weekend crowd was to be denied their powder on the chance, always just a chance, that we could produce an avalanche on our command! I watched the drama enfold. Slowly, the ski crowd started to shift away from the target area toward the WildCat lift. The word was out, and many skiers simply positioned themselves to watch the action. Will Bassett led a control team above the chute, and tossed in the charge. I felt the entire reputation of the Forest Service was at stake. Well, the ski crowd was treated to a spectacular powder avalanche that ran its full path to an area which, an hour ago, had been heavily populated with skiers. Now, that was avalanche forecasting.

Recognizing that skiing in rugged mountain terrain is playing with fire, LaChapelle was not one to take chances when it came to avalanches. During his second season at Alta, LaChapelle witnessed the kind of avalanches that Little Cottonwood Canyon was capable of.

In 1953, a natural avalanche broke loose from Cardiff and Flagstaff, two peaks on the north side of Little Cottonwood Canyon and directly above the town of Alta. It's an alarmingly massive area to all slide at once. According to an account of the avalanche in an Alta Historical Society newsletter published in 2009, a hillside in its path luckily caused the avalanche to split. Both sides careened right over the canyon road. One side came close to hitting the Peruvian Lodge. The other *did* hit the Alta Lodge. It was midday, and Maxine was working at the front desk of the Alta Lodge when the avalanche hit. Luckily the reception desk was in a somewhat protected alcove. Snow and broken glass flooded the reception and dining area, piling up right in front of the desk, but not hitting Maxine.

The avalanche occurred while Junior and Maxine were living in the Alta Lodge, and the room they had been assigned to had windows that had been boarded up prior to them moving in because another avalanche had hit the Alta Lodge the previous season. Junior and Maxine's rooms had been occupied by Alf and Evelyn Engen and their young son, Alan, when the avalanche the year prior hit the lodge in the middle of the night. It was so powerful that it not only broke through the window, but also damaged the side of the building, and completely buried Alan while he was asleep. Luckily Alf had been on the other side of the room and hadn't been hit by the avalanche, but his son was under five or six feet of snow, buried in his own bed. Using his bare hands, Alf dug until he was able to pull Alan out. Junior remembers Alf's hands being bloody afterwards—broken glass mixed with snow.

The Bounouses had a few close calls with avalanches over the decades. Junior has officially been caught in seven avalanches over the course of his life, though he's set off and witnessed many more than that. Luckily he was never fully buried in one. Prior to Ed LaChapelle and a man named John Lawton inventing the first avalanche beacon in 1968, getting buried by an avalanche meant almost certain death. Especially if no piece of you, no ski, nor boot, nor hat, was sticking out of the snow.

Junior's first two avalanches happened with Reed Biddulph and Frank Hirst during some of Junior's early backcountry excursions. He'd had miraculous beginner's luck in both. The next wave of avalanches occurred when he ventured past the boundaries of Alta, often with clients following him like a row of ducklings following their mother goose.

One occurred at the top of Greely Bowl—considered side country at the time. Junior and his class had hiked from the top of Collin's Lift to the ridgeline that divides Collin's Gulch from the neighboring Greely Bowl. It was a beautiful bluebird day and no new snowfall, though Junior remembers that it was a bit windy. Once they reached the top of Greely, they could see that the wind had created a wind drift, or cornice, on the leeward side. Junior, recognizing avalanche danger, told his students to wait where they were while he'd see if he could break it loose. With skis on his feet, he jumped on the cornice. It did indeed break, but instead of breaking a safe distance below him, like he thought it would, it broke above him, almost to where his students were standing. The entire chunk of snow beneath him started moving. He first angled his skis to the right, thinking he'd quickly ski out of it. But there was enough snow moving on that side that he decided to make a downhill turn to try and ski out on the other side. He realized his mistake too late. The entire left side of the hill was sliding too, and he was right in the center of it.

He was able to stay on top of the snow as it picked up speed. There was a pine tree in the path of the slide, and Junior, recognizing it was his last hope, angled his skis toward the tree before losing balance. It was just enough. The avalanche carried him toward the tree, and he was able to collide with it and grab hold of the branches. As the avalanche continued on, it felt like he was in a stream with water rushing over him. He was on top of the snow once it stopped moving, all of his gear somehow still attached. The avalanche continued all the way to the bottom of Greely Hill and into Little Cottonwood Creek—a terrain trap that would have led to almost certain death. His students were still standing at the top of the mountain, calling his name in fear. Junior yelled that he was okay, and he instructed them to ski down the slide path to him. Staying in the slide path the entire way down in case of more avalanche activity, they made it safely back to the resort.

That wasn't the only avalanche Junior experienced in that area of Alta. On another instance he was almost caught and carried while skiing just around the corner with a man named Edwin Gibbs, whose family had built the Peruvian Lodge. They were skiing off Eddie's High Nowhere, just skier's right of Greely Bowl. They set off a slide, and though Junior was able to ski out of it, Edwin was caught and carried more than 100 yards, but thankfully not buried fully. Another avalanche occurred when Junior was skiing for a photographer. He jumped off a cornice into Eagle's Nest, triggering the slide. Junior was able to grab hold of a tree to prevent himself from getting carried, but the slide hit the photographer downhill, not injuring him but sweeping his camera away.

Once, while skiing off Wildcat chairlift at Alta with Jim Shane and Warren Balsevian ("Baldy"), Junior and Shane were skiing on one side of a pitch while Baldy was on the other side. A small slide caught Baldy. Baldy started yelling at Junior and Shane: "Dig for me! Dig for me!" Thankfully his head and shoulders ended up on top of the slide, and there was no urgent need to dig for him.

Another one happened while Junior was hiking with clients. He had led them over Catherine's Pass, skied down toward Twin Lakes Reservoir, near Brighton and what would eventually become Solitude, and then were hiking back up toward Grizzly Gulch, staying mostly in the trees. When they arrived at an open stretch of slope, Junior told his class to wait while he checked to see if the hill would slide. Apparently, Junior hadn't learned much from his previous experience, because, in his own words, "Once again I said, 'Oh, let me go across it first. I'll jump on it.'" A huge slab broke around him. It started moving down the hill as a whole unit, picking up speed, but not breaking apart. Junior remembers it feeling like a tabletop. Knowing he needed to get off the slab quickly before it did break apart, he started skiing across it toward the best exit point.

Junior then experienced a crash course in physics. According to Newton's first law of motion, an object at rest will stay at rest, while an object in motion will stay in motion. As Junior skied off the slab, the combined momentum of the sliding slab and Junior skiing across it meant that once Junior hit the firm snow that wasn't moving, it was a much harder impact than he had anticipated. In his words, "It was like jumping out of a moving car at 40 miles per hour." Momentum not through with him yet, he continued tumbling down the hill, somersaulting end over end. Luckily, once he did come to a stop, that was that; he wasn't carried away by the avalanche, he didn't injure himself, and he didn't try and set off any more avalanches.

Another close call for the Bounouses happened quite a few years later in 1967, though Junior wasn't involved in the actual slide this time. By then, Junior and Maxine had left Utah to work at Sugar Bowl, and they were visiting Alta on that April day. Maxine was skiing with Barry, who was almost 12 years old. She had led him over to an area in Collin's Gulch called Ballroom. Though the run is moderate terrain, it lies right underneath the Baldy Chutes. Ron Perla, no longer a snow ranger, but a full-time ski patroller at Alta, was on top of Baldy, placing dynamite in a cornice that ski patrol was going to do avalanche control work on later. He had a rope tied to him for precautionary purposes, typical of working around cornices, though ski patrol wasn't expecting anything to slide. They were so confident it wouldn't slide that they hadn't even closed the runs beneath Baldy. But slide it did.

The cornice Perla stood on broke, tipping him forward and snapping his safety rope. The slide took him all the way down the face of Baldy and onto Main Street, right across the path Maxine and Barry had skied across about 30 seconds prior. They were the first ones on the scene, and Maxine told Barry to take his skis off and start looking around for a hat, glove, or any other sign of a person. Maxine spotted a glove sticking out of the snow, and soon other skiers joined, trying to dig the buried man out using their poles. Ski patrol and a few ski instructors—including Junior, who had been in a meeting at the Goldminer's Daughter Lodge—were radioed to assist in search efforts and arrived quickly with shovels to dig Perla out. Patrol handed Barry and Maxine probes—long, segmented poles meant for stabbing through the snow to feel if there's a body underneath—and instructed them to start probing in case anyone else had been buried.

Barry remembers the anxiety of that spring day, of walking around the slide area, looking for any sign of another hat or glove or person. On a few occasions, his probe hit a hard chunk of snow under the surface. Whenever this happened about five people would rush to the location and start digging in case it was another body. Luckily, no one else was buried. What Barry doesn't remember is Perla being uncovered. He thinks that Junior and Maxine shielded him from the digging and redirected his attention to look for other potential victims, thinking it might be too traumatic for an 11-year-old to watch without knowing if Perla was dead or alive. Despite his odds, Perla was miraculously okay. The chutes he tumbled down are called Perla's Chutes to commemorate his eventful ride.

Perla, ironically, went on to publish multiple papers about avalanche rescue methods. One paper, published in June 1967, just two months after the incident, was entirely dedicated to the most effective way of probing for victims. The paper is full of technical language, charts, mathematical equations of probability, and discussion of when the search party should switch from coarse to fine probes. Perla had, of course, been knocked unconscious on his way down the 1,000-foot fall, but I wonder, had he been conscious while buried under the snow, if he would have been thinking through his own probability of being rescued and surviving that avalanche and whether the search party was using coarse or fine probes. If his hand hadn't happened to be on the surface of the snow, probing likely would have saved his life if someone's probe happened to hit him.

Another much less eventful but close call happened a few years later while Junior was working at Snowbird. He and his coworker, Jerry Warren, hiked over the ridgeline dividing Gad Valley from White Pine to ski the Birthday Chutes. They entered the chute and cut across it, triggering a slide beneath them. The slide tumbled on without catching either skier and left a strip of undisturbed, deep powder snow on skier's left of the slide path. Junior and Jerry still had a beautiful run that day by skiing directly to the side of the slide.

Junior's and Maxine's avalanche experiences weren't limited to when they were on skis. During one memorable occasion while working at Snowbird, they were driving up a section of Little Cottonwood Canyon that many call the "seven sisters," a series of seven short-radius turns in quick succession with a steep drop-off to the south and cliffs to the north. Snow began streaming across the road, right in front of a bus they were following. The bus came to a stop, and Junior, who had a radio in the car, quickly radioed Hoopi, the mountain manager at Snowbird, and told him that the road needed to be closed ASAP. While they were sitting there, another avalanche came across the road a few turns behind them. They were stuck. Junior got out of their car, shovel in hand, thinking he'd start digging through the snow in front of them. But as more snow continued sloughing off the cliffs and streaming across the road, he thought better of it and got back into his car to wait for a plow.

The most recent (and hopefully the last) avalanche Junior was caught in happened while he was heli-skiing in Big Cottonwood Canyon for a promotional film. He doesn't remember the exact date, but he knows it was after the 2002 Winter Olympics, and he estimates it could have been between 2004 and 2010. Junior was likely in his 70s, perhaps even 80 years old. The avalanche broke around him as he started skiing, ripping one of his skis off. He started swimming through the snow, using his arms to pull himself to one side of the slide. He was uninjured, but his ski was lost. After 30 or 40 minutes of probing for where they thought it might be, Junior told the camera crew that he'd just ski down to the helicopter on one ski, and that their filming was done for the day. They skied beside the path, and about 100 yards down they saw Junior's ski in the debris. If Junior hadn't been able to swim out of the avalanche, there's a good chance the slide would have carried him all the way to where his ski ended up.

The risk of avalanches and the power of the mountain often add allure to resorts. When avalanche danger is extremely high, ski areas will often implement an "interlodge" order, meaning that no one can leave whatever building they're in, not even to walk into a parking lot or visit an outdoor hot tub. Those who have experienced an interlodge know that being stuck inside a building for an indeterminate amount of time can be an inconvenience, but also know the thrill of being at the mountain's mercy without actually being in danger. There is a romantic side of it; watching the snow stack up outside of your hotel's window with a drink in hand, dreaming about the powder skiing you'll get once the resort opens. And knowing that, no matter your previous obligations or desires, everything is out of your control.

Once, in 1954 by Junior's memory, a classic Cottonwood Canyon storm rolled through the Wasatch. There were so many avalanches in the canyon that the road didn't close just for a few days, but for a few weeks. Even after the storm passed and the skies were blue, the amount of snow and debris that had covered the canyon road was such that it took two weeks for plows to get the road open. There had also been heavy snowfall in the valley, and the priority for the plows was to focus on the city roads before clearing the canyon. Junior was living at the Alta Lodge at the time and remembers a small plane nose diving above the resort, pushing frozen turkeys out the plane door so they'd land in the parking lot in front of Alta Lodge for trapped skiers and staff to enjoy.

After two weeks, they were able to plow most of the road up to Mount Superior, but were unable to clear the half mile stretch between Superior and the town of Alta. Some of the guests, whether from cabin fever or having other obligations, decided to hike out, their suitcases in hand as they braved the half-mile stretch of unplowed road. Others, who had been anxious to get up the canyon to ski, hiked in. Chic Morton, the general manager, had an army weasel he brought down to help shuttle guests and employees back and forth. Then, another storm barreled in and closed the canyon for a third week.

Meanwhile, the mountain was open, the skies were blue, and the powder was bitchin'.

"Recently, on a chair lift ride at Snowbird, I overheard two young patrolmen comment, 'Whoever this guy Junior is seems to think every time we rope an area off it's his own personal powder field.'"

— Nancy Kronthauler, Snowbird Mountain School employee

"To watch Junior's soft voice and his causal confidence on skis is phenomenal. There can be a bit of arrogance in the ski industry, but Junior is always so patient and such a good guy that skiing with him is a really humbling experience. He is the epitome of what it means to lead by example, and it's such a pleasure to be around him."

— Dave Watson, Snowbird skier

In celebration of Junior and Maxine's 50th wedding anniversary, Barry Bounous adapted the lyrics of Roy Roger's "Don't Fence Me In" and then performed the song with Steve Bounous.

I once saw Junior looking really down,
Standing by a "run-closed" sign.
And when the patrolman said, "You have to turn around,"
Junior raised his head and cried:

O, give me snow, lots of snow under sunny skies above;
Don't fence me in.
Let me ski through the wide open country that I love;
Don't fence me in.
Let me play in the trees where the powder's sweetest,
Let me take the fall line where the hill is steepest,
I could ski forever where the snow is deepest;
Don't fence me in.

Just turn me loose, let me ride a lift until it disappears into the sky.
In my old boots, let me climb up to a saddle where I see the mountain rise.
I want to hike up a ridge where the sky commences,
Gaze at the mountain till I lose my senses.
Can't look at lift lines and I can't stand fences;
Don't fence me in.

"One day in class when I was in high school, the teacher showed us a video. I was so surprised to see my grandpa in that video! It was all about a group of skiers following their teacher (my grandpa) in a backcountry situation. One of the skiers wanted to go a different way than "the old man" but eventually decided to listen to him. After skiing around, they stopped, and the teacher pointed out what they'd just skied around—a massive cliff. And the one guy was so grateful that he'd listened to the "old man." I remember laughing—who in their right mind could possibly think that any way but Junior's way was best? It wasn't long after that he took me over to Great Scott for the first time. At one point, he paused and said, "Follow in my tracks exactly." Considering the fact that that was something I tried to do anyway—following in his tracks always seemed to make me a better skier—it was easy enough to do. And sure enough, a few turns later, he stopped to show me the large cliff that we'd just navigated."

— EvaLynn Bounous Bolen, granddaughter

"I think Junior's biggest impression is shared joy that he experiences skiing. The way that he inspires me the most is that he's so genuinely excited to ski. That's a contribution that affects nearly everybody that meets Junior. He loves skiing, so how can you have a bad day?"

— Loel York, Snowbird Mountain School employee

Junior with a group of Snowbird instructors after hiking to the top of Twin Peaks from Hidden Peak before skiing American Fork Canyon. Barry is on the left. 1970s.

Junior leading the bootpack up Twin Peaks, with Barry right behind. 1970s.

Cross-country skiing on Timpanogos. 1970s.

Hiking up White Pine with not one but two pairs of skis on his back. (The second is likely a client's or Maxine's.) 1980s.

A shot of Junior skiing powder (no hat or goggles necessary) from a *Powder* magazine article.

Chapter 10

Sweet as Sugar Bowl

Similar to many other ski areas, skiing in the Sierra Nevada of northern California began with Scandinavian immigrants who were pulled toward the mountains of the West by flecks of gold and silver found in the soil and water. The area that would become Sugar Bowl ski resort had a slightly different relationship to the Gold Rush era than other resorts near Lake Tahoe; in addition to active mining sites, the area had one of the more accessible and gentle routes through Donner Pass and the Sierra Nevada. The pass that stretches between two of the mountains at Sugar Bowl Resort—Mount Judah and Mount Lincoln—was part of the California wagon trail now called Roller Pass.

This pass then became the route for the Transcontinental Railroad starting in 1868, though the amount of heavy snowfall and weather conditions made even train travel through the pass difficult. Nearly 40 snow sheds were built to help shield the tracks from the snow buildup. In 1925, a tunnel was blasted through two miles of solid granite rock underneath Mount Judah, and the tunnel became known as "The Big Hole." The massive effort required to accomplish this feat was thought to be justified by the payoff: avoiding the snow.

In 1926, US Highway 40 opened over Donner Pass, and motorized vehicles were able to make the trek through the mountains. Though there wasn't an official ski area at the time, ski enthusiasts began visiting the mountains near a town called Truckee, California, and more specifically a mountain area known as Soda Springs. In order to increase winter use of the train, an ice palace was constructed in Truckee, and the trains began running "Snowball Specials"—train rides that started at the Oakland Pier and took city folk up to visit the mountains. Many of those visitors would also visit the Soda Springs area during their travels, and a couple of rope tows were built to accommodate the enthusiasts.

In 1934, members of the Sierra Club, a land preservation group founded by John Muir, built a cabin nearby, which they called the Clair Tappaan Cabin after one of their members. Two years later, in 1936, two Austrian brothers and ski instructors, Bill and Fred Klein, began operating a ski school out of the Clair Tappaan Cabin. The ski school was immediately a success, and they often had 100-150 students per weekend, some of whom they'd take hiking up Mount Lincoln.

The official creation of Sugar Bowl was catalyzed when 700 acres of land around Mount Lincoln and Mount Judah went up for sale. More than a decade earlier, in 1923, a couple named Stephen and Jennie Pilcher had purchased the land from the Southern Pacific Railroad for $10. They leased the land for sheep and cow grazing until Stephen's death in 1931. In 1937, the Pilchers' daughters decided they wanted to sell the acres of land.

When the Klein brothers heard the land was up for sale, they contacted a man named Hannes Schroll, another Austrian ski instructor and a downhill racer, who was working at a ski area near Yosemite named Badger Pass. Schroll scoped out the northern California land in 1938 and fell in love with it. Born in the Austrian Alps, he had been dreaming of starting a ski resort in North America that would look like a Tyrolean mountain village. By March of 1938, Schroll had agreed with the Pilcher sisters on a price of $6,750, and he shortly after teamed up with a real estate agent from San Francisco, Hamilton McGaughey, to help with the land transfer.

But when Schroll contacted his bank back in Austria to retrieve the funds, he found out that all of his money was gone. The Nazis had just annexed Austria. As McGaughey remembers in *Skiing with Style: Sugar Bowl 60 Years*, "Hannes was told the Anschluss was on—Hitler had taken over Austria. Hannes' money went to Berlin instead of Donner Pass."

Hannes Schroll was born in a small village near Kitzbuhel, in the Tyrol region of Austria, in 1909. Like Junior and many others who learned how to ski in the first quarter of the century, his first skis were barrel staves. Remarkably, Schroll won his first ski race on these barrel staves, and his prize for the win was a pair of hickory skis. Schroll quickly became an avid competitor, and in 1934, he won what was considered the fastest downhill course in the world: the Marmolata course in the Italian Alps. His win caught the attention of the Austrian chancellor, and the following year, Schroll was sent to America to represent Austria in the 1935 US National Downhill Championships at Mount Rainier. Schroll then caught the attention of the world by winning the race, beating Dick Durrance by almost two full minutes.

Besides his talent on skis, Schroll had quite the exuberant personality. He was a professional yodeler and often yodeled while skiing. During the race at Mount Rainier, he apparently yodeled as he raced through the fog. He was described as "the wild man from Austria" by the *Seattle Post Intelligencer*, and he lived up to that name for the next few decades while working at Badger Pass and then Sugar Bowl. Schroll had lasting friendships with celebrities drawn to him by his personality, including Charlie Chaplain and Walt Disney. Disney became enamored with the world of skiing and Sugar Bowl and created a short film in 1941 titled "The Art of Skiing," starring Goofy at Sugar Bowl. Disney recruited Schroll for the film for his yodeling skills. Goofy's iconic "yahoooooo-y" and the yodeling segment were Schroll's vocal contributions.

With his bank accounts plundered by Nazi Germany, Schroll started reaching out to others he thought might be interested in the investment. McGaughey offered to put up some of his own money and convinced George Stiles, an ice-skating champion who owned a ski shop, to put up another portion. Even so, it wasn't quite enough. One of the other potential investors Schroll reached out to was Walt Disney, who had taken ski lessons from Schroll at Badger Pass. Disney sent Schroll a check that was enough to make the endeavor possible, and to thank him, Schroll changed the name of one of Sugar Bowl's three mountains from Mount Hemlock to Mount Disney.

During Sugar Bowl's first snowstorm, on January 4, 1940, the Disney lift officially became California's first chairlift at the newly opened Sugar Bowl Resort, named for the sugary and crystalline quality of the snow. Schroll raised more funding to build a Bavarian-style lodge (named the Village Lodge) and his own personal chalet. Thanks to Disney's involvement, a new train station nearby, and the proximity of the resort to the Bay Area, Sugar Bowl immediately became a hot spot for visiting celebrities, as well as masses from San Francisco and Sacramento. Though the early years of Sugar Bowl had their challenges, Schroll had fulfilled his dream of creating a Tyrolean-style ski resort in North America.

When Junior started working at Sugar Bowl, almost 20 years after its opening winter, the ski resort was still a fairly small operation. By Junior's memory, they had only two or three patrollers and a handful of lift operators. The Village Lodge was still in its original, somewhat boxy state, and they were just starting to build more houses to accompany the three that made up the tiny village. Most guests stayed in the Village Lodge, and there were no roads or motorized vehicles within the village. Initially the resort relied on a bumpy and uncomfortable tractor-drawn sled ride to transport guests from Highway 40 to the resort. That changed in 1953 when Sugar Bowl built America's second and the West Coast's first gondola from the highway up to the village: the "Magic Carpet." There were no roads or cars allowed in the village, so they built at the base of the gondola an underground parking structure where guests left their cars while visiting the resort.

Junior began his career at Sugar Bowl with a negotiation. When he was hired, the manager at the time, Walter Haug, offered him a salary. The amount was already much higher than what Junior had ever made while working under Alf Engen, and he was happy to take it. But Junior could sense an additional opportunity and proposed that he make a commission on profit from the ski school. Haug, though open to the idea, warned Junior that there was zero profit from the ski school. He told Junior that they didn't run the ski school for profit, and that it was mostly just a service for their customers. Junior said something along the lines of this: "Well, let's put it in my contract and see if I can make it profitable." Haug agreed to give it a go. It would prove to be an excellent move on Junior's part.

So, in December of 1958, Junior and Maxine (pregnant with their second child) and two-year-old Barry moved to Sugar Bowl. There was no snow on the ground when they arrived, besides scattered patches among the trees. Even with the opening date up in the air, Junior went right to work creating his ski school. By mid-December he had a full staff of six or seven full-time employees, plus additional help for the weekends.

Haug hadn't found the family a place to stay for the winter yet, so the Bounouses initially stayed in a hotel room. Haug told them he was trying to find an owner with an apartment or house in the main village to rent to Junior and Maxine for the winter. When the family was finally moved into a more permanent residence, it wasn't what they had been hoping for. Unable to find any available rooms in the village, Haug had put Junior and Maxine into a small apartment in a duplex right off the old Highway 40. The apartment was small and miserably run-down. When a few of Junior's instructors stopped by for a visit, they were not impressed. One of them was a painter and offered to repaint the entire place, helped by a crew of ski instructors.

The paint job helped a bit, but the situation was not ideal. Perhaps it wasn't quite as difficult as living in the house at Alta had been, but it had plenty of its own challenges. Sugar Bowl, being fashioned after a European mountain village, was contained at the base of the ski slope. Staying in the village was not only convenient, but also cultivated a strong sense of community. Where Junior and Maxine were, by the highway, there was no real community. And since there were no roads to the village, everyone had to rely on the gondola to get there.

Another challenge was that their apartment didn't have a laundry machine, and the closest accessible one was in the Village Lodge. In order to do the laundry, Maxine, pregnant and experiencing horrible morning sickness, had to load up a toddler and their laundry, walk to the gondola, and then ride the gondola up to the lodge. Then she'd have to wait for the laundry to run through both cycles while watching Barry. Once the laundry was done, she'd gather everything, ride the gondola back down, and walk home. All that just to get a simple house chore done! The one advantage of the duplex was the couple who lived in the other apartment: a man who worked lift operations and a woman who was a nurse. She would bring over pills and remedies to help alleviate Maxine's terrible morning sickness.

Living near Highway 40 was loud and, at times, quite dangerous. There was an instance during that first year when Maxine didn't realize that Barry had somehow snuck out of the house with a level of sneakiness only teetering toddlers are capable of. Suddenly, Maxine heard a cacophony of honking from the highway. Running outside, she saw Barry in the middle of the road. Luckily, a truck driver had seen him and had been able to stop traffic by honking.

Barry wasn't the only Bounous toddler who had a near-death experience while living at Sugar Bowl. When Steve was about seven months old, he followed Barry out the front door and onto the second story landing of the family's condominium in the village. Barry was just four years old at the time, carrying his skis and poles, and forgot to close the door behind him. An open hallway and a staircase connected the landing with the ground floor, and Steve crawled right up to the edge of it, his body small enough that he was underneath the guard rail.

Junior was walking home from work and saw Steve as he sat right on the edge of the two-story drop. Barry remembers walking toward his dad when Junior suddenly dropped his skis and started running. Barry continued on toward the ski hill without a care in the world. Junior, sprinting as fast as he could, watched as Steve teetered backward off the second-story landing and landed on the pavement on his head.

Steve's head was completely smashed in on one side from the impact, but thankfully he maintained consciousness over the next few hours, screaming all the while. Junior and Maxine had to first ride the "Magic Carpet" gondola in order to access their car in the parking garage, and then quickly rushed Steve to the nearest hospital in Truckee, where the doctor told them he couldn't handle something like this. They kept driving to Reno, arriving later in the evening. The doctor on duty told them that he also couldn't handle this bad of an injury. They would have to wait until morning when one of the other doctors came in. They were warned that Steve would likely not make it through the night. They put him in a crib in the hospital while Junior and Maxine attempted to sleep in the waiting room, unable to see him all night.

Steve was still alive the following morning. When he heard Junior and Maxine's voices as they were led into the room, Steve grabbed the rungs of the crib and pulled himself to his feet. His head had swollen up like a balloon. Since he was still so young, his skull was still soft and not fully developed. His skull fractured on one side as it hit the ground, and the impact caused the other side of the skull to fracture as well. This meant that the entire skull could expand with the swelling.

The doctor brought Junior and Maxine into his office after taking some x-rays. He told them that the skull was overlapping in one area, and he wasn't sure whether or not to operate to fix it. Maxine asked him what he would do if it were his child. He thought for a moment, then said that he wouldn't operate and would wait to see if the skull mended itself. So that's what they did.

Steve had a miraculous recovery. Despite all odds, he experienced no brain damage (that we know of), and no scarring or skull deformity. But ever since, as though disappointed in himself for not sticking his first landing, he's had this curious desire to jump off things. . . .

It was such a hard winter with their living situation that the following summer, Junior told Haug that they either needed to find him and his family a place to stay in the village, or he wouldn't return as ski school director the following year. During the off-season, management built the "Snow White" condominiums in the village—some of the first condominiums ever built in the world. They gave the Bounouses a nice two-bedroom unit, which they moved into when Steve was born in the summer of 1959. They lived there for two years until management built an employee duplex meant for the ski school director and head of lift operations.

Life became easier when their living arrangements improved and as Barry and Steve became a little older. Starting their second year at Sugar Bowl, Junior and Maxine had a live-in nanny who would help them take care of the kids, which was common practice at Sugar Bowl at the time. Helpers were often a resort employee's spouse or someone looking for room and board in exchange for childcare and housekeeping. Once Barry and Steve were both old enough to go to school, Maxine was able to be an instructor again, gaining back some freedom she had been missing since Barry's birth.

Besides the living arrangements, there was another factor that made living at Sugar Bowl difficult. Junior and Maxine were no strangers to large amounts of snowfall. They'd had their fair share at Alta. But the volume of snow that could fall in the Sierra Nevada was an entirely different beast than what they had grown accustomed to in the high desert conditions of the Mountain West. Higher humidity levels along the Pacific Coast allows more moisture to gather during storms and fall to the ground. It's unusual, though not unheard of, for a storm to drop 8-10 feet of snow over a few days in Little Cottonwood Canyon. By comparison, it's common for a single Sugar Bowl storm to drop 11-16 feet over a few days. And the quality of the snow there is dense with water content, heavy, and not nearly as easy to clear off of roads and driveways and to clear from doorways.

The snow could be quite paralyzing. The season before Junior started working for Sugar Bowl, an avalanche destroyed one of the ski lifts. According to *Skiing in Style*, in 1951–52, there was such an intense series of snowstorms that Highway 40 closed for 30 consecutive days. An avalanche trapped a passenger train, carrying 223 passengers, in the mountains for six days before they could be rescued. Bill Klein recalls, "I cross-country skied down toward Yuba Gap to help out. The drifts were so big I sometimes stepped over telephone wires." Sugar Bowl recorded more than 900 inches in 1982–83. An article in *Skiing In Style* recorded this:

> *That season more than 75 feet of snow transformed Sugar Bowl into a remote outpost. From March 27 through April 8 a whopping 16 feet was added to the already huge base, an average of 14 inches per day. Houses disappeared. Electrical power from the Pacific Gas & Electric transformers . . . failed. Ice dams backed water up against bridges.*

Doug Stanley, a patroller during that season, wrote this anecdotal account:

> *Most of the senior patrol shared a home close to Sugar Bowl. The house became so completely buried we had to slide down a tunnel from the road to enter the third story. Three times I fell off twenty foot snowbanks in the dark onto the plowed road while on the way to work. Ridges and gullies were covered. We battled the mountain day in and day out, sometimes fighting chest deep in snow. To keep the mountain open you became very connected to it. You felt it even in your sleep.*

When Junior and Maxine arrived at Sugar Bowl, there were still many snow sheds covering the railroad tracks in the Sierra Nevada, some of them a few miles long. One shed spanned the railroad that separated Highway 40 from the Sugar Bowl village. If Junior and Maxine went to grab dinner or attend an event at night in South Lake Tahoe, they often missed the last gondola ride at 10 p.m. The only way to get back up to the village was to climb a wooden ladder over the snow shed in the dark—a climb that took them about 20-30 feet above the ground—then walk across the roof of the shed, and then climb back down another ladder.

Buildings would often get so buried that Junior would have to use a front-end loader to clear a path to their front door of their duplex in the village. The door was Dutch-style, and Junior often had to go in and out of the building by opening only the top half of the door. Barry and Steve preferred taking the high route and would often climb up the snow to access their bedroom on the second floor of their house.

The humid California air meant that the snow wasn't just heavier; it was also wet—wet enough at times that the winter storms wouldn't even deposit snow—just rain. Alex Brogle, the Alta lift operator turned Sugar Bowl instructor who had called Junior and told him about the ski school director opening, had advised Junior that he would need to get a large rain poncho to wear while teaching. Junior, thinking he was joking, asked, "Surely you don't ski when it's raining?" To which Brogle responded, "Oh yes, we do." The wool sweaters they had skied in up until that point were not going to cut it in the Sierra Nevada. Junior recalls a time in the middle of the season when it started raining so hard that there were streams of water gushing across the snow. The water was so intense that Maxine was nervous the boys would be swept away if they played too close to the streams. By Junior's memory, it rained about 15 inches over the course of two or three days during that storm. Then once the temperature dropped, the storm deposited another six feet of snow.

Even when the snow fell as powder, it was so heavy that the snow packed down quickly after a storm. Junior and Maxine realized they needed to update their equipment, since they were on HEAD Standards that had been tweaked for light powder skiing. Many of the ski instructors at Sugar Bowl were Austrian, and they convinced Junior to order a pair of Kneissl skis, made in Austria and marketed as one of the first "carving" skis. Though it's pretty common these days to have multiple pairs of skis for a variety of conditions, this was the start of ski diversity in the industry.

Despite the dramatic snow conditions, it was not powder skiing that Junior improved upon most during his Sugar Bowl years; it was packed skiing. When it wasn't fresh, the snow would compact and create a hard surface. While Junior had run through gates at Alta, he didn't have thorough knowledge of downhill ski racing through gates quite yet. In his own words, he "had the stamina for downhill racing, just not the technique." That was about to change.

By the time Junior arrived in Sugar Bowl, the resort was already known for ski racing. Being a talented downhill racer, Schroll had created a race at the end of the 1940 ski season that he titled the Silver Belt. The name was pulled from a historical record that mentioned how, in the 1800s, Scandinavian miners in a nearby county would hold a ski race, and the winner received a belt studded with silver. The course immediately was considered one of the most challenging and steepest ski races in North America. Since there was no chairlift to the top of Mount Lincoln at the time, all the racers had to hike and sidestep up the mountain to get to the start. The inaugural race was won by Friedl Pfieffer and Gretchen Fraser, and it marked the start of Sugar Bowl's ski racing notoriety. A few years later, Alf Engen would win it, and he encouraged Junior to compete in the race while Junior was still at Alta. Junior didn't compete in it at the time, though he would run and even set the course once he started working in California.

Ski racing was certainly on everyone's mind when Junior and Maxine moved to Sugar Bowl at the tail end of 1958. The International Olympic Committee had shocked the world in 1956 by announcing that Squaw Valley—a tiny and struggling ski area at the northern end of Lake Tahoe with one chairlift and two rope tows—would host the 1960 Winter Olympics. When Junior and Maxine moved to California, the Games were one short season away, and downhill racing was all the rage at Sugar Bowl. Junior began participating in both racing and course setting, gaining more knowledge of the technique required to make quick slalom and giant slalom turns around gates. He helped create Sugar Bowl's first ski team, which was soon known as one of the best in the country. It ended up becoming one of the first ski academies in North America, where children could attend a school designed to accommodate the odd hours and schedules of racers.

In the winter of 1960, the Australian ski team, consisting of two men and one woman, came to Sugar Bowl to train for the Olympics. They didn't have an official coach (the man who had been tasked as their chauffeur wasn't a very good skier), and they asked the resort if it could provide someone to help them set courses and train. Junior was given the task, and in the weeks leading up to the Olympics, he became their mentor, creating courses and giving them advice on how to run through gates. They asked Junior if he would be their official coach for the Olympics, and, recognizing a once-in-a-lifetime opportunity, he accepted.

The 1960 Winter Olympics had an active political backdrop when they occurred. The Cold War and Space Race were in full swing, and tensions between the Soviet Union and the United States were high. Add in the somewhat controversial decision of choosing Squaw Valley as the host area, and the Games certainly had a lot of buzz about them. On top of that, Walt Disney became the chairman of the Pageantry Committee and produced the Opening and Closing Ceremonies, both of which Junior and Maxine got to attend.

Junior was present for all the ski events as the Australian team's coach. A better skier than all three of the racers, he gave them advice on how to run through the slalom, giant slalom (GS), and downhill courses, and even ran the GS and downhill from the top of the mountain through the bottom to show them how to best run it. In the end, one of the men ended up doing quite well, placing around 15th.

The Games culminated in the Soviet Union and US men's ice hockey match. Junior, Maxine, and another ski instructor friend, Roger Bourke, were in attendance. One of the perks of being an Olympic coach was that Junior could get tickets to backstage events and to all the competitions, including what turned out to be one of the most dramatic matches of the century. (Although, they technically were one ticket short, and Maxine had to sit on Roger's lap the entire game.) The Soviet Union's ice hockey team was known for being the best in the world, but the underdog American team had won every single game leading up to the finals, and then it beat the Soviet and Canadian teams to win the gold. The unexpected win, of course, spoke loudly not only on a sport level, but also on the worldwide and political level. (Roger Bourke, who was earning his degree at Stanford to become a rocket scientist while working as a ski instructor for Junior on weekends, would ironically be in the Soviet Union to meet with some of their Mars-roving scientists when the Soviet Union fell two decades later.)

In the wake of the Olympics, Friedl Peiffer founded the International Professional Ski Races Association (IPSRA). Ski instructors, including Pfieffer, had been banned from competing in the Olympics starting in the 1930s, since they were considered "professionals" instead of "amateurs." Pfeiffer wanted to give the "pros" a chance to race and compete for money, and he hosted the first World Pro Ski Tour at Aspen in 1960. When the Tour came to Sugar Bowl for the first time in 1961, Junior had a chance to compete alongside racers like Pepi Stiegler, Stein Erikson, Toni Spiss, and Christian Pravda, who won the inaugural Tour race in Aspen. In *Skiing with Style*, Junior is quoted saying, "Racing against some of the greatest names in skiing was a truly remarkable experience. . . . It made a tremendous impression on my skiing. Those races were another wonderful moment in Sugar Bowl's history when the resort hosted the world's best."

It was an exciting start to a few fun years for the Bounouses in the Sierra Nevada. Sugar Bowl was in the process of expanding, and Junior was right in the thick of it. The Village Lodge was renovated and expanded to include the Beltroom Bar, I-80 was built in 1964 to replace the old Highway 40, allowing for even quicker travel up to the mountains, and the mountain itself was expanding to include more runs and chairlifts. Junior helped design runs on Mount Lincoln, as well as a plan for the newest chairlifts, Christmas Tree and Crow's Nest.

Junior carried these expansion efforts over to his ski school as well, determined to make it less of a "client service," as Haug had referred to it, and more of a money-making business. "Learn-to-Ski" weeks, or more commonly referred to as ski weeks, had become popular in ski resorts with prominent lodges, such as Sun Valley and Alta. After seeing how successful ski weeks were at Alta and recognizing that Sugar Bowl was one of the most accessible and high-end resorts in California, with celebrities skiing and visiting the lodge, Junior knew ski weeks could be a success there as well.

Working with hotel management, Junior helped ski weeks become one of the largest draws for guests starting in the mid-1960s. Clients could purchase a package that included six nights at the Village Lodge, including breakfast and dinner, and five days of ski instruction. The instructors would teach lodge guests how to ski during the day and then eat dinner with them at the Village Lodge and participate in social events like folk dances at night. It created a community-driven week where clients and instructors would mingle and get to know each other well by the end of the week. According to Junior, they had almost 100 percent participation from the lodge guests. And, most importantly, it was fun.

These ski weeks helped solidify the presence of the American ski technique in California, and Junior is credited with being the one to bring the teaching system there. After the creation of the Intermountain Ski Association in December of 1950 at Alta—which Junior became involved in first as vice president, then president, then board member the following years—a desire had been developing within the ski teaching community to create a universal teaching system that could span the country. Up until this time, a skier could have completely different ski lessons depending on whether the resort was influenced mostly by Austrians, or by the French, or by Norwegians. Meanwhile in Europe, ski instructors spanning different countries had managed to create a system that worked across borders. American ski instructors were craving a similar American teaching system.

So, in 1961, Alta ski instructor Bill Lash, along with a few others, including Doug Pfeiffer, created the Professional Ski Instructors of America (PSIA) with the intention of developing a teaching system that could be implemented at every ski area in the country. Junior and Alf had already been tailoring their teaching system while at Alta, and it was this technique that served as the basis for the teaching system described in the 1964 book titled *The Official American Ski Technique*, which Junior helped write while on the PSIA board. The name "American Ski Technique" was later changed to the "American Teaching Method" and then to the "American Teaching System," which it's still called today. Now, a student could take one lesson in California and their next lesson in Vermont and be able to progress within the same teaching system.

American ski instructors finally had the first unified teaching system they could follow. And, unlike the European ski techniques, the system allowed plenty of room for adapting to a student's individual needs. In an article Junior wrote and had published in *Skiing News Magazine*, he explained this:

> *Experienced instructors are well aware that ski school students are individuals; that in order to teach safely and quickly, various approaches are necessary. The U.S. ski system embraces all tried and true exercises which develop good skiers.*

Junior played a large role in helping spread the technique by writing articles while working at Sugar Bowl. A Norwegian photographer friend, Fred Lindholm, would take a series of photographs of Junior skiing in certain ways to showcase a certain type of turn or a wedge, or to demonstrate how to keep one's body aligned in certain snow conditions. Then Junior would dictate to Maxine—who, luckily for Junior, was an excellent writer, grammatical wizard, and superb typist—and she would type up an article to follow each photo series. Junior, who also started working with Rosemount Boots and HEAD Ski Company, became a staff technical writer for *Ski Magazine* and had an article in almost every issue while he was at Sugar Bowl, though of course Maxine was *technically* the technical writer. In Junior's own words, "Without Maxine, I would've never made it anywhere."

By improving technique and publishing articles, Junior was not only making a name for himself. He was also building a ski school that was soon considered one of the top ski schools in the country. He created a teaching program for children, which, as strange as it might seem now, was a rare thing at the time. According to the European ski technique, children shouldn't be taught how to ski until they are at least eight years old. Junior, along with a woman he hired to spearhead the children's program, disagreed. This woman, Glenn Springer-Miller, has been famously quoted as saying, "If they can walk, they can ski." Now, children as young as three years old could begin learning how to ski at Sugar Bowl.

Besides the ski weeks and children's program, Junior's ski school became widely known also for the notoriety of the instructors. Junior cultivated a sense of camaraderie within the ski school. As one of his instructors, Jim Stratto, recounts in *Skiing in Style*, "[Junior] made an effort to get as many instructors as possible to ski together during the week." The camaraderie meant that the guests saw a unified ski school front, and it meant that the instructors themselves pushed each other to be better. The list of people who came out of Junior's Sugar Bowl ski school is indeed impressive. Of his instructors, at least 10 of them went on to become ski school directors of their own programs, and countless others gave their own lasting contributions to the ski world.

- Alex Brogle, who originally tipped Junior off about the job, became Junior's assistant and later took over the ski school at Sugar Bowl once Junior left.
- Toni Marth, a talented racer who became the head coach for the Sugar Bowl Junior Ski Team, co-directed with Brogle before building a chalet in the Austrian Arlberg mountains.
- Jim McConkey, who followed Junior from Alta to Sugar Bowl and would compete with Junior to see who could fly the farthest off cliffs in between lessons, was ski school director for Park City Mountain Resort and then Whistler Blackcomb.
- Mike Wiegele, a spunky young Austrian, ran the ski school at Lake Louise before starting a heli-skiing business in the Canadian Rockies that's still in operation today.
- Phil Jones first became ski school director and then the president and general manager of Park City Mountain Resort, was on the PSIA Interski demonstration team, and became the PSIA chief examiner and certification chairman.
- Emo Henrich became the ski school director at Stratton Mountain Resort in Vermont, where he organized World Cup races and created another one of the nation's first ski racing academies.
- Tom Morgan and Chuck Coiner, friends from Boise, Idaho, both worked at Sugar Bowl. Morgan became the ski school director at Bogus Basin in Boise. Coiner worked at Sun Valley as a supervisor until Sun Valley bought Snowbasin, and then he became ski school director at Snowbasin.
- Bill Briggs, a wild ski mountaineer famous for making the first descent on skis down Grand Teton, became ski school director of Snow King in Wyoming.
- Royal Robbins, who made countless first ascents of various climbing routes in Yosemite, became the athletic and ski school director of the Leysin American School in Switzerland. He and Briggs used to have climbing competitions while at the ski school at Sugar Bowl, during which they'd see who could hang onto a door frame the longest, or climb across the rock wall in the lodge laterally using just one hand and one leg, or do the most pull-ups.
- And though he didn't become a ski school director, Roger Bourke went on to become a rocket scientist for NASA and worked on the Mars mission.

The Bounouses' years at Sugar Bowl were romantic in many ways. Junior was allowed free reign at a ski school of his own. The physical location of Sugar Bowl, with its Tyrolean-style, vehicle-less village, was beautiful and, indeed, romantic. In *Skiing in Style*, Junior recounted this:

> *I was very fortunate to work for Sugar Bowl. The resort allowed me the chance to design and modify a teaching system. I always compared the place to Zermatt (Switzerland) in a small way. Isolated from cars, it is a true alpine environment. And there is as much valid terrain as you can ask for.*

I was once looking at an old skiing magazine with Junior that Roger Bourke had kept all these years. There was an article about skiing that Junior (and Maxine) had written, accompanied by a photo of Junior that took up the entire page. With his poles planted firmly behind him, Junior had swung his skis up and stuck the tails in the snow in front of him. He's looking at the camera and has the most joyous expression on his face, mouth open wide in a laughing smile beneath his dark army-cut hair.

Studying the photo, I said, "It looks like you're having so much fun."

With a smile on his face and the classic twinkle in his eye, Junior responded, "We were. That was a pretty fun time."

Besides the joy of working at Sugar Bowl, employment there also made sense for the Bounouses from a monetary perspective. Besides a decent paycheck, Junior was making commission on all ski school profits. During the season, Junior was also still involved in Timp Haven, somehow still a part-owner, running the ski shop and county-wide ski programs from afar. The extra cash he could make by publishing articles in skiing magazines and contributing to gear development was also helpful. Each year, after the ski season was over, Junior and Maxine would relocate to Provo so Junior could run the family farm in the summer, bringing in another source of income.

Sugar Bowl was a wonderful opportunity, but it had its limitations. The public school system there was very small, and Junior and Maxine started noticing that Barry, especially, wasn't being challenged enough. So, after eight happy years at Sugar Bowl, Junior decided it was time to relocate. He applied for the ski school director position at Park City Mountain Resort. During the interview, they told him what his salary would be, but when they officially offered him the job the amount was significantly less than what they had promised him, and he turned it down. McConkey, upon hearing this, immediately applied for the job and became Park City's ski school director instead.

Junior decided that Timp Haven, though he had decided to sell his ownership portion before returning, still had the most to offer to him and his family. He had continued to help run both the ski school and the ski shop from afar, and he knew that making his way back into the Timp Haven world would be seamless. Junior also sensed the resort was teeming with opportunity, and he was eager to see what he could accomplish with the contacts he had already established and his new knowledge of running a ski school. And, if he and Maxine were being truthful to themselves, the Wasatch Mountains were, and always would be, their true home.

"The Olympics came to town during the winter quarter of my senior year of college at Stanford. I played hooky from my classes for two weeks. (Got some lousy grades.) I didn't have a car so [I'd take the train out to Sugar Bowl, then] I would [drive] with Junior . . . from Sugar Bowl to Squaw. The opening ceremonies were quite memorable. It was snowing when they started, but as the skier carrying the torch came down the hill, the sun came out."

— Roger Bourke, Sugar Bowl instructor

"He likes to take you to places that you'll be okay with, but you go, 'Woah, where did we just go? Did we just do that?'"

— Rick Hodas, Snowbird Mountain School employee

"An incredible quality about Junior is his standards don't change. The way he is on the hill and the way he was as a ski school director to train us and teach us about how we need to teach a good ski lesson and interact with our students—that's the way he lives his life."

— Jerry Thoreson, Snowbird Mountain School employee

Junior with Sugar Bowl general manager Ed Segal in the 1960s. Junior is wearing a sweater Maxine knitted for him.

Junior in an advertisement for Sugar Bowl in the 1960s. Junior's ski school was always full, so the ad must have worked!

Junior looking suave in one of the Sugar Bowl Ski School uniforms (hat was his own addition). 1960s.

Barry, Junior, and Steve (head looking nice and round—prior to his fall) at their condo in 1959 or 1960.

Junior promoting Rosemount boots, which he helped design in the 1960s. Junior's wearing a sweater that Maxine knitted for him. Note how perfectly flat his crew cut hairdo is.

An old proof of Junior showing off at Sugar Bowl in the 1960s. Soda Springs can just barely be seen on the opposite side of the lake in the background.
From Junior's private photo collection

Junior with a batch of students in front of his Sugar Bowl Ski School sign. Note that they shortened Junior's name to "JR" on the sign.

Junior skiing off Mount Lincoln. Photo featured in an article about Sugar Bowl in the 1960s.

Chapter 11

Skiing Onto the Big Screen

Sometime in the year 2010, I was riding on the subway while visiting a friend who was attending college at Boston University at the time. She had invited a few of her friends to go to a bar with us, and I was sitting across from a young man who, by my memory, had grown up in the greater Boston area. Hearing I was from Utah, he asked me a couple of questions that quickly had us talking about skiing. I can't remember if I told him my last name, or maybe I mentioned my grandpa, but somehow there was a moment in our conversation where he said, "Bounous? As in, Junior Bounous? I grew up watching him in Warren Miller films!"

This was not an isolated incident. Growing up in Sandy, Utah, I had plenty of schoolteachers recognize my last name. When I moved into my house in Millcreek and introduced myself to the neighbor across the street, he immediately asked if I was related to "the Bounous from all the ski films." Even when I was traveling far away in Australia, I met a man who also connected the dots.

While Junior made a name for himself in the local ski communities by being a prominent force on the mountain itself, his national—and even international—presence came from articles and photographs published in ski magazines, and, of course, ski films.

One of the first photographers to capture Junior on film was a Norwegian man named Fred Lindholm, who would be a constant companion and inspiration to Junior for decades. Many of the iconic photos of Junior were taken by Lindholm, including several that are in this book. It was Lindholm who took the photo of Junior and Maxine that wound up on the cover of the first issue of the newly renamed *Skiing* magazine in 1956. Other shots of them ended up being used for marketing purposes, like the one of Maxine that was used for a whiskey ad. Lindholm once caught a photo of Junior as he jumped off a rock on the Baldy shoulder, carrying so much air and speed that he soared about a third of the length down the hill without intending to. It's still named Bounous Rock.

Lindholm was also the one who had the idea of taking a helicopter to ski on Mount Timpanogos. Helicopters had been invented in the first half of the 20th century and started being mass produced in 1944 for military purposes. About 20 years later, helicopters became more widespread in the public realm, and it was not long before some skiers had the idea to use helicopters to access terrain normally only accessible only by a long, and potentially dangerous, hike.

When the first helicopter arrived in Utah in 1961, Lindholm contacted Junior and Jim Shane and proposed a heli-skiing day. It was early season, probably late October or early November, as Junior remembers, and there wasn't much snow in the mountains yet. They needed a location that was high in elevation (though below the chopper's altitude limit of 12,000 feet), with an aspect that would retain as much snow as possible and an area where it would be safe to ski with only 15 inches or so of snow. Being well versed in Wasatch terrain, Junior knew of a place. It was a rock-less, steep pitch in Provo Cirque.

And that's how Junior, Maxine, Elfriede Shane, and Jim McConkey became the first to heli-ski on Mount Timpanogos. The photos that Lindholm took, with Jim Shane at his side as a second shooter, are possibly some of the most iconic skiing photos ever taken on Timp. One is especially memorable. A massive rock face looms behind the group, blue and magnificent. The four skiers' tracks have cut across the side of the slope, and all four are skiing down the pitch. Three skiers are skiing abreast, while one is out in front of the pack. That one is Maxine, living up to her nickname "Fast Max." Junior would heli-ski on Timp five or six times before it would become a designated scenic and wilderness area, and choppers would no longer be allowed to land on it.

Lindholm was born just 600 miles south of the North Pole on the Norwegian island of Spitsbergen. His father worked for the Great Norwegian Coal Company. When his dad died and left his camera to him, Lindholm moved to the United States with the intention of becoming a photographer. His first gig was shooting bathing suits in Los Angeles, a stint that introduced him to another photographer named Peter Green. Green was the Alta photographer in the 1950s. When Green was drafted by the army, he contacted Lindholm to tell him about the job opening. Lindholm wisely chose a lifestyle centered on skiing rather than bikinis.

Lindholm worked in the basement of the Peruvian Lodge during his few years at Alta. He had numerous pictures printed in and on the cover of a variety of ski magazines. He started bouncing all over the United States taking ski photos of the most famous skiers in their natural habitats. Many of the most classic shots of skiers like Stein Erikson, Alf Engen, Ted Johnson, Robert Redford, and Jim McConkey were taken by Lindholm. Lindholm quickly became known for his iconic black-and-white ski photos and for using a certain Polaroid filter that made the sky dark once developed.

While working at Alta, Lindholm happened to be in the right place at the right time to capture one of the first photo series of an avalanche. He had been taking photos of McConkey skiing down a pitch, with Ed LaChapelle a stone's throw away from them, when a wet avalanche broke above LaChapelle. Lindholm was beneath them on the slope but a safe distance away, and snapped shots as the avalanche grew larger, almost burying LaChapelle. Luckily, LaChapelle was able to stay on top of the heavy snow until it stopped moving. The series of photos were featured in *Sports Illustrated*.

Not long after, Lindholm was asked to be one of the official ski photographers for the 1960 Winter Olympics in Squaw Valley, and then again for the 1964 Olympics in Innsbruck, Austria. His iconic shot of Alan Engen in 1963 became the official HEAD Ski Company ad for the Innsbruck Olympics, and a shot of the French skier Jean-Claude Killy made the cover of Newsweek magazine. Lindholm became the official photographer for Sun Valley in the 1960s, where he captured celebrities like Louis Armstrong and Steve Wynn. He was a photographer for the Freestyle Skiing World Tour in the 1970s, shooting photos of Suzy "Chapstick" Chaffee. He even caught Michale Grazier and Roger Evans doing the first hand-in-hand backflip in competition in 1973. Lindholm's quick notoriety led him to become one of the leading ski photographers of the day. I'd wager a guess that anyone who has ever skied in North America has seen some of his prints on the walls of ski resorts or on promotional material. Many of the most circulated and iconic "old school" action ski shots were taken with his lens.

Perhaps the first exposure Junior had to the fresh, developing world of ski films was through Sverre Engen. Sverre had developed an interest in ski films while working at Alta. He skied in, and may have even helped produce, two promotional films for Alta in the 1940s: *Ski Aces* and *Margie of the Wasatch*. As mentioned earlier in this book, *Ski Aces* featured the three Engen brothers skiing at Alta and was apparently one of the first films in Technicolor ever made by 20th Century-Fox. *Margie of the Wasatch* differed from *Ski Aces* in that it had a plot. In the storyline, Sverre, the leading male, tries to win the heart of Margie, a guest at the Alta Lodge. He's unable to convince her to join his ski class, and when he searches for her after she gets caught in a storm while skiing up on Baldy and has to spend the night in a cabin, it's another search party that finds her. Sverre finally wins her over when she loses her ski toward the top of the mountain and he's able to retrieve it.

Once Sverre started making his own ski films, Junior was a prime person to feature for decades to come. Steve was featured in a few of them, too. During one memorable shoot, Steve insisted that he and Junior ski a chute off Baldy that had never been skied. The reason it hadn't been skied yet is because it's not actually accessible by skis. With Steve leading the way, the two stepped their way across a cliff face, skis still on their feet, holding onto rocks to aid them. To their knowledge, it hasn't been skied since. R. I. P. to their skis' edges.

While at Sugar Bowl, Junior crossed paths with a few different directors. During his first year at the resort, he met an Austrian named Hans Gmoser. Gmoser would go on to start a heli-ski business in the Canadian Rockies called "Canadian Mountain Holidays," more commonly known as CMH. But when Junior first met Gmoser, he was traveling, mostly around Canada, and promoting ski films he had made, including one with Junior in it. It was also during Junior's stint at Sugar Bowl that he collaborated with Warren Miller the most, though their paths would first cross prior to his Sugar Bowl years.

Warren Miller started his film career in the 1940s with short surf and ski films that he narrated live for his friends. It was a recipe he would become famous for, traveling and accompanying his ski films with his live narration. Junior doesn't quite remember the first time he crossed paths with Miller, but it was sometime while he was working at Alta. When Miller would come to Salt Lake City to show his films, he'd get tickets for Junior and Maxine. Afterward, they'd go to a local ice cream shop in Sugarhouse called Snelgrove Ice Cream for banana splits—Miller's favorite. Miller, unwilling to leave his two rolls of film anywhere they could be stolen, would always bring the film into Snelgrove's in a carrying case that he kept strapped on his shoulder.

Junior can't remember all of the Warren Miller films he was in, though it seems as though, for a period of time, Junior had a powder sequence in almost every film that came out in the 1950s, even if he wasn't considered a "featured" skier in each one. In *The Color of Skiing*, filmed in 1974, Junior and his Snowbird coworker Jerry Warren were featured in nearly 10 minutes of ski footage. Miller had sent one of his videographers to Snowbird to film them, but they weren't able to film anything for a few days because of a raging snowstorm. After three or four days, the videographer started going stir crazy, claiming he couldn't just sit there and wait for the storm to cease. He decided he would try to film some footage in the storm to see what they'd get, and then he'd leave the following day. But when the following day was bluebird, Junior told him that he couldn't leave yet. So, the trio headed back out onto the mountain. Miller liked the footage from both days so much that he included almost 10 minutes in the film.

Once Steve became a strong enough skier, Miller started using him in films as well, referring to the father-and-son duo as "Junior" and "Junior Junior." In *Skiing in the Sun*, Steve is featured jumping off cliffs around Snowbird, while Junior, his hair by this time turning its iconic shade of silver, charges through chest-deep powder without a hat.

In a memorable clip in *Winter Fever*, Junior and Steve were skiing for Miller's team at Mike Wiegele's heli-skiing company up in British Columbia. The film crew proposed that Junior, Steve, and one of the heli-guides ski side by side through a narrow chute. After looking at the chute, Junior decided to sit this run out. Steve and the guide started down the pitch, and the snow broke around them immediately.

Since they had started skiing near the top of the peak, Steve knew that the fracture line couldn't be too far above them, and the slide likely wasn't very deep yet. He immediately maneuvered his skis so the tips were pointed toward the side of the slide, while sort of flipping himself over and reaching his arms through the moving snow. He knew there was a hard layer of snow beneath him—a crust from a recent bout of rain. He punched one of his hands through the rain crust, letting it drag through to create resistance to slow his momentum even as the slide around him threatened to pull him down the hill. The slide popped him back up onto his skis, which pulled his arm out of the stable snow, but he punched through it again, and perhaps again a third time. It did the trick; Steve was able to halt his momentum enough that he was able to ski out of the slide the next time it popped him up. After the slide had settled, they could see lines in the rain crust where he had punched through the snow: "claw marks" where Steve had clung to the snow for dear life almost by the tips of his fingers.

The guide was not so lucky. He was swept down into the chute and partially buried, but thankfully got out okay, despite the avalanche debris being an estimated 8 to 10 feet deep. In the film version, however, which captures the start of the avalanche and Steve punching his fist into the moving snow, the avalanche sequence ends with just one hand (apparently the hand of the man caught in the avalanche) sticking out of the snow, waving for help. Another man (apparently Steve, who avoided the avalanche) skis up, but rather than assisting the hand in need, he takes the wristwatch off the hand and then skis away—classic Warren Miller humor.

The last film Junior skied for was one titled *Bounousabuse: 80 Junior Years*. Produced by the Keller and MacLean families, the film was made to celebrate Junior's 80th birthday. On March 13, 2004, a helicopter took

Junior, Barry, and Steve to the top of Pipeline Chute at Snowbird, the chute on which Junior had taken the inaugural run in 1972. Junior and his sons then skied Pipeline together, 79-year-old Junior not realizing it was for his surprise birthday film.

"He was up on Germania one day, and he decided that he wanted to try skiing a little different way. . . . He stepped out of [his skis], switched his feet around so the skis were going backwards, and then proceeded to ski all the way down the mountain backwards. And everybody that was watching him would say, Who in the world is this man?'"

— Alan Engen, Alta skier and historian

"When I was a teenager, my mother was a librarian at the Provo City Library. She was happy to inform me that they would show weekly ski films by Warren Miller featuring our neighbor Junior Bounous. I watched the movies each week and felt like I got to know Junior from his personable descriptions of his ski experiences. I fell in love with the beauty of what was shared in those films—the mountains, the snow, and Junior's powder skiing."

— Debra Bounous, daughter-in-law

"To be able to ski some of the most spectacular places on earth with my dad in various Warren Miller films was super special for me. I'll always cherish the experiences we had skiing and filming together."

— Steve Bounous, son

". . . [Junior] was always one of the most laid back people in the ski industry. And when I showcased his ski ability on my films, some people said, 'Wow, that looks a lot more fun than going through the bumps and things.' And I went out of my way to put him in the films for a long time because he was so much better than anybody else."

— Warren Miller, ski film producer and legend

"I found him and Jerry Warren in deep powder one day, and I had this camera that would shoot 400 pictures a second, so it was about 15 [or] 20 times slower than normal. And when it came back, it was just some of the most beautiful stuff I had ever seen in my life. Anyway, when you think of powder you think of Junior Bounous. End of story."

— Gary Nate, photographer who worked for Warren Miller

"I've spent decades skiing with him, and each time I learn something more. His unending patience, his generosity, his kindness and optimism—they all play into him being such a great teacher. But the times I made the most growth were when he'd just encourage me to go for it. For instance, I learned to turn quickly simply because of his love for finding the powder in the trees. 'Follow me!' he says and disappears into the thick of it, and next thing you know it's turn or else! And turn I did!"

— EvaLynn Bounous Bolen, granddaughter

"I started working in Alta in the late 1980s, but I already knew of Junior during my younger days skiing in New England and Pennsylvania from seeing incredible pictures of him skiing in Little Cottonwood canyon. I dreamed of skiing the deep powder of Utah as a kid, and Junior's apparent ease on skis in the deep snow inspired me to learn.

[While working at Alta] I often hitchhiked on the canyon road going to and from to ski or work. On numerous occasions, Junior picked me up and gave me a ride up the canyon, often all the way to Alta even though his destination was Snowbird. It's hard to describe the feeling of meeting the deep-snow legend Junior Bounous, but I think the word 'awe' comes to mind. . . . He comes across as genuine, cultured, and easygoing, which I think reflects in his skiing style . . . His [style] is a true deep powder icon."

— Nathaniel DuPertuis, Alta skier and employee

Maxine and Junior on the cover of *Skiing's* first issue in 1958. Photo taken at Alta by Fred Lindholm one or two years before the issue came out, off the Baldy shoulder.
Fred Lindholm

Maxine skiing the Baldy shoulder at Alta for a whiskey advertisement around 1954.
Fred Lindholm

Barry tagging along for a ride at Alta in the late 1950s. These photos, captured by Fred Lindholm, were taken using Kodachrome film, which produced some of the first high-quality colored photos in the mid-20th century.
Fred Lindholm

Jim McConkey, Elfriede Shane, Junior, Fred Lindholm, Maxine, and Jim Shane, during a heli-ski excursion on Mount Timpanogos. Around 1961.

Junior doing what he does best: skiing powder in the sun. He's wearing the iconic orange Snowbird ski instructor uniform from the early 1970s. Junior and Jerry Warren, wearing these uniforms, were featured as the main skiers in one of the more iconic Warren Miller films, *The Color of Skiing* (1974). In one of the segments, Junior and Jerry, both in their orange uniforms, float through bottomless powder, blue skies behind them, accompanied by Antonio Vivaldi's Op. 8 No. 4 in F Minor: I. Allegro (otherwise known, appropriately, as "Winter" from Vivaldi's "The Four Seasons").

Warren Miller and Junior at Sugar Bowl in 1964. Note the low-cut boots (before Junior helped design the Rosemount boot). The deck of The Lodge at Sugar Bowl is in the background.

Barry and Steve catching a ride at Alta during a photo shoot. This photo was used in an advertisement for a Polaroid camera (which Maxine is holding). The ad covered an entire wall in a New York City train station. Early 1970s.

Junior jumping in Canada for Warren Miller's film *Winter Fever*. 1979.

Steve and Junior skiing in sync for a photo shoot for a *SKI Magazine* article about skiing powder. Early 2000s.

Chapter 12

Give 'Em the Bird

By the time Snowbird Ski Resort lifts began running in December of 1971, Junior had been involved in Utah's ski industry for 30 years. He was a confident leader, a phenomenal skier, a dependable contributor to multiple ski magazines, and one of the country's most inspiring ski instructors. He had spent the past few decades developing new ways of skiing, improving current techniques, and crafting methods of teaching these to others. It would be incorrect to say that Junior didn't continue doing all of these things during the following decades, but he had also reached a pinnacle of professionalism by the time he committed to a career at Snowbird. It was as though he had been climbing up a mountain the past three decades and, upon finally reaching the peak, found that there was much exploring to do. And the top of that peak was, of course, Hidden Peak, Snowbird's iconic summit.

The area that became Snowbird had long been a side-country and backcountry destination for skiers, many from Alta who would hike over the ridgeline dividing Collin's Gulch and Peruvian Gulch, or over Sugarloaf Pass into Mineral Basin. Avalanche danger was often a concern when skiing there. Dolores LaChapelle almost lost her life in an avalanche in Peruvian Gulch, and the Bounouses' future in-law, Grant Culley, almost lost his life during a slide on Regulator Johnson. The only thing sticking out when the snow settled was his thankfully prominent nose.

Over the years, the area had caught the attention of a man named Ted Johnson. Born in 1926 along the beaches of southern California, Ted's first passion was not skiing, but surfing and road biking, the latter of which he competed in and won junior titles. He worked for a stint in Hawaii as a lifeguard manager at Waikiki, and then became involved in one of the earliest cotton harvesting machines to hit the farming market. His venture was quite successful monetarily, but it didn't satisfy Ted's craving for adventure. Intrigued by the skiing fad—relatively new at the time—he visited Sun Valley sometime after World War II and immediately fell in love with skiing. Then someone mentioned Alta to Ted as he was headed to Sun Valley again, and he decided to make a detour to Utah. That detour changed the course of his life forever. Willing to trade in his financial success to lead a lifestyle he loved, he sold his cotton harvesting machine and moved up Little Cottonwood Canyon in 1954.

In order to support his skiing obsession, Ted became a man of all trades, working as a handyman and maintenance man at times, a photographer at other times, and then as a part-time ski instructor. He began working his way through the ranks, managing the Watson Shelter and both the Alta and Rustler Lodges. It was while he was working at the Rustler Lodge that he hired his soon-to-be wife, Wilma (whose nickname "Wilbere" is the namesake of the Wilbere chairlift at Snowbird). Then in 1964, he set his sights down the canyon from Alta, to Peruvian Gulch, Hidden Peak, and Gad Valley.

Like Alta, much of the land had been used for mining purposes. According to an article published in a 1972 edition of *Sports Illustrated*, "In all, about $37 million worth of ore was packed and chipped and tunneled out of the sides of Little Cottonwood Canyon." There was still some active mining at Snowbird around the middle of the 20th century, though it had been losing steam when Ted started looking at the land.

Ted knew that he would have to own the majority of the mining claims in Peruvian Gulch and Gad Valley in order to propose another ski resort to the US Forest Service, so he quietly began hunting down the mining companies and individual miners to offer them cash in exchange for their claims. The first of these claims he purchased in 1965 was the Blackjack mine for $30,000, for which the Blackjack run at Snowbird is named after. It took him quite a few years to track down the owners of 95 other abandoned mining claims, the last of which was owned by a retired miner living in a trailer in California, whom Ted paid $18,500 for the claim.

In the meantime, Ted started approaching others in hopes of finding 20 limited partners willing to give Ted the capital required for the development. In exchange for $20,000, they and their families would get lifetime season passes to Snowbird, as well as a set of rooms to own at the first hotel. The first of these partners to commit was Grant Culley. Ted sent him over to Hidden Peak via helicopter with a few other folks, including his 12-year-old daughter Suzie, to scope out the area and ski some powder. Apparently undeterred by his near-death experience, Grant eagerly told Ted that he was in.

Grant Culley played an integral part in Snowbird's development (and not just because he was the author's other grandfather, though indulge her as she dedicates a moment to him). Grant was born to a ranching family in the greater Los Angeles area. He became a radio jammer in World War II, and then he attended Stanford University (gambling to pay for his tuition), where his roommate was a man named William LaFollette. William invited Grant to join his family vacation at Sun Valley over Christmas one year. It was there that Grant met William's younger sister, Suzanne LaFollette.

Suzanne, a concert pianist, violinist, and model, had recently returned from a trip to Norway, where she had accepted a man's proposal for marriage. According to Grant, Suzanne wore her engagement ring the first night. After they met that first night, the ring was nowhere to be seen. Not unlike Junior and Maxine, Grant and Suzanne's relationship was kick-started by skiing together. Not long afterward, the two were married on September 18, 1952.

They built a house in Portola Valley, California, and would often travel to Sugar Bowl to ski in those early days. While at Sugar Bowl, Grant became aware of the renowned ski school director named Junior, and though they didn't interact directly too much during that time period, Junior's presence made Grant aware of a ski resort in Utah where the powder was deep and light and the skiers were some of the best in the country. Pretty soon, rather than embarking on the relatively short four-hour drive to Sugar Bowl, Grant began packing up his family, which now included three young girls—Robyn, Suzie, and Maryly—and making the much longer trek to ski at Alta.

Grant became the first monetary investor in Snowbird in the 1960s, and from then on, the Culleys became a persisting presence at the new resort. Our family still owns the original set of four rooms at the Lodge that Grant picked out as part of that early investment. Suzanne insisted on lugging a grand piano into one of the rooms, and there are some who still remember hearing her piano music echoing down the halls on the sixth floor (the piano is still there).

During Snowbird's first Christmas, Grant, a bit of a pyromaniac and a licensed pyrotechnician, put on a firework display near the plaza on both Christmas Eve and New Year's Eve. After doing it by himself for the first few years, he recruited ski patrol to assist. It's a tradition the resort still has to this day. Being the devious trickster he was, Grant would also sometimes set off fireworks that hadn't necessarily been approved by resort management. It was not uncommon to be sitting at an outdoor dinner table with Grant and suddenly have a round of firecrackers go off at your feet. And he'd often recruit his soon-to-be son-in-law, Steve Bounous, to participate in these stunts. During one memorable display, Grant and Steve set off a large rocket near the Lodge Bistro, which has floor to ceiling windows at ground level. Steve remembers that the sound waves were so intense that all the windows reverberated with the force, nearly shattering. Lucky for them, Grant was good friends with the manager of the Bistro at the time. Rather than calling the authorities, the manager urgently beckoned them into the restaurant to take haven before they could get into real trouble. Having received the approval of Grant, Steve married Suzie Culley at the Cliff Lodge in 1985, thus joining the Bounouses and Culleys as one family.

(And in 2021, I married Colin Gaylord—grandson to Bud Gaylord and Mary Ellen Shumway, the couple who built the original Cliff Lodge in 1971.)

Grant kept skiing until an aggressive cancer took his life in 1993. For our family, it's the highlight of our year to watch the fireworks accompany the torchlight parade on Christmas Eve. It might seem like a normal holiday occurrence to most, but for us it's a celebratory nod to Grant and Suzanne, who, like Junior and Maxine, were iconic members of the early Snowbird community. Watch for us on the plaza deck every Christmas Eve—we'll be in Suzanne's and Grant's old neon ski outfits, singing Christmas carols in harmony at the top of our lungs.

Even with the limited partners he had acquired, Ted knew he would need more capital to develop a new ski area. In 1969 Ted connected with Dick Bass, the heir of a very successful Texas oil family. Intrigued by the idea, and already an investor in Vail Associates and Aspen Ski Corp, Dick agreed to visit the area. It was early season when Dick arrived in Little Cottonwood Canyon, but Snowbird already had a significant amount of snow on the ground, so much that it actually somewhat hindered their tour of the mountain. Ted was quick to point out that other ski resorts in the West, like Sun Valley and resorts in parts of Colorado, were still lacking snow on their slopes. Dick was convinced, and by 1970, Ted was ready to approach the US Forest Service and propose the creation of the new ski area: Snowbird.

Collecting mining claims, raising capital, and finding investors turned out to be only half the battle for Ted. Despite many who were excited by the idea of another resort up Little Cottonwood Canyon, there were many who were not. The Wasatch Mountain Club, still dedicated to backcountry skiing excursions, was opposed to building chairlifts in the beautiful backcountry. One of the Wasatch's most prominent conservation groups today, Save Our Canyons, was formed to quash the resort, believing it was corporate America overstepping by placing dollar signs on the Wasatch's wilderness and environment. The group began circulating an illustration of a massive gorilla with a pair of skis on his shoulder and a money sign on his shirt, greedily hiking up the mountain between tram towers. In addition, many of the higher-ups at Alta were worried that Snowbird would take their business. Much of Ted's time was consumed by participating in debates and discussions about the environmental impacts of what a new ski area would bring.

These groups were not incorrect that the creation of a new resort would alter the mountain's landscape. Ted had designs to build a tram to the Hidden Peak, one of the longest tramways in the world at the time, which would not only provide a stunning vista to customers, but also be an eyesore on top of a once pristine peak. Ski areas, of course, need runs for clients to ski down, requiring large swaths of land to be cleared of trees, shrubs, and bushes. Service roads had to be cut into the side of the mountain and widened for moving machinery and work vehicles. Ted also decided that the resort required the canyon's first sewage pipe that would run the entire length of Little Cottonwood Canyon—an enormous undertaking that required boring and blasting through solid granite rock. The five-year process of getting permission and funding, not to mention the complicated process of building it, led to the system being named the "Ted Johnson Memorial Sewer Line."

Junior had known Ted for some time before Snowbird was built. The two had overlapped briefly at Alta, Ted working part time with Junior and Alf as a ski school instructor before Junior left for Sugar Bowl. During one visit to Alta while Junior was living in California, Ted approached Junior and asked him if he would like to become one of the 20 limited partners. Though he was financially better off than he had been his entire life, Junior still couldn't afford the $20,000 price tag and had to decline. A few years later, in the early spring of 1971, Junior was at Alta competing in the National Gelande Championship. Ted approached him again with a different proposition. Junior had been hired as a development consultant for multiple ski areas in both Utah and California by this time, and Ted wanted to hire him to design the runs for Snowbird. The resort was scheduled to open in December later that year, and it would be a large undertaking to get all the runs cleared and ready to go before then. With his work at the Sundance ski school wrapping up in April, Junior accepted. (Perhaps it was the excitement of this new venture that caused Junior to fly farther than anyone else at the competition that day and, at the age of 45, win the National Gelande Championship.)

Junior already knew the area from decades of backcountry skiing, and Ted had already mapped out where the chairlifts would be. Junior's job was to figure out how to get skiers from point A—the top of Hidden Peak and the various chairlift terminals where skiers would unload—to point B—the chairlift terminals where the skiers would onload, as well as Snowbird Village, where the base of the Tram was being built. To anyone who hasn't aided in the run development of a ski area, it can be easy to take designated ski runs and cat tracks for granted. Getting a mountain ready for skiing is challenging, which Junior knew as well as anyone, having helped open a few and having served as a consultant for many others. But Snowbird was exceptionally difficult. As Junior says, "Ski areas in Colorado and most areas had it easy compared to what we did at Snowbird. It was a rough mountain to open for skiing."

Junior's work for Snowbird Ski Resort began in an architect's office building in downtown Salt Lake City that spring. He was hired on full time at the end of April, and he immediately began pouring over topographic maps of the area, analyzing where each chairlift would unload skiers and how to get those skiers down the mountain. He and a man named Kent Hoopingarner (nicknamed "Hoopi"), who was in charge of avalanche mitigation and working with ski patrol, spent a month and a half working on several tasks. They had to figure out where they would need cat tracks, design a variety of beginner, intermediate, and advanced runs based on the natural features of the terrain, and hire trail crews to get ready for the summer push. These crews included a man named Tedd Cloward—a ski racer whose father was a lumberer and who became Junior's right-hand man during the next few months. After Junior would analyze an area on the topographical maps thoroughly, a helicopter would drop him off around the mountain, still covered in snow at that time, so he could ski down and examine the would-be runs for himself, making note of the natural features, checking to see that the topographical maps matched the actual terrain and what would be underneath the snow, and verifying what would have to be done to make it skiable.

The winter season of 1970–71 had been a big snow season, and there was still a foot of snow on the ground by the time Junior's trail crews started chain saw work on June 10, 1971, at the base of what would soon become the Wilbere chairlift. They started their work in the lowest elevations, having to wait until the snow melted more before moving to the higher elevations. The base of Wilbere was mostly aspen trees, which could be handled by a crew with chainsaws, but Big Emma, which was soon to become the main beginner-intermediate thoroughfare for almost any skier in Gad Valley, was a thick tangle of 20-foot-tall willows that proved difficult to get rid of. Junior hired a friend of his from Provo, Ernie Tucker, to work a bulldozer in the area, but even so, it took great effort to get that part of the mountain ready for skiers.

Clearing runs near the Gad 2 chairlift turned out to be the area that required the most amount of tree clearing. It was a challenge to figure out a way of getting skiers from the offloading area of the Gad 2 lift toward Mid Gad Restaurant and Big Emma. The two runs that they designed—Election, which was solely Junior's idea, and Bassackwards—were heavily forested with pines. To clear them, Junior had to work closely with the Forest Service, which had initially limited how wide the runs could be. Both runs were very narrow, but after a few years, the Forest Service realized how dangerous these narrow, bottleneck runs were, and the agency allowed the runs to be widened.

While the higher reaches of Regulator Johnson were naturally clear of trees, the bottom of Regulator, near where Grant Culley was caught in an avalanche, proved to be tricky as well. There was no natural route off the pitch. It was all rock and pine, and Junior had to design a banking right turn to get folks from the bottom of Regulator to the top of Bassackwards.

Peruvian Gulch wasn't quite as difficult to clear as Gad Valley. Much of Chip's Run was already devoid of dense trees, which is why it was such a popular backcountry skiing area. And since service roads had already been made through the gulch for machinery to access the top of Hidden Peak to build the tram, Junior's crew didn't have to work as hard to get onto the hill as they did in Gad Valley. But Peruvian Gulch had its own challenges. Blackjack had deep stream beds that had to be culverted, Anderson's Hill proved to need some tree clearing, and the steep gully at the bottom of the Cirque needed to be smoothed into a more gentle bowl shape. Since they had needed to dedicate so much effort to Gad Valley during the majority of the summer, much of the work done in Peruvian Gulch happened later in the fall.

Partway through the summer, Junior realized that there needed to be some sort of connecting road for the crews to navigate from Gad Valley to Peruvian Gulch and back. He also knew that once the resort opened, there needed to be a way for skiers to get from Chip's Run to Gad Valley without having to ski all the way to the base of the mountain and traverse. Junior proposed another cat track that would accomplish both things, and Ernie Tucker built Rothman's Way using his bulldozer.

In late November, as the opening date approached, Junior sent a crew to start clearing a run that would be the farthest northeast run on the entire mountain, a bit down the canyon from Alta's Wildcat chairlift and near the Blackjack area. Junior and his team began at the base and worked about a third of the way up the run when a large snowstorm rolled in, depositing a couple of feet of snow. Knowing that trying to clear it anymore would be pointless with winter on the way, Junior called off the effort. So, when Snowbird opened about a month later and the run hadn't been fully cleared, mountain operations wondered who had begun clearing the run but hadn't finished the job: who'd done it? Who dunnit?

As Junior says, "I would've told them that I did it, but no one bothered asking me."

So next time you ski the run named Who Dunnit, you'll be able to answer the mountain's question. Who dunnit? Junior dunnit.

It was tough work. Junior and his crew labored 10 hours a day, from sunrise to sunset, six days a week for two summers. On Sundays, their one day off, Hoopi would spend his day cleaning the chainsaws and resharpening them, so they were ready to go on Monday. And Junior, still a husband and a father of two down in Provo, commuted about two-and-a-half hours each day to drive up to Snowbird and back down.

The mountain itself was unlike any other terrain he'd skied before, and Junior was getting to know it more intimately than almost anyone else. It intrigued him. Designing runs requires taking a lot of factors into consideration. First, there's the type of terrain: the bedrock, the soil, the vegetation, the pitch. Then there's the way the terrain lends itself to a potential ski run: the way the land turns, the fall line of water, the run-out from a steeper pitch into a flatter area, any natural bottlenecks. Then one has to determine what is required to make it skiable: vegetation clearing, culvert building, widening, perhaps explosives if an area is too rocky, a cat track to cut from point A to point B. And finally, one has to consider how people would ski it: the level of ability required to ski it, whether it's an essential run to get to the base of the mountain, and if so, whether true beginners ski it, and if not, the alternate ways beginners can get down.

Junior grew to love the challenge of working with the mountain, not trying to flatten and force it into a skier's submission, but building the resort to weave its way as naturally as possible around the mountain's curves. Despite the obvious environmental impacts necessary to develop a ski resort, Ted had been firm that no tree be cut down that could be left standing and no stream redirected unless there was no other option, in order to keep the mystique of the mountain that he and so many others had originally fallen in love with. Junior, too, had fallen in love with the place, and, though he didn't know it yet, was about to commit the next five decades of his life to it.

Junior's early dedication to the mountain before the resort was open was one of the reasons Junior accepted when Ted Johnson approached him that fall and asked him to be the ski school director. Not many people realize that Junior's initial involvement at Snowbird had nothing to do with the ski school whatsoever. Junior hadn't even applied for the job. He was running the ski school and county programs and ski shop at Sundance, which was significantly closer to his house and family in Provo, and he had no inkling of a desire to change that. If Ted had approached him a year earlier with the same job offer, he likely would have politely declined the position. After spending months getting to know the intricacies and challenges of the mountain, however, that changed. Junior was able to witness firsthand how long of a season Snowbird could have, having to deal with a foot of snow at the mountain's base in June, and knew the quality of snow from his days at Alta. Junior was enthralled by the possibilities.

As for Ted, he had received 10-15 applications for Snowbird's first ski school director. But no one had caught his eye like the man working tirelessly from sunup till sundown, leading crews of workers through thickets of willows and aspen, who somehow managed to balance a dedicated work ethic with a gentle presence and humorous outlook on life. Who better to take on the role of Snowbird's first ski school director?

Ted and his mountain crew's efforts paid off. Despite the incomplete Who Dunnit (or perhaps because of it, in a way, since the early snowfall that halted its development served as a good snow base for the first season), Snowbird Ski Resort started running its lifts on December 23, 1971. The red tram and the blue tram, installed by a team of Swiss engineers, were polished and ready to carry 125 passengers per load to the top of Hidden Peak. There were three double chairlifts—Wilbere, Gad I, and Gad 2—and a myriad of runs to get skiers from the chairlift terminals to the base. At the heart of it all was the Snowbird Center, complete with shops, food options, a bar, and a skier's bridge spanning from the village's third-story plaza to the ski runs. The first hotel, The Lodge, was ready to tempt guests with an outdoor pool with uninterrupted views of the mountain.

The first few weeks of Snowbird's existence were full of the "who's who" of the ski industry. Ted Johnson invited any celebrity he could get a hold of to come ski the official opening day at his new resort—about 10 days after the resort started its lifts running. All three Engen brothers were in attendance, as were Stein Eriksen, Robert Redford, and Jim McConkey. As Junior and Jim stood on the summit of Hidden Peak that day, Jim asked Junior what terrain hadn't been skied yet. Junior pointed to Pipeline—a long, narrow, steep chute off the crest of Twin Peaks and a tantalizing opportunity. Junior radioed down to Ted to get his approval, and Ted sent one of their work helicopters to pick them up from Hidden Peak and drop them off at the top of Twin Peaks.

Despite the two friends' good-natured competitiveness to be the first to ski new terrain, Jim, recognizing the significance of the moment, yielded the honor of "first run" to Junior. But not by much. Junior recalls charging down the chute and looking over his shoulder at one point to see Jim barely a turn or two behind him. The knee-deep snow was soft, and the skiing was beautiful.

From the first day the resort opened, Junior Bounous Ski Incorporated (which would later transition to the Snowbird Ski School and then be renamed the Snowbird Mountain School when snowboarding lessons were added in the 1990s) was ready to teach. Junior had a quiver of ski instructors—including Jerry Warren, soon to become Junior's second-in-command—who eagerly signed up to work for Junior at Utah's newest ski resort. Instructors emerged from the woodwork, coming down from Alta, up from Sundance, even from other states. Junior brought to Snowbird the bus program he had created in Utah County while at Sundance. Every weekend at 10 a.m., 500 students would unload from the buses at the base of Gad I lift, where 100 instructors would be ready to greet them.

It was tricky teaching students that first year. Today's classic Snowbird beginner run, Chickadee, had yet to be developed. Students would meet their instructors in the corral at the bottom of Gad Valley, which wasn't well-equipped for crowds of that size. Instructors would teach their students how to snowplow and stop on a gentle slope near where the race timing shack is now. Once the students got the hang of that, instructors took them up the Gad I chair, unloaded at the midway point, then took West 2nd South to the bottom. Junior's instructors' goal was to get the student onto the lift by the end of a two- or three-hour lesson. Once Chickadee opened the following year, they moved many of the beginning lessons to Chickadee, though their numbers were so great that many lessons continued in Gad Valley as well.

Junior recalls bumping heads a bit with the marketing team at Snowbird during those early years. Ted intended Snowbird to be a higher-end resort, catering to professionals and the "who's who" of the ski world. Having hundreds of beginner skiers in the corral wasn't the look the marketing team was going for, and Junior got some pushback. But Junior knew the importance of teaching others how to ski. It was an essential part of building the resort's clientele. Teach young adults and children how to love to ski at Snowbird, and they are likely to come back for decades, bringing their own families and friends. Junior was quite right about this. Anyone who has spent a significant amount of time skiing at Snowbird has likely noticed that it has a generational, family-like feel to it.

Creating a strong children's program was one of four factors that Junior credits to the development of Snowbird's reputation as having one of the best ski schools in the country within just a few short years after opening. A second factor, though it may sound obvious, was the mountain and the snow. The quality of the snow in Little Cottonwood Canyon was already well-known from Alta, and it didn't take long for accounts of the exciting terrain to spread through the North American ski community. The tram, only the second of its kind in the United States, was a factor as well. Within just seven minutes of boarding the tram, a skier could have access to 3,000 vertical feet, which, if the skier was skiing fast enough, could be skied down in the seven minutes it took for the tram to return to the base. The pace of play for skiing was fast, and instructors would be required not only to ski these conditions themselves, but also to teach others how to do so.

Another factor that contributed to Snowbird's reputation was the quality of the ski instructors who immediately applied to work for Junior. Because of the hype around Snowbird's opening and the rumors surrounding the terrain and snow, some of the best ski instructors in the country wanted to take advantage of the opportunity. Junior had no shortage of excellent instructors vying for the chance to become a Snowbird ski school instructor. While some ski school directors might feel uncomfortable and shy away from hiring instructors who are better skiers than they are, Junior did not. In his words, those high-performing skiers were "feathers in his cap," and he welcomed them with open arms.

The fourth factor was how these instructors were trained. Junior's approach to the ski school was that public relations was more important than profit, and his goal was 100 percent customer satisfaction. The Snowbird instructors were known for being able to teach a student how to ski on a wide variety of ski conditions and terrain, from firm and steep pitches to powder in the trees. To make sure that his employees were up to date on the latest teaching techniques, Junior would take instructors onto the hill to show them new teaching techniques, and to help them improve their own skiing.

A fifth important factor that contributed to the school's success, though he'd be hard-pressed to acknowledge it, was Junior Bounous' role as the captain of the ship. His presence certainly added to the ski school's allure. Staying true to his past and the teachings of Alf Engen, Junior preached that the role of the instructor was to keep students safe and to teach them to enjoy skiing and the mountain. A phrase that gets passed around our family, the ski school, and the race team rings true: "Learn to love skiing and the rest will follow."

A few years after Snowbird's opening, Junior found himself spending time with a couple of true celebrities. Robert Redford had driven up from his cabin at Sundance to spend the day at Snowbird, and he'd brought a couple of friends: Paul Newman and Barbara Streisand. Redford and Newman had starred together in *Butch Cassidy and the Sundance Kid* in 1969, and Redford and Streisand had just been costars in *The Way We Were* in 1973. Redford was arguably one of Hollywood's most recognizable actors at the time, and Junior was standing in the Gad Valley corral with him, as well as Newman, and Streisand, when a man approached the group. The man asked if Junior was *the* Junior Bounous and then asked for his autograph. The man said that he was from Tooele, a rural town west of the Salt Lake City airport, and excitedly told Junior that Junior was the second celebrity he's ever met—the first being Earl Miller down in Provo. Without a second glance at Robert Redford, Paul Newman, or Barbara Streisand, the man thanked Junior profusely and skied away.

Soon Snowbird instructors were recognized on a national level. Every few years, the PSIA (Professional Ski Instructors of America) selects a few individual ski instructors from around the country to be part of their demonstration team. These team members are supposed to exemplify the ideal qualities of a ski instructor, and they visit ski resorts around the country to teach clinics. In 1975, Snowbird instructors PJ Jones, Chris Ryman, and Jerry Warren were all named to the demo team (then called Interski). They were the first of many Snowbird instructors that would be named to the PSIA demo team in the following years and decades.

Jerry became an integral part of the Snowbird ski school. He had already proved himself to Junior while they were at Sundance. He was a decent skier and had a great personality, and from the start, he expressed a desire to get better. His skiing continued to improve, as did his ability to teach others. Once Junior brought him to Snowbird, Jerry matured into a management role. He was excellent with clients and even better at training other instructors, particularly how an instructor could teach a variety of techniques to clients. Junior found that he could trust Jerry in any situation that got thrown at him. Junior and Jerry both lived quite far from Snowbird—Junior in Provo, and Jerry down in Springville, a town south of Provo—so it quickly became routine for Jerry to pick up Junior on his way to Snowbird, and the two would spend the hour-long commute discussing their ski school. At the end of the day, they would spend another hour talking about how the day went. It was as though they had a casual, two-hour meeting together each day. It added to the apparent seamlessness of their work relationship.

Soon there was a powerful sense of community seeping out of Snowbird's mountain school. From the very start, Junior worked tirelessly to create camaraderie and a sense of family within his ski school. One of the ways he did this was to have the ski school instructors take the last tram together at the end of the day, similar to how the instructors at Alta used to take one last adventurous run together on Collin's chair. These last trams, which happened after the mountain had closed to the public, were "follow the leader" excursions, where Junior was the leader. He'd take them wherever he saw fit that afternoon.

Quite often on a last-tram run, Junior would lead them in a clinic, showing them different drills that they could teach their clients, and he sometimes invited guest teachers. Once he invited his son Steve, who was racing for the US Ski Team at the time, and a couple of Steve's friends who raced for the Canadian national team. Starting from the top of Regulator Johnson, Junior staggered his ski school down the side of the hill. Then the racers, all World Cup skiers, would make GS or Super G turns all the way down the pitch while the ski school instructors observed. The entire group would then move to the next part of the mountain, ending with Big Emma. While everyone else was still at the top of Big Emma, Steve was the first down, cruising into the Wilbere corral at breakneck speeds before coming to a halt.

A ski patroller named Marty Hoey saw Steve skiing past as she was working to close down the mountain for the day, unaware that he was part of a ski school clinic. By the time she skied up to him, she was irate. With Junior still up at the top of Big Emma, there was no one to convince Marty that the seemingly hot-headed 20-something wasn't just free skiing like that for the hell of it. Marty skied away before Junior or anyone else could come and vouch for Steve. She apparently tried to get Steve kicked off the mountain for good. Luckily for Steve, he was later tasked with having to spend a day on Big Emma telling other people to slow down as his punishment, rather than receiving a permanent ban. At the end of his shift, Marty skied up to him and told him to take a lap with her. Over the course of the next hour skiing together, the two were able to develop mutual respect for one another.

Besides being on ski patrol at Snowbird, Marty was an excellent mountaineer. She was considered one of the best female mountaineers in North America, perhaps in the world, during the early 1980s. She and Dick Bass became friends while working at Snowbird, and when Dick decided that he was going to try to be the first person in the world to summit the seven highest peaks on each continent, he knew Marty would make a great companion for the Mount Everest excursion.

In 1982, an ambitious group, including Marty and Dick, arrived in Nepal with the intention to be the first people to summit Everest's North Wall. It would not be the only "first," if their mission were successful. If she prevailed, Marty would be the first woman from North America to summit Mount Everest. But a strap on the leg of her harness that wasn't double-backed proved to be her Achilles' heel. Slipping out of her harness while moving to the side to make room for a climbing companion, Marty tragically fell an estimated 6,000 feet down the face of the Great Couloir to her death. Shaken by the loss of one of their best mountaineers, the rest of the trip members decided to turn back. Three years later, when Dick successfully summited Mount Everest, he dedicated his feat to Marty.

Sometimes, the last-tram runs could be full of "Bounousabuse," where Junior would lead them into a narrow gully in the heart of Peruvian Gulch that even the instructors had never skied before, or into the devious chute known as Great Scott, or sometimes across resort boundaries into side-country terrain. During their in-bounds skiing, Junior would instruct his employees to follow closely behind him. Those able to keep up with his tight turns were often saved from humiliation. If someone wasn't following behind Junior closely enough, they might come around a blind corner and not make a tight enough turn, winding up headfirst in a snowbank. Junior enjoyed keeping his instructors on their toes, sometimes subjecting them to some light ski "torture."

A particular feature at Snowbird became notorious for Bounousabuse. In Peruvian Gulch and near the top of Hidden Peak, between Great Scott and upper Silver Fox, is a series of cliffs, over which the tram passes directly. One particular cliff feature looks daunting if you were to stand on top of it. But because of the wind in the area, once the season has progressed, snow fills in much of the landing, almost right up to where a skier might jump off the cliff, creating a steep but filled-in landing. From the top, however, it looks as though the landing is some 70 feet beneath you (rather than the actual distance of 30 to 40 feet), which is how Junior came to dub the cliff "Psych-Out Rock."

As a somewhat psychologically cruel initiation, Junior would lead his ski instructors to the top of the cliff with the intention of jumping. He would then comment about the landing, how soft the snow looked, how quickly someone would have to turn before they'd be in the trees. The instructors would also psych each other out up there, and once it was time to jump, they'd be so freaked out that, in Steve's words, "they'd already be falling before they'd have even jumped, they'd be so flipped out."

(Though when it came to Steve, of course, Psych-Out Rock was just the appetizer. In fact, he called it "Little Psych-Out Rock." Steve would use Little Psych-Out Rock as a "beginner" cliff that he'd teach kids to jump off. He, himself, would hit "Big Psych-Out Rock," which would send him rocketing well over 100 feet down the hill before his skis made contact with the snow again.)

During their ventures out of bounds, Junior often would lead the group over the ridgeline above Gad 2 and into the neighboring Birthday Chutes or Scotties Bowl, back into Mineral Basin (then undeveloped) or Mary Ellen Gulch, or up and over the Twin Peaks toward American Fork or White Pine. These excursions often involved steep hikes that were physically taxing. In those cases, Junior would often carry two sets of his skis on his back, drop them off at the top of the hike, and then loop back and take two more pairs of skis from the last two instructors at the back of the group. Many of the faster instructors would do the same. Once the terrain had been skied, the group would hike back to Snowbird or take a previously arranged shuttle. Junior would sometimes coordinate with the current Alta ski school director, PJ Jones, and arrange for Alta instructors to join them.

During one memorable and exhausting spring excursion, Junior led his Snowbird group, along with PJ and a group of Alta instructors, in a hike up and over Twin Peaks to ski down toward the Silver Lake Dam in the upper reaches of American Fork Canyon. They then hiked back up to the ridgeline above White Pine, assuming they were done for the day. But Junior had other plans. Unbeknownst to the instructors, he had been in communication with PJ to keep the Supreme lift at Alta running for them after the rest of the lifts had closed. Junior had shuttles waiting for them in the White Pine parking lot once they skied down, and the instructors were driven up to Alta. Junior recalls many of them being flabbergasted at the idea of taking more runs at Alta after already hiking over Twin Peaks and back up into White Pine. But instead of skiing the groomed runs down from Supreme, Junior instructed the instructors that they were going to hike east toward Catherine's Pass. When they got there, he told them once again to keep hiking. Junior's final destination for his instructors was the top of Patsy Marley, which they reached around 5 or 6 p.m., right on time to see the sun begin its descent across the Salt Lake Valley. The group was treated to beautiful, spring corn snow from the top of Patsy Marley, all the way down to the base of Alta. But the day wasn't even over, then. The shuttles picked up the crew and brought them back to Snowbird, where they were treated, among other snacks and drinks, to champagne and chocolate-covered strawberries.

Champagne and chocolate-covered strawberries became quite a tradition with the Snowbird Ski School. The ski school's reputation wasn't built on skiing only. Especially in the early days, when the school wasn't as regulated and subject to liability, the ski school also became known for its parties. Junior and another instructor named Sally Koskinen-Kuledge were responsible for the planning and execution of these parties. (Sally, otherwise known as Sally Snowbird, is credited with associating the Chickadee bird with Snowbird, often starting off snow reports on the radio by saying, "Tweet, tweet, here is Sally Snowbird calling," and greeting people at the airport in a large bird costume.) As time carried on, the Snowbird Ski School parties gained notoriety for their wild costumes, wild participants, and often wild behavior.

The first parties hosted by the ski school were innocent enough. Children enrolled in ski school were treated to ice cream on Thursday afternoons, and there were always leftovers. So, it became a tradition that instructors and patrollers would gather every Thursday to enjoy the remaining ice cream and hang out. They also had themed parties around the holidays—Christmas, New Year, and Easter being some of the most memorable. After the Thursday ice cream gatherings lost steam, Junior, who by then was (and is still to this day) known for loving a good floral-print, button-down shirt, began hosting "Aloha Fridays," where everyone would come to work in Hawaiian-themed attire and wear leis around their necks. Once the clients had all cleared out of the building around 4 p.m., Sally Snowbird would bust out the champagne and chocolate-covered strawberries, and the party would begin.

Junior and Sally often enjoyed adding a bit of a surprise element to their parties and adventures. On one special occasion, Junior told his ski school that they'd take the last tram to have a clinic. They all arrived at the tram loading dock, only to have the mountain manager, Kent Hoopingarner ("Hoopi"), storm onto the loading dock with a sour expression on his face. In a rough, carrying voice, he asked what was going on. The instructors responded that they were participating in a clinic, and then he demanded they all leave their skis on the plaza. He told them that he didn't want anyone skiing down that afternoon. So, grumbling, the instructors boarded the tram ski-less.

Once on the summit, Junior led the instructors to look into Mineral Basin. There wasn't a lift there yet, but Junior distracted them by telling them about the potential development and pointing out where the proposed lift terminals would be and where the runs might go. Meanwhile, Sally was at the tram dock, loading the tram full of shrimp cocktail, cheese hors d'oeuvres, crackers, wine and beer, and, of course, champagne and chocolate-covered strawberries. As Junior kept his instructor's eyes away from the tram terminal, Sally rode the tram and put all the drinks on ice as she cruised to the top of Hidden Peak. Once ready, she gave Junior the signal, and he led the instructors back over to the tram. They were greeted with a tram car full of delicious treats. And champagne and chocolate-covered strawberries.

They partied at the top of Hidden Peak for a while, and then boarded the tram to head back down. Knowing that there would be a tram operator in the other rising tram, a few folks decided it would be an excellent idea to moon the operator. The instructors all lined up along the windows facing the other tram and dropped their ski pants. Junior, who had remained upright with his pants still buttoned at his waist, was the only one looking at the other tram as the two passed. Turns out, it wasn't just a lift operator in the opposite tram. A large number of ski patrollers were inside as well. And, knowing that the instructors had been up at the summit partying, the patrollers decided that they would moon the instructors. So, like two ships passing in the night, the instructors and patrollers all faced away from the windows to moon each other, and Junior was the only witness.

As time went on, the parties got wilder. Junior was known for showing up to meetings with something ridiculous on his head—be it a conehead or buffalo horns—and conducting the meeting in a serious manner, confusing everyone as to whether they were supposed to take him seriously or not. For one Christmas or New Year party, Sally decided that they should dress Junior up a bit. She magicked up a tutu and feminine blouse and dangled Christmas baubles all along his shoulders. That was the start of the parties that became known as "Queenie contests," when all the rookie instructors dress up in drag and the designated judges determine who has the best outfit. Another time, for PJ Jones' birthday party, they hid Junior in a box and wrapped it up in ribbon. When PJ opened the box, Junior popped out of it and surprised PJ with a slice of cake in his face. After an especially memorable moment when two instructors set off a fire extinguisher in the staff locker room and had to spend all night cleaning up, Junior decided to rein in the parties a bit. Even so, the instructors were widely regarded as the fun, and occasionally wild, "aunts and uncles" of Snowbird.

While the Snowbird Mountain School was the largest and most common operation at Snowbird, Junior has headed up other successful programs during his time at Snowbird. The most prominent programs, still around today, are the competition program, Snowbird Sports Education Foundation (SBSEF), and the adaptive sports program, Wasatch Adaptive Sports (WAS).

SBSEF

When Junior started SBSEF in the 1970s, then just an alpine race team, he intended it to be similar to his mountain school; it would be one of the best in the country, the coaches would be given the tools required to create a unique and welcoming atmosphere, and participants would feel like they were part of a family. Right from the start, Junior snagged two phenomenal coaches to lead the race program: Beat von Allmen, a Swiss Olympian, and Jean Saubert, a two-time US Olympic medalist in GS and slalom and a Sundance Ski Team coach. The program, which started off relatively small, had a mix of athletes from the Sundance team, including Barry and Steve, and new ones from the Salt Lake Valley. As the competition program grew over the next few decades, it took shape in a way that was unique to ski racing culture at that time.

Alpine ski racing, which had been a sport largely dominated by Europeans, gained momentum in North America during the mid-20th century. Even with the increase of skiers, it took a few decades for alpine racing to gain traction. The inaugural Winter Olympic Games, held in Chamonix, France, in 1924, included only Nordic events—cross-country, ski jumping, and the combined event. Alpine racing was added to the Winter Olympics in 1936, and the United States had only one true contender—Dick Durrance, who placed 10th in the event (a combined downhill and slalom race). It wasn't until 1948 that the United States brought home its first Olympic medals in downhill skiing from Gretchan Fraser of Sun Valley, which still had a strong European presence at the time, and it wouldn't be until 1964 that any men would bring home Olympic medals in alpine ski racing.

If the 1950s were the catalyst for ski weeks and mass winter recreation in the United States, then perhaps it was only natural that the 1960s became the catalyst for an interest in ski racing, starting with the 1960 Olympics in Squaw Valley (when Junior was the coach for the Australian race team). As skiing became more accessible to the masses, children were enrolled in programs that would simultaneously keep them entertained, while allowing their parents some freedom on the slopes. Race teams for children popped up all over the country as American families watched the first true wave of American alpine racers bring home international medals.

This increase in alpine racing popularity showed up in pop culture. New media was created around the sport, like *Ski Racing* magazine in 1968. Robert Redford, recently discovering a love for skiing in the 1960s, married a woman from Provo, purchased Timp Haven, and attached himself to a ski film called *Downhill Racer*. Not yet a strong skier, Redford took lessons from Junior in preparation for the role. In 1968 Redford spent a few weeks traveling around Europe with the US Ski Team to get a feel for what life on the road for a ski racer was like, allegedly even riding in their buses and sleeping in hallways. The main character whom Redford portrayed, David Chappellet, was loosely based on the most notable male American ski figures of that decade—Buddy Werner of Colorado, Spider Sabich of California, and Billy Kidd of Vermont. Released in 1969, the film, which film critic Roger Ebert said was "the best movie ever made about sports—without really being about sports at all," portrayed the wild and dangerous sport of downhill racing, as well as the romantic dedication yet lonely life required by professional international ski racers.

When Junior founded SBSEF, racing programs around the country mimicked Robert Redford's mentality in *Downhill Racer*: the objective of ski racing is to ski fast and get results. The head coach of the US Ski Team in the 1960s, Bob Beattie, was quoted in a 1982 edition of SKI *Magazine* advising his racers: "When you think you're going too fast, *accelerate*." This mentality was especially felt on the East Coast, where ski academies, starting with Burke Mountain Academy in 1970, were being built to accommodate the difficult balance of year-round ski training and schooling for high school age kids.

Despite Junior's brief but successful stint as a competitor, his approach to all sports was that the individual should compete to have fun, rather than to be on a podium. (Though Junior was an excellent long-distance runner, he preferred beating his own time running to the top of Hidden Peak and back down—his record time was one hour and five minutes round trip—to beating other people's times in more official races.) As the Snowbird race team developed, he encouraged the coaches to have the same approach.

As Steve became one of the top racers in Utah and interacted with many other athletes from different programs across the nation, he saw that SBSEF differed from the others. Following in his father's ski tracks (literally), Steve was just as good at jumping off 50-foot cliffs around Snowbird as he was at racing through slalom gates. Freeride skiing, which emphasizes skiing down the raw terrain of a mountain rather than through gates, was not a competitive sport yet. Snowbird athletes, perhaps because the rugged mountain lent itself so well to this type of skiing, were equally capable of powder skiing off the Cirque as they were racing gates, which certainly wasn't true of many ski racers from other programs.

Steve started racing for the University of Utah ski team straight out of high school, though he refused to train with them at Park City and insisted on training at Snowbird instead (which upset the coaches, but Steve was an "All American" and top alpine freeskier of his generation, so he got away with it). Not long after, he was picked up by the US Ski Team and began his career as a professional ski racer at the World Cup. Even as he traveled internationally, Steve brought the holistic approach to ski racing that SBSEF had taught him. Steve, weighing only 145 pounds while racing professionally, could tell if he'd do well on a racecourse depending on the terrain. If it was a steeper course, which requires more technical ability, Steve knew he'd perform well. If it was a flatter course, which requires more weight to carry one's momentum through the gates, he knew he'd easily be smoked by men weighing 50 pounds more than he, even though they possessed less technical skill. Whether or not he'd do well in a race, once Steve would free ski with his fellow racers in their free time, it was no question who was the overall better skier. (Yes, I realize I'm *quite* biased here. But I doubt anyone who has seen Steve free ski, even today over 60 years old, would question this claim.)

Though Steve raced for the University of Utah's ski team, he had received a scholarship for water polo rather than for skiing. Since the university's ski team was one of the strongest in the country, the team had plenty of great athletes but not enough scholarships to go around. Rather than receiving a skiing scholarship, Steve and another ski racer were given water polo scholarships, even though they had never played water polo. In order for this to work, the skiers had to compete in at least one water polo match per season, with a certain amount of time played.

Steve, who had been on the swim team at the country club, was a strong swimmer. He had practiced a few times with the water polo team in preparation for the match he'd be participating in, and while he didn't quite understand all the nuances of the game, he was a natural competitor. However, he wasn't prepared for the brutality of the sport like getting pulled underwater and held there by opposing players and punched in the ribs. Nevertheless, he was at least a good enough swimmer to keep up with the pace of the game (unlike the other ski racer turned temporary water polo player, who had to rest by hanging off the side of the pool every few minutes).

At one point, when he was near the goal, Steve got passed the ball. He went up to try for a goal, and, expecting a fast throw, the opposing goalie kicked himself out of the water to block the pass. But the goalie had over anticipated Steve's talent as a water polo player. As Steve threw the ball, the ball slipped over the top of his wet fingers, so instead of a fast, firm throw, Steve ended up unintentionally lobbing the ball slowly toward the goal. The goalie fell back into the water before the ball had reached him, the ball went into the goal, and Steve had his one, glorious moment as a water polo player.

Even as Steve competed, first for the US Ski Team and then as racer for the Raichle Molitor Pro Team in the mid-1980s, Junior kept bringing him back to Snowbird to help coach clinics for SBSEF. Taking notes from his father, when Steve led clinics, he rarely had his students work on just running gates. He had grown up under the wing of Junior and Alf Engen, who emphasized safety, fun, and learning, in that order, and he worked to incorporate that as he transitioned from racing to teaching.

When Jim Gaddis and Steve Schowengerdt approached Steve to offer him the position of the director of SBSEF in 1989, Steve knew that he would carry on Junior's legacy and add his own flair to it. On powder days he released his racers and coaches from their normal training to go and get "face shots." He instructed his coaches to take their racers off piste so they could practice skiing in variable conditions and go off jumps while wearing GS racing skis. When a freeride team was formed, Steve made sure the freeriders learned how to lay an edge and developed the skills necessary to run gates. It was this holistic approach to skiing that led to SBSEF creating some of the most well-rounded skiers and snowboarders in the business. While other programs emphasized winning, Steve had his athletes set smaller, more attainable goals, and measure their success by those.

Both Junior and Steve knew that, when it comes to training athletes, as much as skiers learn from their coaches and instructors, they learn the most from the mountain itself. The East Coast, with its smaller mountains but steep and icy slopes, lent itself perfectly to ski racing, and, once it came around, to snowboard racing. Snowbird lent itself to the type of adventurous skiing it's today known for all over the world. The athletes from Little Cottonwood Canyon are some of the best in the world in what they do—be it freeskiing, alpine racing, or snowboarding—because the mountain presents the best teacher they could want for. The physical terrain of Snowbird is challenging, and it's fun to ski. When discussing why he and other Snowbird competitors return to Snowbird both to train and to freeski during their off times, Steve said, "We use the 'Bird' as a recharge. Snowbird was made for that. It's why we produce the best to this day."

Today the program, just 45 kids and 5 coaches when Steve took over, is now capped at 300 kids and 70 coaches and still produces some of the greatest racers, freeskiers, snowboarders, and general mountain lovers in the nation. Under Steve's guidance, it expanded to include snowboarding and para snow sports. Some athletes, such as Brennan Rubie and Bryce Astle, were picked up by the US Ski Team, while others, including Jared Goldberg, Bella Wright, Sondra Van Ert, and Faye Gulini, have competed in the Olympics. Brenna Huckaby won two gold medals in the Paralympics in snowboard cross and dual banked slalom, and Paralympic skier Maggie Brehle took home a bronze, and Paralympic snowboarder Brittany Coury, a silver. Brother-sister duos Angel and John Collinson and Jacqueline and Andrew Pollard have dominated the Freeride World Tour.

What's more impressive than these decorated athletes, however, is the scope and depth of how Steve and Junior, through SBSEF, instilled not just a love for racing in a ski team, but a love for skiing in a community that has permeated through Little Cottonwood Canyon. Their focus was not just building habits to make the athletes better competitors, but on building habits that would help them become lifelong skiers. And, in an individual sport that can at times feel lonely with teammates who race against each other, they created yet another Snowbird family.

WAS

The creation of Wasatch Adaptive Sports was a collaboration between Junior and a man named Peter Mandler. Peter had been an instructor up at Alta who transitioned to Snowbird in the 1970s. In 1972 he came to Junior with a request. He had an acquaintance who had a developmental disability and wanted to teach him how to ski, and asked Junior if he could reserve a time slot every week to work with him. Junior told Peter that he could, and that Junior would pay him through the Snowbird Ski School. Through teaching this student, Peter realized a significant portion of the population was unable to appreciate winter sports because of existing disabilities, such as blindness, amputated limbs, brain trauma, or severe autism. There weren't many adaptive sports programs at that time, and those that existed were very expensive.

The widespread creation of adaptive sports programs around the world coincided with the end of World War II, when many men were returning home as amputees. Some of them knew how to ski before losing limbs and had a desire to continue participating in the sport they loved. Others were more fortunate in their injuries but knew many others who were not so lucky. In the United States, members of the 10th Mountain Division, like Jim Winthers, became ski instructors and ski school directors, but watched as their amputee friends were no longer able to participate in activities they used to love. As a result, adaptive skiing programs began popping up in North America and Europe.

New equipment was soon developed to cater to this new ski clientele, and with new equipment came techniques to use the equipment. In the 1940s, a one-legged German amputee named Franz Wendel attached short skis to the end of his crutches to aid him in skiing with one leg, creating the first adaptive ski equipment now known as "outriggers." Due to the three tracks left behind by the one leg ski and two arm skis, the technique is known as "three-track skiing." The term "two-track skiing" indicates that the skier can stand on their own two legs, but needs assistance from a guide to get down a slope—often due to impaired vision or autism. Sit-skis (also known as "monoskis") were developed for those who can't stand on a ski at all, and they allow for the user to sit, strapped into a chair on top of a single ski, with outriggers in their hands.

Adaptive clinics started to share teaching techniques with instructors. Later on, soldiers returning from Vietnam created even more incentive to have systemized programs, and in 1967 the National Amputee Skiers Association was founded. Adaptive skiing soon expanded to include those with other disabilities besides amputations, and in 1974, the first World Disabled Alpine Championships were held, followed by the world's first Paralympic games in 1976.

Peter approached Junior again with another proposition. Could he head the charge to create a new program at Snowbird, one that would train instructors to teach people with a disability how to ski? Junior thought it was a great idea and pitched the idea to Snowbird management. Dick Bass thought it was a fantastic idea as well, and Wasatch Adaptive Sports was created.

As Peter began training other instructors, he quickly realized just how expensive adaptive sports were for those who wished to participate. Many of the people who could take advantage of the program were already dealing with massive hospital bills and medication costs. And sometimes their loved ones had to quit their own jobs in order to help take care of them. Peter knew that to make the program successful in every aspect, he'd have to get the funding to subsidize the cost for the students. They hosted the first of what would become an annual fundraiser, at which Dick Bass, a huge advocate for the program his entire life, purchased almost every item.

It wasn't too long after the creation of the program that it received plenty of positive attention. Only a few years after Peter took on that first student, he was approached by NFL quarterback Steve Young, who, having been born in Salt Lake City, had heard of WAS and wanted to collaborate. Together they created the Steve Young Ski Classic, an event that included a ski race, live and silent auction, and banquet dinner that would be a fundraiser for WAS. Steve Young brought in celebrities, from football players to Olympic competitors, to participate in the event, racing against adaptive athletes in a ski race on Chickadee. The ski classic was a huge success, and about a decade later, in 1993, Steve Young created the Forever Young Foundation that would continue to provide services to children facing challenges around the world.

Wasatch Adaptive Sports has continued to expand as the years have passed. Besides the classic mono-skiing, bi-skiing, and outrigging, the program now includes year-round activities like yoga, hiking, mountain biking, kayaking, and paddleboarding. In 2010 a veteran-specific program was added, catering to veterans with all levels of ability. The focus of the program was not just to teach veterans a new skill, but to create a community and support system centered around the outdoors.

WAS instructors are trained to teach a wide variety of students—people experiencing blindness, deafness, PTSD, depression, autism, limb differences, neurological disorders, and traumatic brain injuries. When a student arrives at WAS, every lesson is catered to the individual. Instructors receive information about their students ahead of time, and once they meet the student, they conduct an assessment to make sure the lesson is structured to help the student be successful. The goal is to help the student be as independent as possible, which varies greatly, depending on the student. Unlike SBSEF, which has a lot of turnover as the athletes grow into adults and leave the program, many of the WAS students don't "outgrow" the program and some continue with WAS for more than a decade.

Today, WAS is composed of a kaleidoscope of folks from all walks of life. It's a community that seems to have no boundaries. Peter and Junior may have not known exactly how many lives they would end up changing back in 1972, but they did have the sense that their new program would have a ripple effect through the disability community. From the start, they knew that being in the mountains would have a therapeutic effect on these clients. It doesn't matter if the student doesn't progress quickly in the sport because there are so many other benefits that contribute to the individual's wellbeing, such as balance, social skills, getting outside, being pushed out of their comfort zone, and being welcomed into a supportive outdoor community.

The program has proved to be incredibly rewarding for the instructors as well. My sister, Tyndall, has been both a ski coach for SBSEF and an instructor at WAS for the past few years. As much of a family as SBSEF is, Tyndall says that WAS has an even more intimate feel to it. While SBSEF instructors are rewarded by watching children turn into strong skiers, some of whom might become the best in the world, WAS instructors get to interact with those who have experienced the lowest of lows, yet are still able to find joy and hope in life. WAS students are often in the program for years or even decades, since their challenges are lifelong obstacles. Perhaps more than anything, the WAS community is one of beautiful resilience.

The SBSEF and WAS programs gained strength and esteem within the community until they were as integrated as the mountain school, and as years quickly turned to decades, as they tend to do when one is having fun, Junior's role at Snowbird stayed largely the same. Junior first was the "father" of this Snowbird family by being a constant, charming, and welcoming presence on the slopes and around the village in the early years, and then he became a "grandfather" figure, his dark hair speckled with more and more white until it became the silver wave it is today. His yellow helmet became a common sight on the ski hill, his wicked grin familiar to those who dared follow him across the mountain. Seeing him was sometimes like seeing a mystical presence, like catching a glimpse of Sasquatch on the slopes—except that Junior was there every day, was approachable, and loved to ski a few runs with whoever asked. He is the local living legend.

At 70 years old and after 20 years as the ski school director, Junior was ready to relinquish some of his responsibilities. So, in 1992, Snowbird created a new position for him: director of skiing. The title was slightly honorary; he would take on fewer responsibilities as the director of skiing, though he'd still be an integral figure for marketing purposes. He would continue to take on private lessons and teach the occasional clinic, but he wasn't involved with day-to-day management of instructors, nor involved in the hiring process.

Junior, now a senior citizen himself, wanted to focus on catering to an older ski clientele. He had noticed that many older skiers stopped skiing, not necessarily because they weren't still strong skiers, but because they didn't have friends to ski with. As the director of skiing, Junior started "Junior's Seniors," a group for folks more than 65 years old, as a means of creating community in the older crowd. It was a free group open to all ability levels, though if there was a weaker skier, Junior would take the extra time to work with them while the rest of the group skied on. Folks not only got to ski with the legendary Junior Bounous, but also got to form friendships with each other that would encourage them to keep skiing into their later years.

Recognizing another need, Junior then started another group called "Silver Wings." This group was for folks who were 50 years old or older. Unlike Junior's Seniors, this group did have a minimal fee to join. Junior had seen how many people wanted to ski with him but couldn't afford the hefty price of a full-day private lesson, so they were allowed to participate in two-hour group lessons for much cheaper. Oftentimes, Junior's old colleague from Sugar Bowl, Roger Bourke, who had purchased a house near Grizzly Gulch and spent part of the year at Alta, would participate with these groups and became a sort of assistant to Junior.

Although wildly popular, both programs unfortunately lasted only a couple of years. Snowbird management sensed the programs had the potential of being cash cows with Junior as the hook. They implemented a fee to join Junior's Seniors, despite Junior's adamant objections. Junior believed that having access to a supportive skiing community that would encourage more older folks on the hill shouldn't be a commodity that they had to pay for. Management disagreed. But once there was a fee involved, the group's participation rate dropped significantly, and Junior's Seniors was eventually disbanded. Management also bumped the cost of Silver Wings from $20 for two hours to $95, and the same thing happened. Then, they tried to increase Junior's private lesson rate to be twice the cost of other instructor rates. Junior fought tooth and nail against that one and won, keeping his rates at a reasonable price.

In 1996, a group of people, led by Chuck Rowan and Herb Lloyd, submitted Junior's name to the US Ski and Snowboard Hall of Fame. To no one's surprise, they accepted him immediately. When he was invited to the induction ceremony in Ishpeming, Michigan, he realized that he, Maxine, Chuck, and Suzanne had planned a trip to the Galapagos over that same weekend. He told the organizers that, as much as he'd love to attend, there was no way he was going to miss the trip. They told him not to worry and that they would push back his induction another year, so long as he made sure not to plan a trip over next year's induction dates. When Junior and

Maxine made it to Michigan the following year, Junior recalls they had an excellent experience and were treated as though they were on the red carpet the entire time. A few years later, in 2002, Junior was inducted into the Intermountain Ski Hall of Fame as well.

That same year Junior had the opportunity to participate in something he never anticipated: the 2002 Winter Olympics in Salt Lake City. Bringing the Winter Olympics to Salt Lake City had been somewhat of a pipe dream for many enthusiasts for a few decades. The first bid attempt in 1966 for the 1972 Olympics went to Japan. The second bid attempt in 1973 for the 1976 Olympics went to Innsbruck, and the third and fourth attempts went to France and Norway, the fifth to Japan once again. Finally in 1995, Salt Lake City won the bid for the 2002 Winter Olympics.

While there was some pushback from the Salt Lake community for hosting the Olympics games, Junior was in favor of bringing the games to Salt Lake City, writing the occasional article and opinion piece published in local newspapers to show his support. In the year leading up to the games, his son Barry had an idea. He approached a Coca-Cola representative (the Olympics were sponsored by Coca-Cola) who lived in his Provo neighborhood and asked about submitting Junior's name to be an Olympic torchbearer. Junior's application went through, and Junior was named an official torchbearer for the 2002 Salt Lake City Olympic Games. When Barry's Coca-Cola contact asked if Barry would want to be an assistant torchbearer (otherwise known as a torch runner, who would run next to a few torchbearers and take the torch if they needed a break), Barry gave the honor to his brother, Steve. In Barry's words, "Steve had worked toward this all his life."

So, on a cold, snowy evening in February of 2002, just a few short days before the Opening Ceremonies, our family and a large group of Snowbird Mountain School instructors bundled up and headed down to Provo. As I recall, the stretch of road where we stood was packed with people. We waited in the dark, jitters from both the cold and the excitement. Then all at once, we could hear noise coming from down the road, a cheering that grew louder and higher in intensity as it moved closer. The flashes of cameras illuminated the street as a caravan of police cars and motorcycles passed, and there they were. Dressed in the white-and-blue uniforms of torchbearers and runners, Junior and Steve were running down the street side by side, holding a slender, silver torch between them.

Junior and Steve recall running through what seemed to be a tunnel of people—walls of sound and light and energy on either side of them. It was surreal. Twenty years later, they're both still awestruck when talking about it. Barry, responsible for the whole thing, said, "It is one of my happiest memories seeing Steve and Junior run that torch up Center Street in Provo."

The Olympics were followed by slower years for Junior. He was headed into his 80s and had spent the majority of his career making the long commute from Provo to Snowbird and back, nearly every day of the week. As the years passed, Junior took on fewer clients in exchange for more time spent skiing with his family. There were fewer non-stop tram laps and more runs on Wilbere and Baby Thunder, leading grandchildren through hidden tree runs or guiding them on mountain-wide scavenger hunts on Easter. In the blink of an eye, Junior was coaxing great-grandchildren down Chickadee.

Despite the slower pace, Junior continued to take on clients until he was nearly 90 years old. These weren't beginner skiers that he taught; most of his clients were already proficient skiers and didn't hire him to learn how to ski, but to refine their skills. One of his clients, Jay Grossman, used to hire Junior for a half-day private lesson three or four days a week for 10 years. But according to Junior, Jay may have hired Junior six days a week, if he could have. Other families, like the Kellers and MacLeans, would hire him for a week or two at a time when they came into town.

I once asked Junior why people continued to hire him even if he wasn't teaching them how to ski. Why was he such a hot commodity? I refused to believe that it was just because of his local "celebrity" status; these were people who were good friends with him, who weren't starstruck or hiring him for the novelty of it. Junior told me that he thinks it was his knowledge of the mountain and his intuition when it came to understanding his students that kept so many people interested in skiing with him.

It seems so simple and so subtle, but once I thought this through, I realized that I understand this well. It's why, on deep powder days, I prefer following my father, Steve, around Snowbird rather than skiing by myself. Even though I know the mountain better than many, I prefer skiing behind him because he has a more intimate feel for the mountain, and he understands my ability as a skier. He knows where the little pockets of powder will be depending on the snow conditions, which terrain I'll feel comfortable skiing in and which terrain will be challenging and push me to become better. When I ski with others who are less familiar with Snowbird, they ask the same things of me; they want me to lead them to where the good snow is, to places they may not have been before, and they trust me to keep them in situations where they'll feel comfortable for their ability level or to push them out of their comfort zone, if that's their desire, though not going so far that they can't ski down.

In other words, it's the sense of attainable adventure that so many people love about skiing with Junior Bounous. Some go so far as to call this "Bounousabuse." It's what has kept Junior so popular well into his 90s, and it's what made him such a good instructor for almost 80 years. It's the knowledge that adventure isn't found only in the steepest chutes or on the topmost peaks; depending on the level and desire of the skier, adventure can be found within the hidden gully the student has never seen before, or in a beautiful tree run on a low-angle slope. It's finding a balance between familiarity and excitement for each student, between helping them stay within their comfort zone and also having realistic goals they can reach to increase their confidence. It's creating a confluence between mountain, snow, gravity, and student in a moment that seems surreal. And once the moment is over, you develop a craving for it, and you want to do it again, and again, and again. This is the Junior Bounous recipe for experiencing the joys of skiing.

Little Cottonwood Canyon has become a magnetic field for many. Anyone who has skied in the canyon recently knows this. As Junior's pace of skiing slowed, the overall pace of the ski community in the Wasatch has increased 100-fold. Those who skied at Snowbird and Alta a mere two decades ago will remember when powder stashes could be found for days after the latest storm. Now, if you don't time the rope drop perfectly, you might miss out on the untracked. I hear a lot of people grumbling about all the newcomers to the canyon, about how crowded it is, how cutthroat skiing has become today. I grumble about it myself. But I also find it incredibly beautiful when I ride Peruvian chair on a powder day and listen to all the hooting and hollering and screams of pure delight beneath me. Witnessing a Mineral Basin rope drop might feel like watching the herd of wildebeest stampeding down the canyon walls in The Lion King, but it's also witnessing hundreds of happy souls in motion.

Those powder pioneers, Alf and Junior, helped make powder skiing more accessible to the masses over half a century ago. They did it because they had discovered the joys of skiing and wished to pass on those joys. More than passing along a technique, it's passing along a feeling of confidence and accomplishment. That's what the best teachers do—they desire to pass on their knowledge so others may appreciate it. While I don't necessarily love sitting in a massive line at the bottom of Mineral Basin after a rope drop, I also can't hate it. It's proof that my grandfather succeeded in sharing the joys of skiing with as many people as he could over his life.

After 45 years of working at Snowbird and just shy of 90 years old, Junior finally retired. Though that certainly didn't mean he stopped going to work; Junior is as much of a presence on the hill today as he was when the resort opened. Many folks within this Little Cottonwood Canyon community marvel at how Junior has continued skiing so far into his 90s. Many credit him for this accomplishment, and while his passion for skiing and good health have certainly played a large role, there are many others who should also receive credit. The act of skiing isn't the hardest part for Junior—it's the travel, dealing with the equipment, and the logistics behind the scenes that is the most challenging. Driving upward of an hour in each direction, putting on ski boots, walking in them down and up stairs and through parking lots and snow, getting a pair of heavy skis onto the hill—these are obstacles that most 96-year-olds would be unable to manage, and it's through the generosity of others that it's been possible for Junior to jump these obstacles.

Barry and Steve, as well as their wives, Debbie and Sue, have become incredible pillars of support for Junior in the last few years. They organize ski excursions for him, drive with him, carry his equipment, help him put on and take off his boots. Countless friends do the same when they ask to join him on ski days, which they do so often it makes it nearly impossible for his own grandchildren to find free days to ski with Junior. These friends want to sit next to him on chairlifts and follow close behind him on runs, listen to his stories and hear his laughter. They pull him to Snowbird, Alta, Sundance, and Deer Valley, and make sure that he always has someone to ski with. They keep the excitement of skiing ripe. Those who work at ski shops have provided Junior with equipment that make his life significantly easier, such as rear-entry boots. Doctors and physical therapists have helped him manage injuries and pain that might otherwise prevent him from doing what he loves.

Equally responsible for Junior's success are Snowbird employees. Folks like Dave Fields, Snowbird's general manager, make it possible for Junior to continue being a key figure in Snowbird's continued history and make sure it's financially possible for him to continue skiing. Others, such as lift operators, ski patrol, and mountain school instructors make sure that he is well taken care of on the hill. Powderbird employees helped Junior accomplish becoming the world's oldest heli-skier in 2021. I also want to give an extra special nod to the employees at the Lodge. In the 2020–21 and 2021–22 seasons, Junior essentially lived in his room at the Lodge the entire winter. Lodge employees worked tirelessly to ensure that Junior had a place he could truly call home up Little Cottonwood Canyon, going above and beyond their typical duties. Those who work the front desk go out of their way to accommodate and check in on him, while those at the bell desk help him carry his skis and luggage and make sure his car is always free of snow. Those who run the shuttle pick him up from Alta when his legs are too tired to ski back over to Snowbird. And in April of 2022, a housekeeper who rode next to him on the bus in Gad Valley carried his skis all the way up to his room at the Lodge so he didn't have to carry them himself.

While Junior can seem almost superhuman, his ability to keep skiing is not just because of his physical capabilities, but because of the ski community that has risen magnificently to make sure that he succeeds. Like the saying that it takes a village to raise a child, it has taken a village to keep a 96-year-old skiing. The Bounous family thanks them for helping our grandfather accomplish this feat. Keep an eye out for his yellow helmet between the blue and green Snowbird wings.

"Junior running with the Olympic torch was the most appropriate thing that I could imagine. I mean, talk about a true champion. You're taught the Olympic moment [is] when people are striving to be their best. Who is a better symbol [to carry the torch] than the person who pushes you to reach for your highest potential all the time. That's Junior Bounous. . . . The image of Junior running with the torch in the Olympics—it's just a natural fit. It was meant to be."

— Adrian MacLean Jay, family friend

"Junior had 'follow me' time, where we'd follow him down the mountain. There were a bunch of instructors skiing together, and Junior was leading the pack. He took us down someplace I had never been, on the Peruvian side and basically down a creek bed with a bunch of snowbanks. We were all following as closely as we could and went down that creek bed one after another. I was watching Junior closely because he could be very unpredictable—especially when he had a little smile on his face. I saw Junior prepare for a turn, even though it didn't look like you needed to turn. And all of a sudden, he made a hard right turn, so I followed and did a hard right turn too. If you weren't watching closely, you'd end up where the little stream ended, which was this big snowbank of soft snow. The following three guys embedded themselves in that thing, just one—two—three! Totally into the snowbank. Junior had stopped really quickly and turned around to watch the carnage and was laughing like he couldn't believe it. Of course I was laughing too because I had narrowly avoided that same fate. These guys picked themselves up out of the snowbank, and everybody was shaking their hands, tears of laughter on their faces. It was a lot of fun."

— Gary Powers, Snowbird Mountain School employee

" . . . Fast forward to January 11, 2021, I was skiing with Junior and some friends at Alta. It was a beautiful, sunny day, and the slopes were groomed to perfection. After a couple of hours, I said to Junior, 'Junior, we gotta slow down. We're creating our own wind chill factor, and I'm getting cold.' He just smiled. That's the way you ski with Junior—fast, just a few turns and you can only follow him because no one can catch him. He's a hero and a mentor to so many of us."

— Cheryl Kidder, Snowbird Mountain School employee

"We were skiing with Junior off of the tram one day. My son, Sam, was just starting his first year working for the Mountain School. Junior took us to the top of Regulator, and . . . [said], 'So what we're going to do is see how many turns we can make down Regulator. . . . Follow my line.' So we take off and there are 12 of us, and Sam and I are near the front of the pack, close to Junior. He did like 178 turns. . . . We get down there and we're trying to get the group all back together—they were all over the mountain. Once we get everyone back together, we take another tram and do the same thing. Our numbers dropped from 12 to 7. Junior says, 'Let's take another one.' By the end of the next run, the only people left in the group were Sam and I. The group consisted of mostly younger instructors, and everybody dropped out. Junior's over 80 years old. He very graciously and sweetly ran them into the ground."

— Dave Watson, Snowbird skier

"When I first got hired at the Snowbird ski school, another instructor, Jim Spielman, told me, 'There's one thing you want to know about Junior. At some point, he's going to take the rookies out for a ski run. Be on Junior's tail when he does that; go exactly where he goes.' So I said, 'Okay, I'll do that, if I can.' So we went up the tram with Junior, and none of us rookies knew the mountain at all. All I knew is what Jim had told me. So I stayed on Junior's tail and now looking back, we must've gone down Nirvana, or something like that, 'cause we ended up coming out onto Big Emma. And I stayed literally right in his tracks; I didn't vary from his tracks at all. He skied down and we're going down through the trees and the rocks and all over the place, and we came out onto Big Emma and stopped, and we both turned around, and there were instructors just scattered all over the mountain. I took the right advice. It was Junior's little way of kind of introducing instructors to the mountain by first-hand experience—a classic Junior moment."

— Ed Chauner, Snowbird Mountain School employee

"One time we were out in a clinic, and we're going down out in Little Cloud somewhere, and he turned to all the group before we started in, and he said, 'Follow my tracks.' And he went down through a group of trees and kind of launched over a little cliff barrier, and I wanted to get freshies, so I went about two feet to the side of where he landed [and I landed right on a rock.] Just popped right on a rock. And he turned around and said, 'I said to stay in my tracks; I knew that rock was right over there!' I learned to stay right where Junior told me to go."

— Lane Clegg, Snowbird Mountain School employee

"I came down from British Columbia and wanted to visit and ski with Junior. And we got off at the top of the tram there, and I looked over and saw this thing they call the Pipeline. And I said, 'What's that like to ski?' And Junior said, 'Well, it's never been skied before.' So I said, 'Well, why don't we ski it?' And Ted says, 'I'll pay for the helicopter if you guys will ski it.' And so we called the helicopter, and up came the chopper and picked us up and took us up to the top. And I remember he couldn't even land the helicopter there—there wasn't much room. And he had to maneuver there just about it, and we stepped off and put our skis on, and that was the first time the Pipeline had ever been skied."

— Jim McConkey, ski legend

"Junior leads through example. I thank him for teaching me patience in life, all the while I never knew it was being taught."

— Sue Bounous, daughter-in-law

"Back in the early '80s we had race camps in Little Cloud in late May and June. Junior would set the courses for us. Early one afternoon, a thunderstorm rolled in while we were setting a GS course in Mark Malu Fork. There were no drills in those days, so Junior was pounding in the holes for the bamboo gates with a heavy metal pole. As the lightning got closer and it started raining and hailing on us, we voiced our concerns that maybe we should quit until the storm passed. Junior said he wasn't worried and continued to post holes for the gates. However, those of us on course duty with Junior eventually bailed and ran for cover, leaving Junior alone with a metal post and the gates in an electrical storm in a wide-open bowl at roughly 10,500 feet. I am not sure, but lightning may have actually struck the Little Cloud lift that day. When everything cleared, there was Junior, still setting up the GS course. He stayed out there through the entire storm. It was then that we all decided that the man had nine lives or someone from above was protecting him or he was just 'plum crazy.'"

— Jo Garuccio, Snowbird Mountain School employee

Junior getting a face shot shortly after Snowbird's opening in the early 1970s. Taken while shooting promotional footage for the new resort.

Junior and two unidentified skiers at Snowbird. Likely taken in the 1970s.

Junior, Ted Johnson, Stein Eriksen, and Jim McConkey on the Snowbird plaza. Early 1970s.

Junior and his staff on Big Emma. Early 1970s. *Snowbird*

Junior, Steve, and Maxine at Snowbird on the tram dock. Seventeen-year-old Steve had just won the slalom at the North American Junior Alpine Championships in Alyeska Resort, Alaska, in 1977. It was his first major win against an international field, against racers much older than he was. Steve emerged from the second seed of racers to take a surprise win—not unlike his father 30 years prior when Junior pulled out his surprise win at Brighton in 1946.

Snowbird Ski School poster. Late 1970s.
Snowbird

Snowbird Ski School brochure.
Snowbird

Suzy "Chaptick" Chaffee and Junior skiing at Snowbird. 1970s.

Barry bootpacking up Twin Peaks on a beautiful spring day. 1970s.

Steve running through Giant Slalom gates before the days of required helmets. 1970s or 1980s.

Maxine and Junior during one of the Snowbird ski school's "Aloha Friday" parties in the 1980s.

Junior teaching a ski school clinic at the top of Hidden Peak in the late 1980s.

Maxine and Junior wearing a classic Snowbird ski instructor uniform. Likely in the late 1980s.

A few members of the notorious Junior's Seniors, ready to cause some mischief. From left to right: Bill Ross (as Chewbacca), Junior, Ed Amende (Darth Vader), Suzanne Culley, Jan Amende, Grant Culley, Ann Ross, Gekko Kidwell, Kim Fletcher (Yoda), Marilyn Fletcher. Around 1990.

Junior and Steve running with Junior's Olympic torch at the top of Hidden Peak. 2002.
James Kay Photography

Suzanne and Grant Culley in their classic ski suits at one of their classic champagne picnics at Snowbird in celebration of Grant's 70th birthday. 1991.

Junior and his successor (director of Snowbird Mountain School at the time), Maggie Lorring, at Junior's 90th birthday celebration in 2015.

Chapter 13

Bounouses Abroad

Junior and Maxine became extensive international travelers over the course of their lives, and Junior credits Maxine for this. Junior was driven and a hard worker, but he also tended to be content with whatever situation life threw his way. He enjoyed staying close to home, be that in the Wasatch or the Utah desert, and visiting haunts he knew like the back of his hand. He quickly became intimately acquainted with certain landscapes and continued to revisit them time and time again, comfortable with the familiar things around him. It wasn't that Junior didn't want to travel, but he was also satisfied spending summers in places he was familiar with. Junior had a very settled vibe about him, rooted to the land and to who he was as a person.

Maxine, on the other hand, seemed always to be searching for more, focused on improvement, and desiring to experience new things. She had the yearning to visit places she had never been before—to experience new cultures and see new landscapes and architecture. Maxine had wanted to become a flight attendant after graduating from high school, but she had been told she couldn't because she was too short. The minimum height requirement for flight attendants was five feet, and Maxine stood a quarter of an inch below the requirement. Instead, she ended up working as a travel agent for some time, which fueled her desire to travel abroad.

Canada

The first time Maxine and Junior crossed an international border, they were on a road trip to western Canada in their first few years of marriage. Junior remembers not even needing a passport to cross the border back then; they just had to flash their driver licenses and they were let in. They drove their station wagon through Glacier National Park, Calgary, and then the Canadian Rockies, camping out of their car along the way. They visited Banff and then took the Icefields Highway up to Jasper National Park. It was the first of many trips to Canada.

About 20 years later, Mike Wiegele, the young, spunky Austrian who worked for four years for Junior at Sugar Bowl, started a heli-skiing business in the Canadian Rockies in the early 1970s. Junior, Maxine, Mike, and his wife, Bonnie, had a tight-knit friendship that would continue bringing the Wiegeles to Snowbird and the Bounouses to Canada almost every year from the 1970s until the late 2000s. Mike would remain a dear friend until his passing in 2021.

The first time Junior went heli-skiing with Mike was two or three years after Mike got his company off the ground, around 1975. The idea arose while Junior was skiing at Snowbird with a friend, Paul Van Anda. Junior had been Paul's ski instructor since 1949 when Junior worked at Alta, and he had continued as Paul's private instructor at Snowbird. Paul expressed his interest in heli-skiing with Mike Wiegele, and Mike had told Paul that he was welcome to come skiing on the condition that he bring Junior as his private guide. When Junior and Paul arrived, Mike was running his business out of a somewhat run-down hotel in Blue River, a small logging town in the heart of the Rockies. Every evening, Junior and Paul were entertained by observing loggers and railroad track workers playing billiards in their hotel, and they got a kick out of how enormous the portion sizes were to accommodate the workers' appetites. There was just one narrow staircase leading to the second floor where the rooms were, and Paul, accustomed to searching for emergency exits wherever he stayed, told Junior that "this hotel is a death trap."

Since Paul was a slow skier, Mike arranged to have Junior be a guide for the time they were there, decking him out with a radio and avalanche gear. So as not to rush Paul, Junior and Paul would take one easier run while the rest of the group took two, and both groups would have the same helicopter pickup. There was a thick layer of clouds when Mike had the helicopter drop them on a ridgeline for their first run. Mike assured Junior that, though they couldn't see much, the run below them was safe, had a low angle, and would lead them right to the pickup point. Then the chopper took off from the ridge, leaving the two of them alone.

Junior started leading Paul down the hill through some trees, unable to see what the pitch looked like. The snow was deep, and once Junior started skiing, he could tell the hillside was steep. With his first turn, Junior's skis sent sluffs of snow sliding through the trees beneath them. The pitch was too steep for Paul to be able to connect his turns, so Junior had them take one kick turn and then traverse as far as they could before they could make another. Junior even had Paul sit down a few times so he could switch the direction of Paul's skis. Once they were able to see downhill a little bit better, Junior noticed the snow was sliding around them even when they weren't moving, creating very dangerous conditions.

Eventually Junior heard the helicopter passing near them and quickly grabbed his radio. He radioed up to Mike and described the situation. Mike, realizing his mistake, told them he and the helicopter pilot had accidentally dropped them in the wrong place, unable to see the correct ridgeline because of the thick clouds. Mike advised Junior that it was difficult terrain, but if they could make their way down, they would eventually meet up with the run Mike was taking the second group on, and they might be able to see the second group's tracks. Junior remembers, "I found the path where they skied down and followed. It was much more open and gentle than what we had to ski our very first run. Thanks a lot, Mike."

Despite the rocky start, the duo had a great time heli-skiing. Paul would typically tire out after four or five runs, and Junior would be able to join the main group for some more challenging skiing. It was the first heli-ski trip of what Junior estimates was at least 15 trips with Mike—12 of them in the winter, 3 in the summer. Mike would invite Junior and Maxine to heli-ski and heli-hike for free every single year, and they often accepted. They brought Barry and his wife, Debbie, along once, on the condition that Barry and Debbie would "sing for their supper." Barry and Debbie performed a couple of songs in German one evening for a large group of Germans visiting for a special trip, and Junior recalls that "the Germans got a kick out of it."

Mike's business took off in the 1980s, and he reached out to a few film producers to see if anyone could help him make a promotional film. Warren Miller agreed, and Junior and Steve were brought up north to ski for the film. This was when Steve and one of Mike's heli-skiing guides were caught in the avalanche, and Steve was able to punch through the rain crust and hang onto the hill by the tips of his fingers.

The relationship between Mike and Junior, and more generally, the operation out of Blue River and Snowbird, was a symbiotic one that lasted for decades. Mike, Bonnie, and their daughter, Michelle, would come and ski at Snowbird with them over Christmas almost every year, staying at the Goldminer's Daughter Lodge as guests of Jim and Elfriede Shane, who also frequented Blue River. Mike and Junior would often free ski together, getting Mike in skiing shape for the season, and Michelle and Bonnie would race gates and train with Steve and the Snowbird Ski Team. Mike was interested in expanding his avalanche knowledge and spent some time working alongside Snowbird Ski Patrol, often inviting them up to the Canadian Rockies to heli-ski as well. Mike even tried to convince Steve to become the manager of the business, but Steve politely declined, wishing to remain in Utah.

Mike and Bonnie loved hosting events and would throw parties every time they reached a significant benchmark in their business or personal lives. Over the years, Mike had developed a relationship with the folk singer John Denver, letting him heli-ski for a week for free in exchange for one performance for the guests while he was there. During one memorable celebration for the company's 25th anniversary, Denver gave a performance, and the Bounouses ended up at a table right in front. At the end of his set, Denver announced that he was just the warm-up act. The true performer of the night was Moe Dixon, a fiery solo guitarist known for getting après-ski crowds dancing. And dance that crowd did.

South America

Junior and Maxine's first significant international trip (meaning that they had to fly, rather than drive) was to South America. It was also significant in a few other ways. While working at Alta, Maxine had become pregnant with what would have been their first child, but they had a terrible complication at the end of the pregnancy. The experience was heartbreaking, though it did open a door for the young couple. Friends of theirs had invited Junior and Maxine on a trip to South America for the following July, which they had declined because they were expecting to be taking care of a newborn and the farm. That following spring, a late frost killed all the cherry blossoms, the significant July crop for the Bounous farm. Junior and Maxine suddenly found their summer free.

In order to get passports, they had to provide their birth certificates. This is the moment when Junior, assuming his given name was Junior and that he was born on August 23, 1925, discovered that he wasn't given a name at birth and that he had been born on August 24.

The friends who had asked Junior and Maxine to join them were Bill and Janis Levitt. The Levitts had built the house up at Alta with the Bounouses and had been ski students of theirs for some time. Janis and her brother had inherited a large ranch outside of Santiago, Chile, and her brother was living there at the time. The Levitts' plan was to first visit the ranch, and then go to the Portillo ski area. This is why they had invited Junior and Maxine: it was a South American ski trip, and the Levitts wanted their favorite ski instructors to tag along.

The Bounouses first stop was New York, where they spent a few pleasurable evenings seeing shows and enjoying the city. Then they flew south, taking boats and trains through Peru and Bolivia before winding up in Santiago to visit the ranch. Containing an enormous herd of cattle as well as orchards full of grapefruit, apples, and oranges, the ranch was massive: about 30,000 acres, 30 miles long, and 15 or 20 miles wide. In Junior's words, "It was as big as Utah Valley, practically."

When they left the ranch to travel to Portillo, it was in the nick of time. The country was experiencing civil unrest, and the railroad workers went on strike. Portillo could not be accessed by roads during the winter, only by train. As the Bounouses and Levitts approached Portillo, hordes of people were leaving the ski area so they wouldn't get stuck. The Bounouses and Levitts, used to getting stuck up Little Cottonwood Canyon quite often, didn't mind the risk and managed to hop on the last train to Portillo.

There Junior got to see an old acquaintance: Emilie Allais, the famous French ski racer and instructor Junior had previously crossed paths with. Allais was the ski school director for Portillo and invited their group to dine at his table every night. A big storm rolled through the area, closing the lifts for a couple of days. But once the storm had cleared, the lifts didn't start running. Unperturbed, Junior, Maxine, Bill, and Janis began hiking around the resort on their skis, packing down certain slopes to ski on. Allais showed up, shovel in hand, to join them. Together they built a gelande jump with different levels so everyone could jump it depending on their ability.

Finally, Allais and Junior went to one of the lifts to investigate why it hadn't started running days after the storm. They saw all the parts torn out of the machine and lying on the snow. Laughing at the sight, Junior and Allais realized the Peruvian Lift operators didn't know enough about their equipment to get the lifts back up and running. The group was resigned to the fact that they would likely be hiking for their skiing most of the time, but they didn't mind.

The rest of their 30-day South American trip was spent making their way back up to Peru to see Machu Picchu. They visited Lake Titicaca and traveled mostly by single-car trains that were common on railroad tracks at the time. Junior remembers having quite a time trying to travel by these; fallen logs forced them to stop on one occasion, and then another time, one jumped off the railroad tracks and became severely delayed.

Another memorable trip to South America was in 1996, for which Junior skipped his initial National Ski Hall of Fame induction. Of the Galapagos, he recalls how amazing the exotic birdlife was. Many would fly and land so close to them that they could have touched the birds. Once a blue-footed booby walked right up to Maxine with a stick in its mouth as if it were a dog looking to play fetch. It hung around Maxine so persistently that Maxine finally tried to take the stick out of its mouth, but it waggled its head back and forth as if saying no. The bird wouldn't leave her side.

Central America

Junior and Maxine's first international trip with Barry and Steve was a trip to Mexico. After finishing up one ski season at Sugar Bowl, the family loaded up their station wagon, strapped a tent and sleeping bags to the top of the car, and drove south to Mexico. It was the first time the boys had seen the ocean, and Junior remembers them having a grand old time during the first stop—a town called Guaymas on the shores of the Sea of Cortez.

They rented a motel room and became friends with their neighbor, a man from Texas. He invited Junior and Maxine to go deep-sea fishing with him and they accepted. When Junior eventually pulled up a mahi-mahi, the Texan was thrilled. That evening he cooked the fish over a charcoal grill, promising them that mahi-mahi was the best fish for eating. They had never tried it before, and Junior remembers it as a special experience, especially since he was the one who had reeled in the fish.

Another memorable moment from that trip was when a random snorkeler caught a scallop and offered it to Maxine, telling her she should cook it and her family could eat it. Back then, scallops were not such a common delicacy as they are today. Junior managed to get the meat out of the shell, and Maxine, unsure how to cook it, boiled it for 30 minutes. It was so overcooked and rubbery that no one could even take a bite.

Junior and Maxine would visit Mexico and Central America many times over the next few decades, with many different people. They returned one time as part of an RV brigade with Ray and Ava Stewart, driving for a solid month down to Mexico City and back. They camped on the shores of Magdalena Bay to witness calving whale populations. During a cruise in the Bahamas with their friends Chuck and Suzanne Rowan, the cruise ship held a windsurfing competition for the guests. There was just one problem: there was no wind. However, Suzanne had mastered the art of "pumping," using one's arms to pump the sail back and forth to create an impersonation of wind. Suzanne's strong upper body won her the windless windsurfing race.

During one eventful trip to Mazatlán, Junior rented a small sailing catamaran called a Hobie Cat to take out for a spin. The folks renting it to him gave him instructions on how to get out of the break and how to sail it, but they neglected to teach him how to bring it back to shore. When it was time to come in, Junior pointed the Hobie toward the shore, accidentally catching a wave. The wave carried him in, twisting the boat and flipping it in the break, tumbling Junior and the sail craft over and over. Junior emerged uninjured; the Hobie Cat did not. Junior wound up having to cover the damages to the broken daggerboard, mast, and sail.

Since Maxine particularly enjoyed the music and dancing of Central America, having taken many types of dance lessons at BYU, the couple frequented dance spots whenever they traveled to Central America. Once, they stumbled upon a dance floor in Puerto Rico, filled with incredible dancers. By Junior's recollection, they were dancing to bossa nova music—a form of Brazilian music that emerged from the 1960s and is known for its unusual syncopation. Junior and Maxine didn't dare get on the dance floor and instead watched from their table, trying to learn the moves through observation. A young man approached Maxine and asked her to dance. In no time, he was teaching her the movements and she was mimicking them perfectly. As Junior recalls, "Within three or four minutes he had her doing this beautiful dance, and my gosh, I was so impressed. The way she could imitate and control her body like that—she was so good."

Europe

The first time the Bounouses decided to ditch their kids and visit Europe was when they went to Italy to see the place where Levi Bounous was born and to meet a few of Junior's Italian relatives. It would be the first of many trips they would take to Europe. Over the decades, the two of them visited the quaint countryside and towering cathedrals of France, the Tivoli Gardens in Copenhagen and tulip fields in Amsterdam, the fjords of Norway and Sweden, world-famous art pieces like Michelangelo's *David* in Italy, and the Rock of Gibraltar on the Iberian Peninsula. They saw an excellent performance of *Les Misérables* while in London, hiked all around the Scottish highlands, took up boat up the Danube river in Germany, and visited Berchtesgaden, where they saw the infamous Eagle's Nest and the museum documenting the rise of Adolf Hitler and the Nazi party.

One especially memorable trip was when they returned to Italy with their son Barry. Barry had spent two years in Italy while serving a mission for the Church of Jesus Christ of Latter-day Saints, and Junior and Maxine met up with him once his service was complete. The three of them, along with Junior's sister Stella, visited distant Bounous relatives in both Italy and Paris before heading to Greece. They brought tents and initially camped much of the time, though they stopped camping once they caught on to how cheap and convenient hostels were. Then they visited Madrid, where they went to a cafe one night to watch a couple of Spanish guitarists. At one point, the performer handed Barry his guitar, and Barry performed a few of his own songs for the crowd.

Junior and Maxine would also have the pleasure of seeing parts of Europe with Steve. When Steve took over as director of the Snowbird Sports Education Foundation, he began hosting summer ski camps in Zermatt, Switzerland. Maxine and Junior took the opportunity to join the camps. They'd often spend upward of three weeks in Zermatt, where they'd ski on the glaciers around the Matterhorn, hike the rugged terrain that surrounds the quaint mountain town, and counteract all the calories burned during these excursions by eating their weights' worth of raclette, fondue, and gelato.

One of Junior and Maxine's final, big trips to Europe was when they visited Turkey at almost 80 years old with Bill Schwartz and Jo Ann Givan. They visited the ancient Greek city of Ephesus, known for its classic Greek architecture and the Temple of Artemis—one of the Seven Wonders of the Ancient World. Ephesus was an important sea town, though an enormous volume of silt deposit from the nearby Cayster River has caused the coastline to extend miles out from the location of the ruins. Junior remembers looking at some of the remnants of docks in the middle of what seemed to be the desert, astounded that the sea could have been in such a vastly different location as it is today.

Another exceptionally memorable visit was in Cappadocia, where they were able to see the dwellings of early Christians who carved two- and three-story buildings into the soft rock cliffs starting in the first century CE. Becuase of a series of attacks and invasions during the next few centuries, the communities started moving underground, chiseling their multi-level buildings and cities deep into the rock beneath the earth's surface for protection. These dwellings were meant for protection from sieges lasting upward of six months. They had complex ventilation systems to provide fresh air to their inhabitants and release smoke from cooking fires. Wells and cisterns provided water for drinking and for toilets. Some communities had monasteries, churches, and even prisons. Nearly 40 of these underground cities exist, with many largely unexplored and perhaps still some yet to be discovered. Visiting these dwellings was one of Junior and Maxine's favorite things they did in Europe.

Hawaii and Alaska

While it wasn't international travel, it certainly felt like travel abroad when Junior and Maxine went to Alaska and when they spent significant time visiting Hawaii. During her short stint in California, Maxine had been tempted to move to Hawaii when one of her friends, Marilyn Morley, moved there. Maxine had already purchased a boat ticket, but she backed out at the last minute after receiving a letter from a young man back in Provo, Utah, imploring her to return to the Wasatch so they could be together. After giving up the opportunity to move there, Maxine wanted to at least visit Hawaii.

It was Junior and Maxine's time at Sugar Bowl that catalyzed their first trip to the islands. They became good friends with Dr. Frank Gabodi, who was on the board of directors for the ski area. Gabodi had married a woman who grew up in Hawaii and whose family owned a significant amount of land around the Diamond Head volcanic cone on Oahu. Her family was connected to another man from Hawaii named Abe Waterhouse, who also skied at Sugar Bowl. After meeting Junior and Maxine, Abe invited them out to visit after the ski season ended, and they eagerly accepted.

Leaving Barry and Steve in California, they met up with Maxine's friend Marilyn in Kailua, where they excitedly went on their first beach walk after wintering in the Sierra Nevada, and they got sunburned from head to toe. After a few days with Marilyn, Abe took them up a mountainside above Honolulu. His family owned a large swath of land that seemed to stretch halfway up the mountain on a historical road called Round Top Drive. The Waterhouse family was incredibly accommodating. They gave Junior and Maxine one of their cars to use during their time there and let them stay in a carriage house on their property. Abe introduced them to his mother, who was almost 100 years old and still an adept golf player. Her family had moved to Hawaii a few generations back and owned a cattle ranch that stretched all the way down to Honolulu. She delighted Junior and Maxine by showing them old photos and giving them an elaborate history of her family's time in Hawaii.

It was beautiful up on the side of the mountain, if occasionally wet and rainy, though Abe assured them that it didn't matter if it was raining up at the house; all they had to do was drive down to the beach where it was always sunny. He took them to the family's beach house on Kailua Bay to go surfing. It was a quaint, two-story house that didn't have plumbing when it was originally built. The following year, Junior and Maxine returned to Hawaii with Barry and Steve in tow. Rather than staying in the carriage house, the Waterhouse family let them stay in the house on Kailua Bay. From then on, the Bounouses almost always stayed there. The Waterhouse family continued to allow Junior and Maxine to return and stay at the Kailua house for half a century, even after Abe had passed away. Abe also owned a beautiful condo in Aspen to which he invited the Bounouses many times.

Junior and Maxine's connections at Sugar Bowl also led to them visiting a friend in Alaska in 1973. With a camper on the back of their truck, the family began their five-week journey by driving north through Wyoming and Montana, stopping at Glacier National Park before crossing the border into Canada. They passed Calgary to hop on the Alaska Highway, a gravel road constructed during World War II to connect the border of the contiguous United States with Alaska. The rugged road winds its way through more than 1,300 miles of some of the most remote terrain in western-central Canada. The entire roadway was made up of gravel, which they had to routinely knock out of the tread of their tires to prevent a flat. Even with their efforts, they still had to change a tire on their return journey. Once in Alaska, they spent a considerable amount of time in Denali National Park (then called Mount McKinley National Park), camping right at the base of Mount Denali where mountaineers began their long trek. There they admired the majestic scenery and most exciting animal life they had ever seen. Their trip fell over the summer solstice, and the sun stayed in the sky the entire night as they tried to sleep.

Then the Bounouses headed south and west, taking a ferry to Juneau, a coastal city inaccessible by roads. There they left their camper for a few days and boarded a small plane that took them to Yakutat, a small logging and fishing community along the coast and where their friend from Alta and Sugar Bowl, Alex Brogle, had a fishing cabin he lived in during the summer. Brogle was a fishing ranger in charge of checking fishing permits. The Bounouses had arrived at the start of the salmon fishing season, and Alex treated them to a few fishing excursions and took them to see the stunning glaciers of the region.

After returning to Juneau, the family loaded their truck and camper onto a ferry that carried them south through the Inside Passage, dropping them off on the mainland north of Vancouver, so they could finish off their northern adventure, watching as pine trees turned to silver sagebrush outside their car window.

Indonesia

Starting in the late 1970s and into the 1980s and 1990s, one couple that became one of Junior and Maxine's most steadfast travel companions were Chuck and Suzanne Rowan. They were eager international travelers, often organizing the trips they took with Junior and Maxine. One such trip was to Indonesia—one of the most culturally interesting places Junior has ever been.

Because of Indonesia's placement as a critical location along many ancient trading routes, it is a mosaic of many different cultures. Four major religions—Christianity, Buddhism, Hinduism, and Islam—are all quite prominent. Junior remembers the presence of these religions being a defining point of their trip. He and his travel companions visited a few religious temples, which required them to don certain clothing in order to enter.

A memorable moment from their time in Indonesia was when they were invited to visit a deceased woman in a small village they'd have to hike to. Junior, Maxine, Chuck, and Suzanne were the only ones from their group to accept the invitation. They were led into a house and into a room with a bunch of children seated on the floor and an old woman propped up in a rocking chair, looking as though she were sleeping.

The Torajan people of Indonesia, who live in mountainous villages on one of the islands, believe that the soul remains in the body and on earth until the body is cremated. They have a unique way of preserving the bodies of loved ones for months, years, and even decades after they pass, often feeding them and giving them cigarettes to keep their soul content until the village can hold a mass cremation ceremony for the community members who've passed away. The woman whom Junior and Maxine had the opportunity to see had been 100 years old when she had died and had been dead for a few months.

Africa

Another trip the Rowans organized was an excursion to Tanzania and Kenya in the 1990s. The group's intention was to climb Mount Kilimanjaro and Mount Kenya. They started training for the excursion while in Utah, summiting Mount Timpanogos and other local peaks, acclimating themselves and getting their legs in hiking shape. They departed the United States in the spring, which is the end of the rainy season in Africa. They flew into Tanzania and immediately headed to the base camp of Mount Kilimanjaro. They had wisely decided to get their biggest hike out of the way at the start of the trip, while they were still in their best shape and most used to being at high elevations.

The plan was to reach the Uluru summit of the 19,341-foot mountain—a 16,000-foot climb from its plateau base—after the course of three nights. Mount Kilimanjaro has five unique climate zones hikers pass through: cultivation, rain forest, heather and moorland, alpine desert, and arctic. Beginning their climb in the dense rain forest of the cultivation and rain forest zones, they had such a dense layer of fog and cloud around them that they didn't even see the mountain until their second day hiking when they entered the heather and moorland zone. From then on, they would have spectacular views looking up the mountain and looking down to a sea of clouds beneath them. They climbed quickly during their first two days, traveling their farthest days at lower elevations and slowing their pace the higher they climbed. They spent the nights in wooden huts along the way, with porters shuttling their sleeping bags, food, and water. They reached 17,000 feet late on the third night after a long, brutal day passing through the desolate alpine desert zone. They ate a light, specialized meal in preparation for the next day, tried to get three or four hours of sleep despite the elevation, and woke up at two o'clock in the morning to begin the final climb.

They started the trek in the dark with headlamps, hiking up steep switchbacks through enormous scree fields—hillsides made of small rock debris, often hard to walk on. They employed a mountaineering technique known as the "rest step." Before taking a step, they put one leg in front of them but keep their weight on their back leg and rest briefly before stepping up on their front leg and picking up their back leg, all while synchronizing their breath with each movement. This technique helped them pace their physical energy with the little amount of oxygen they consumed. They had packed extra gear for hiking on snow and ice, but it was a low snow year, and it turned out they didn't need it. They reached the summit in six hours, spent less than an hour on top, appreciating the view and the feat, and then hightailed it back down the mountain. What had taken them three days to summit took them only two days to descend, quickly dropping six or seven thousand feet in elevation before they rested for the night.

The group then embarked on a camping safari with guides who packed food and water into trucks for them, and the travelers pitched tents and set up cots on the plains every night. They saw some of the classic geological features of the Olduvai Gorge region and visited the Ngorongoro Crater, where Junior remembers millions of pink flamingos around the lake at the crater's base. Since the group had visited during migration season, they also witnessed millions of animals, mostly zebras and wildebeest, moving across the plains. At one point they drove through a migration that was 17 miles wide.

They also had the opportunity to visit a Maasai tribe. While there, Junior and Maxine saw a man wearing a beautiful bead necklace. Hoping to trade him something for it, they began talking to him through an interpreter. The man initially didn't want to trade, telling them that his girlfriend had made the necklace for him. But he stuck around, which their interpreter told them usually indicated a willingness to trade, but they just hadn't offered him the right item yet. Junior had brought along his Snowbird Ski School vest, blue and red and white with the Snowbird patch on the chest. Junior offered it to the man, and he accepted. Junior and Maxine left the village with the necklace, and the Snowbird vest remained on the Maasai man.

They finished the trip off by summiting Mount Kenya. Junior recalls bringing postcards to stick in a mailbox high up on one of the mountains, being told by their guide that they could use the box to send postcards home. But the postcards never made it to Provo.

South Pacific

In 1985, Steve and his soon-to-be-wife, Suzie Culley, started an international travel business called Bounous International. Having spent the past few years traveling with the US Ski Team and competing all over the globe, Steve was familiar with the lifestyle of ski racers: visiting amazing mountain towns and landscapes but being so focused on training and racing that they rarely got to truly appreciate the places they went. He also had spent a few years as a private ski coach to help skiers from non-racing backgrounds improve their skiing by learning how to run gates. He decided that he wanted to start a ski business that would combine these experiences—finding clients who wanted to improve their skiing while having international adventures—and then hire professional skiers to accompany them and become the clients' coaches. And on top of that, he wanted to add in all sorts of wild adventures to make the experience memorable.

Bounous International's inaugural trip was to New Zealand's South Island, with Steve and Junior as the coaches. Most ski teams training in New Zealand during the 1980s trained at Mount Hutt, but when Steve tried to book accommodations there, everything was full because of school holidays. Uncertain how to proceed, Steve happened to have lunch at the Forklift Restaurant at Snowbird with a New Zealander named John Murphy. John told Steve to look into a rural ski area called Treble Cone, which was still "off the map" and wasn't a well-known ski holiday destination. John promised that the nearest town, Wanaka, was just as beautiful as more popular towns like Queenstown.

The main group, numbering about 12 guests, flew into Christchurch to meet Steve and Sue, who had flown in early to make sure that everything was in order. It was a good thing they did because their original accommodation choice was so run-down that they had to relocate before the main group arrived. Traveling separately from the main group, Junior and Maxine flew with Chuck and Suzanne Rowan. Junior and Maxine, having never been to New Zealand, didn't realize when they rented a car that folks drive on the left side of the road there. Chuck had had some experience driving on the left side in England, so he offered to be the driver. Junior remembers the tires of the car constantly running onto the narrow, winding road's shoulders during their drive from Christchurch to Wanaka.

John Murphy had been right about both Wanaka and Treble Cone. Wanaka was a sleepy little town on the shore of New Zealand's fourth-largest lake, Lake Wanaka, with stunning views of the mountains. Treble Cone was certainly a bit rustic, with limited facilities (the only bathroom available to guests was essentially an outhouse at the base of the runs). The road up to Treble Cone, which they nicknamed the "White Knuckle Express," was quite rugged. Steep, narrow, and unsealed, the road was always a bit of a harrowing ride for the guests, especially while attempting to drive on the "wrong" side of the road in winter weather.

Determined to create a truly unique experience for their guests, Steve and Sue planned a variety of activities. Guests ran through gates Steve and Junior set up and received tips on how to improve their technique. For a fun adventure, the group got dropped off in a farmer's field to be picked up by a helicopter to go heli-skiing (Steve recalls the wind from the helicopter sending sheep droppings rolling across the field). They mountain biked along the shores of Lake Wanaka, took a jet boat ride on the Shotover River, and went bungee jumping. "Triathlon" days, which they drove to Queenstown for, were marathon days of eating, drinking, and shopping. Steve and Sue also scheduled excursion days.

One of the most decadent excursions was a day that began with the group getting picked up by a helicopter before the sun had risen. They became the first commercial group to ski on Roy's Peak as the sun was rising and had a few bottles of champagne to celebrate afterward. The group was then loaded up into small planes and flown out to Milford Sound, where they boarded a boat. They had a lobster lunch out in the middle of the magnificent fjord before flying back to Wanaka.

Another time they boarded a boat on Lake Wanaka, crossed the lake, and got picked up by helicopter on the far side to ski terrain that had never been skied by anyone (that peak would later be named "Bounous" in honor of the inaugural excursion leader). Steve recalls everyone struggling to climb down the boat's ladder in their ski boots. When they came back from skiing, they had a big bonfire on the beach, complete with Olympic silver medalist Christin Cooper (one of the coaches for a later ski camp) opening up beer bottles with her teeth.

A few years after their first camp, one of their camp attendees, a wealthy Guatemalan man named Alfredo Rego became a large monetary investor in the company that owned both Treble Cone and the main heli-skiing company there. Acting on Alfredo's behalf, Steve and Junior were brought to New Zealand to be advisors on how to expand the ski area. They were taken by helicopter to check out a peak that Treble Cone wanted to expand onto (and which they did). Steve was taking video out of the open helicopter door with a handheld camcorder. After checking out the resort terrain, the pilot, a man named Sir Tim Wallis (a local kingpin who is credited with starting New Zealand's helicopter deer hunting industry) took them right up to an icefall. They got so close that Steve couldn't get the icefall in the camera's frame. Afterward, the helicopter took them up to hover above the peak of Tititea / Mount Aspiring.

Besides spending two weeks in New Zealand, the Bounous International itinerary included flying to the little Fijian island of Vanua Levu, where Sue's family, the Culleys, owned a small coconut plantation called Namale (now owned by famous life coach Tony Robbins). There the group would swim, snorkel, participate in kava ceremonies, scuba dive, surf, kayak, windsurf, and take part in tennis tournaments that required the competitors to dress in silly costumes. The whole adventure came to a close with a night of skits and songs. During Bounous International's first year, Chuck and Suzanne entertained everyone with a skit that involved them getting dressed in almost every single article of clothing they brought on the trip, with their ski layers on top. They pretended as though they had gotten ready for the day's intended activity (skiing) and were about the leave their hotel room when they got a call from Steve or Sue, saying that the mountain was "socked in" and that they were now going mountain biking instead. So, Chuck and Suzanne stripped off their ski layers to reveal mountain biking clothes underneath. But then the pretend phone would ring again. It was Sue and Steve, saying there was a change of plans and they were actually going to Milford Sound now. So, Chuck and Suzanne would take those clothes off to reveal others underneath only to get another call that they were going shopping in Queenstown, and so on.

The last significant trip Junior and Maxine took to the South Pacific was when they visited Tahiti with Bill Schwartz and Jo Ann Givan around the year 2000. While in Tahiti's capital, Papeete, they visited the daughter of Maxine's long-time friend Marilyn Fanoimoana. She recommended a restaurant for them to try, up the side of the mountain. Junior, Maxine, Bill, and Jo Ann were seated next to a large picture window with a view of the ocean. They were in awe of the sunset, and right as the sun was disappearing behind the horizon, Junior decided to stand up to watch its completion.

It was at this moment that Junior saw the rare phenomena known as the "green flash," which occurs in clear, undisturbed air when the sun's light is refracted as though in a prism, creating a green flash for a split second. A few other folks in the restaurant saw it, though unfortunately, no one else in Junior's party got to witness it. It was one of Junior's most memorable moments.

Nepal

Junior and Maxine spent their lives doing almost everything together, from when they got married in 1952 and right up until Maxine's passing in 2020. Perhaps the only significant thing during that time period that they didn't do together was a five-week trip to Nepal that Maxine took with Grant and Suzanne Culley and Steve and Sue Bounous to celebrate Grant's retirement. They invited Junior and Maxine, but because the trip was five weeks long and during prime ski school training season, Junior was unable to make it. Maxine would be a companion for Suzanne, who loved watercolor painting instead of doing the more intense hikes, while Grant, Steve, and Sue would tackle the difficult terrain.

The group flew into Kathmandu, right in time for a three- or four-day rainstorm. Water gushed down the narrow streets, and business owners attempted to shovel the water out of their shops. The group didn't get much of a chance to truly appreciate the city because the flooding in low elevations was severe. Since their trip was mostly based around trekking in the Khumbu region, they boarded a small plane that flew them up to Lukla, home of what's considered one of the most dangerous airports in the world. The airport sits on sloping ground on the edge of a 9,000-foot drop-off, planes landing there have to angle their wings up at the last second to get up on the runway. Planes taking off have to go downhill before they're able to get their plane airborne. Add in any wind or weather, and the airport can be treacherous. Steve remembers seeing the wreckage of other planes scattered on the side of the runway.

The storm that had hit Kathmandu had also hit the mountains. Some areas received more than 12 feet of snow, and avalanches had killed quite a few people. Steve was sitting at the Lukla airport and remembers seeing an English man telling a policeman that his wife had been killed in the tent right next to him when an avalanche came down. The couple had been at the base camp of Island Peak, which is where the Culley and Bounous group was headed.

Luckily for them, their timing was such that their excursion was free of tragedy. The snow was still so thick that the sherpas had to dig out spots for their tents every night. Yaks, looking for warmth and grass to munch on, would try to lay on the exposed ground where the tents were, resulting in tents practically collapsing from the weight of the yak leaning into them. They spent Halloween at the Hotel Everest View, known for having one of the most spectacular views of Mount Everest. The group slept at Everest's base camp and made it to the top of Gokyo Peak, which at 17,575 feet was the highest any of them had ever been. Grant had been hiking with a large straw hat, which blew off at the top of Gokyo. He wasn't disappointed in the loss of his favorite hat; he was so excited to be so high up that to him it felt like an offering to the mountains.

Because hiking and sleeping at such high elevations are tough on the body, the group assumed that Steve and Maxine, having grown up and lived at a higher elevation their entire lives, would be more suited to the elevations than the Culleys, who lived nearly at sea level in Palo Alto. In reality, the opposite ended up being true. Maxine, a tiny person sleeping alone in her tent, got so cold and had such a hard time getting enough oxygen that Steve had to start sleeping in her tent with her to keep her warmer. Steve also got altitude sickness at one point and had to abandon their goal of summiting Island Peak.

When it was time to leave the Khumbu region and fly back to Kathmandu, another storm rolled in, causing delayed and canceled flights. There was a general sense of panic at the Lukla airport, and a man allegedly threatened air traffic control with his ice ax in order to get on a plane. Grant, Suzanne, and Maxine had already flown back to Kathmandu, but Steve and Sue had remained in the mountains to do more hiking and climbing. When the couple finally managed to get on a plane, a worker pulled Steve off at the last second because the plane had too much weight on it. Since they had gotten separated as they loaded and the plane was full of travelers, Sue didn't realize that her husband wasn't on the plane until landing in Kathmandu. He had all of their money and her passport, and she had no idea when he'd be able to get another flight. Luckily a tour bus driver helped her get to the hotel where the group was staying.

After their stint in Nepal, the group went to Thailand for a night before flying home. Those who travel internationally know that travelers are often advised not to drink tap water in other countries. All five of them had managed to avoid getting sick for over a month. The morning that they were flying out of Bangkok, Steve walked into Maxine's hotel room just in time to see her finishing a glass of water from the sink. She started feeling a bit sick on the flight home, but it was when they landed in Salt Lake City that the water caught up with her. As she and Junior were reuniting after almost six weeks apart, she started throwing up.

Junior had taken time during Maxine's absence to get things done around the house that had needed to be done for some time but Maxine had been indecisive about them. When they got home from the airport, Maxine was so sick that it took her a few days to realize Junior had given much of their house a face-lift while she had been gone. Framed paintings on the wall and new appliances weren't the only new things in the house that week. Junior recalls that Maxine brought home with her the smell of yak in her clothing and gear—a stench so strong that it lingered around their house for at least a week after she returned home.

Bill Levitt, Maxine, and Junior in Portillo, Chile, in the mid 1950s.

Steve and Junior competing in a "Powder 8's" competition in New Zealand. Mid-1980s. *James Kay Photography*

Junior visiting Wanaka, New Zealand, in 1984.

Sue, Steve, and Maxine on the deck of the Everest View Hotel with Mount Everest in the background. 1987.

The Bounous International Ski Adventure group in Fiji in 1984.

Maxine skiing through gates at Treblecone Ski Area while attending a Bounous International Ski Adventure (nicknamed "Kiwi to Fiji"). Lake Wanaka is in the background. 1984.

Hiking Mount Kilimanjaro in the 1990s. Maxine is third from the right, Junior far right.

Junior and Maxine at the summit of Mount Kilimanjaro in the 1990s.

Junior, Liz and Jim Irwin, Suzanne Rowan, Wilma Johnson, Maxine, Chuck Rowan, Teddy (last name unknown), and a safari guide on their African safari in the 1990s.

Junior, Maxine, John Denver, and Suzanne Culley in Blue River, Canada, during Mike Wiegele Helicopter Skiing's 25th anniversary in the 1990s.

Visiting a Maasai tribe in Kenya. Wilma Johnson in blue, Maxine and Junior with their backs to the camera. Junior had just given his Snowbird Mountain School vest to a Maasai tribe member in exchange for jewelry. 1990s.

Junior and Maxine in Tahiti, in front of the window where Junior witnessed the phenomenon known as the "green flash." Around 2000.

Chapter 14

The Desert Song

South of the Wasatch Mountains is a landscape that knows erosion more than almost any other landscape in the world. Like a snake shedding its skin, this red desert sheds its layers at such a rapid pace that even the fleeting life spans of humans can sometimes witness the change. Despite the softness of the sandstone that sweeps across the Colorado Plateau, this landscape is unforgiving and not for the faint of heart and body. Entirely different from the lush emerald and diamond hues of the Wasatch, the arid juniper brambles and deep salmon-colored sand of southern Utah were equally important landscapes in Junior's and Maxine's lives. And, much like powder skiing, one of their favorite things was to share the landscape and their experiences with friends.

Capitol Reef

The first time that Junior went south to the land of stone was while he was in high school at Lincoln High in Orem. He was president of a group known as the Future Farmers of America (FFA). The group was composed mostly of children of farmers in the Provo and Orem area, and they spent their time learning how to repair tractors and do other agricultural tasks. In his junior year of high school, Junior organized a fishing trip in south-central Utah at Fish Lake. He planned a few excursions during their trip, including a drive through Capitol Reef. Back then, prior to Highway 24 being built, the road through Capitol Reef was a hike known today as Capitol Gorge. It winds through a deep and narrow slot canyon, passing petroglyphs and what is known as the "pioneer register," a rock wall with the names of pioneers who traveled through the area. Junior and his friends took the truck along that rough and sandy route, and Junior witnessed his first glimpse of the red and dusty wonderland that would become a second home to him for the rest of his life.

His next trip south was with Frank, Lorraine, and Maxine—prior to their marriage. It, too, was to Capitol Reef to see the Waterpocket Fold, a wrinkle of rock that stretches nearly 100 miles from north to south, ending close to where Lake Powell is today. They stayed in a motel in Fruita, a small orchard community surrounded by red rock, and spent their days hiking around the area to see the natural caches of rainwater that provide valuable water in the arid land.

Canyonlands: The Maze

It would take a few more years for the couple to return to the desert again. Their friends Dick and Donna Johnson knew of a spot called the Maze Overlook (which would soon become one of the four districts of Canyonlands National Park upon the park's creation in 1964). Having been warned that they would need a car with four-wheel drive to access the location and knowing that their little red farm jeep wouldn't cut it, Junior borrowed a jeep from Jim Shane. They packed the vehicle full of camping gear, crammed Barry and Steve, still quite young, in the backseat and made the trek to one of the more remote areas in Utah and the continental United States.

They camped on what seemed to be the edge of the earth. From their perch on the rim, they could see how the landscape beneath them was a boiling cauldron of erosion. The name "The Maze" couldn't have been more accurate. The canyons beneath them were so intricately intertwined that it almost appeared as though onlookers were looking at a formicarium—an ant farm sandwiched between two panes of glass. And towering high above the deep labyrinths were thin and tall formations that seemed too delicate to exist, protruding sheets of dark rock known as the Chocolate Drops.

Dick had frequented the Maze often and had begun to trailblaze some of the earliest routes around the Overlook and down into the canyons. Junior recalls that he found a route from the Maze Overlook down to the Chocolate Drops, and he built cairns to mark the routes he found. Though they didn't venture down into the proper Maze until their next trip, Junior and Maxine loved following Dick around the desert.

Besides their shared love of the outdoors, the Johnsons were a good match for the Bounouses because they, too, had two young children. Steve and the Johnsons' son, Scott, who was a little older than Steve, used to go out adventuring on their own while the adults would be cooking dinner or taking care of camp business. During one such excursion, when they were camping in the Maze proper, Steve and Scott left camp with a small, nylon rope and the intention of using the rope to get into places they wouldn't be able to get into otherwise. They used the rope to lower themselves into a deep waterpocket that had an overhanging rim. When they tried to get back out using the rope, they found that they couldn't get up and over the overhang. The boys were stuck.

As the sun set at the campsite, the adults became worried. Steve and Scott hadn't told anyone where they were going, and the adults had assumed the boys had just gone on a short adventure near the campsite. They began searching the surrounding area, calling out the boys' names and quickly realizing the seriousness of the situation. As the search party expanded their territory, they came across Steve stumbling back through the dark. He told them that he and Scott had gotten stuck in a water pocket, and that Scott was still in there. When it had started getting dark the two boys got desperate. Scott, the taller of the two, had tried standing on Steve's shoulders first, unsuccessfully. But when they had switched and Steve had been on Scott's shoulders, Steve was able to hoist himself out of the hole and go to get help.

Steve has loved getting his friends stuck, and then unstuck, while rock climbing in Utah ever since.

That wasn't the only scary thing to happen to the kids during that Maze trip. Dick's daughter, who was only three or four at the time, was walking behind her parents on a trail when she suddenly cried out that something was on her. Her parents turned around to see a rattlesnake hanging off their daughter's dress, its tail dragging along in the dirt behind her. As she had passed the snake it had struck and gotten stuck in her dress, the fangs sinking into fabric and luckily not flesh.

Over the course of the next few decades, they would take many trips to the Maze, camping at the base of Lizard Rock and hiking down into the labyrinth of rock beneath them, or across to the Chocolate Drops, or camping in an area known as the Dollhouse and hiking down to Spanish Bottom, where the sandstone meets the Colorado River.

The last time Junior and Maxine went down to the Maze was with a group of Snowbird ski instructors, and they were well into their 80s. Junior can't recall the exact number of times they made the lengthy drive to the Maze Overlook, but he estimates it's around 15 times.

Canyonlands: The Needles

After their first trip to the Maze, the Bounouses' next trip to the desert was into the Needles District of Canyonlands National Park, across the Colorado River from the Maze. Quite different from the Maze, the Needles are rock gardens that point straight up into the sky, making the visitor feel as though they are a small bug in the midst of many crimson-and-cream striped potato sprouts and white-capped mushrooms.

Knowing they needed a reliable four-wheel drive vehicle of their own if they wanted to continue these desert excursions, the Bounouses bought a new jeep for this trip. It was a good decision. They tested out the new vehicle by driving it over Elephant Hill, a notorious four-wheel drive route in Canyonlands, and then they camped with Dick Johnson and Jan Billings on the far side of the feature. The took the trip during the Easter holiday, and Junior and Maxine hid eggs all around the Whale's Head campground for Barry and Steve to find.

Before the area became a national park, there were no rules regarding where vehicles could or couldn't go. Junior and Maxine drove their jeep on a cattle road through Chesler Park, which is now a beautiful grassland recovering from decades of erosive cattle grazing. Junior put Steve, only three or four years old at the time, on his lap and let him hold the steering wheel. Driving the jeep through Chesler Park is one of Steve's earliest memories. They took that jeep throughout the region, driving up past Dugout Ranch to where Salt Creek Canyon begins. Thankfully, the Needles Outpost, a small family-owned "store" with limited supplies, was around even in those days and had a 500-gallon tank for storing gasoline, so they didn't have to worry about running out of gas during these excursions.

Though the Needles didn't start off as one of the locations they'd return to every year, after Steve took over the Snowbird Ski Team in 1989, Junior and Maxine began frequenting the Needles almost every fall. Steve started organizing "dryland" camps—when athletes, ski racers in this case, start getting in shape for the upcoming season by participating in other physical activities—at the Needles every October. He'd reserve a group site where kids and their parents could camp, and then he'd lead hikes, yoga, and rock climbs throughout the weekend. It's a cherished tradition that the Snowbird Ski Team still does today, where the kids can run around the rock playground while the parents have just as much fun drinking frozen margaritas at sun set and hot toddies around the campfire (not to mention Bailey's in their morning coffees before the day's activities). Junior and Maxine participated in these camps for many years, as well.

On Halloween weekend of 2020, Junior, Steve, and his wife, Sue, took their RVs to camp for a week. Taking their RVs rather than camping in tents was a smart move—they promptly were snowed on. Rather than putting a damper on the trip, the few inches of fresh snow across the landscape added to the allure of the landscape, and Junior had an amazing time hiking through the snow. The following fall in 2021, Steve and Junior embarked on what unexpectedly turned into quite the adventure traversing eight miles from Elephant Hill to Squaw Flat Campground—both Steve and Junior receiving a bit of their own Bounousabuse.

Lake Powell

When Junior and Maxine began visiting Lake Powell, it was during a unique time in the location's history. The United States had gone on a dam-building rampage during the first half of the 20th century, and Utah rivers were no exception. After a sneaky trade-off, it was decided that the Colorado River would be dammed near the start of the Grand

Canyon, creating a reservoir in a little-known area called Glen Canyon in exchange for preserving the more widely known Echo Park, which would become part of Dinosaur National Monument. Once people started visiting Glen Canyon after the decision had been made, however, many of the environmental conservationists realized their mistake. David Brower, head of the Sierra Club at the time and one of the main folks who fought to save Echo Park, felt deeply the weight of the loss and wrote this in *The Place No One Knew*: "Glen Canyon died, and I was partly responsible for its needless death."

Junior and Maxine were able to witness the final breaths of Glen Canyon while experiencing the earliest flooding of Lake Powell. Features that they would visit during one summer would be submerged the next summer. And while it was devastating to watch arches, caverns, Native American ruins, and willows disappear beneath the water, the rising lake also opened up new areas to explore. Despite its bleak beginnings, Lake Powell became one of the couple's favorite places to visit during their lifetime, in part because of the cool and deep sandstone-enclosed waters.

Their first trip to Lake Powell was more of an adventure than they had anticipated. Dick and Donna Johnson and Max and Jan Billings had visited three months prior, strapping two canoes together to form a sort of pontoon, then sticking an engine on the back to cruise more easily around the lake. They took photos of their trip and invited Maxine and Junior to their house in an attempt to persuade the couple to join them on their next trip. It didn't take much convincing. Soon after, Junior asked his brother Barney if they could borrow his 12-foot, flat-bottomed fishing boat.

On the eve of their vacation, Junior dropped the boat and trailer off to get serviced and then rode his bike back to the service station the morning of the trip and threw the bike into the back of the boat. He drove back home to pick up Maxine and the kids, and they left Provo around noon, the forgotten bicycle still in the back of the boat. Interstate 15 was undergoing construction, so the road was rough and filled with potholes. When they were about 150 miles outside of Kanab, they noticed the trailer wasn't driving well and pulled over. One of the tires had been stripped down to the hub cap, and it became clear that they needed a new wheel. With no other option, the family left the boat and trailer on the side of the road and drove the rest of the way into Kanab, where the Johnsons, the Billings, and another friend named Harman Steed had rented them a room for the night at a motel, arriving around midnight.

They began the search early the next morning, visiting almost every store in the small town to try to find the right wheel. Junior had brought the destroyed wheel with them, and no place in town had one to match. Then someone from their group passed a place that was selling a boat and noticed the trailer underneath had a very similar wheel and tire. The problem was the boat was for sale—not the wheel of the boat's trailer. Luckily for Junior, Harman had been the head of a bank in Kanab and had been jokingly called the "mayor" of Kanab for a few years (later winning the actual title of mayor by just two votes) and knew almost everyone in town. Harman somehow convinced the store owner to let Junior borrow the one wheel from his boat trailer, with the promise of returning it after their trip.

Now with the right tire, Junior left Maxine and the boys at the motel while he drove three hours back to where he had left the boat on the side of the road, switched out the wheel, and drove another three hours back to Kanab. Their friends had left Kanab long ago, having given Junior and Maxine directions to where they would be camping. By the time the family reached Wahweap Marina, it was late in the afternoon. There was nothing around the boat ramp except for a very small store, where they picked up a map of the lake and a flashlight, since they hadn't packed one. It was a smart move.

Their destination that night was Last Chance Bay, about 30 or 35 miles away. The family loaded the camping gear into the boat (leaving the bicycle with the car) and set off as soon as they could manage, in immediate awe of their surroundings as the rock walls rose around them. Being autumn, the sun began setting around 8 p.m., and the night around them quickly became darker than dark, with no hint of a moon to illuminate rock walls and no lights on the fishing boat. Junior and Maxine debated whether they should find a place to camp. Junior looked at the flashlight and the map, and, in his words, "Bounousabuse said, 'Oh, let's keep going.'"

So, with Maxine standing at the bow of the boat with the flashlight in hand, illuminating only 20 or 30 feet in front of them, Junior drove the boat at speeds barely more than an idle. It was so dark that they couldn't tell when the canyon turned, so they would just go straight until they hit a rock wall, then consult the map and decide if they needed to turn to the right or to the left. Then they would drive straight until they hit another wall. In this manner they zigged and zagged for hours through completely unknown terrain, until they finally came across the buoy in the middle of the channel that read "Last Chance Bay."

The journey wasn't over yet, however. Last Chance Bay is a very wide channel, and they didn't know exactly where their friends had decided to camp. Whenever they saw a campfire, Junior and Maxine would call out one of their friends' names to see if there was any response. If there wasn't, they'd continue on. Finally, they came across a camp that called back to them.

The rest of the trip was quite memorable. The Bounouses were enthralled. Lake Powell was a playground of sorts for kids and adults. They taught Barry and Steve how to water ski by pulling them by a rope along the shoreline. Their friends had brought a few fast speedboats and used them to venture farther up the dizzying canyons. During one excursion, they were surprised by a heavy downpour. Not expecting the rain, they had left all of their food, sleeping bags, and supplies out on the beach. They returned to their camp to find that one of their friends who had stayed back had gathered all of their belongings together in a pile that he then sat on top of in a fruitless attempt to keep them dry. They had laid their sleeping bags out in the natural concave stream beds along the shore, not thinking about how those stream beds would become funnels for water if it ever rained. The entire trip was, to say the least, a learning experience. On a positive note, they found an abandoned army surplus tent that was broken in a few places. They took it home with them and repaired it. It would become their main camping tent for years to come.

Despite the difficulties of their first trip to Lake Powell, the family was hooked. After camping on the beach for quite a few years, Junior, Maxine, and a few other couples decided to go in on a houseboat together. Their friend Dean Wheadon found an old rental houseboat for sale out of Bullfrog Marina around 1972. It was a bit of a dingy thing, and since it had only 35 horsepower, they couldn't venture too far up the ever deepening fingers of the lake. Being one of the better mechanics of the partners, Junior recalls spending much of his vacation repairing the boat. Rotating through the four couples, each couple would get seven days on the houseboat. So every four or five weeks, the Bounouses would head south for a week at the lake. They called it their "poor man's Hawaii."

Once they discovered certain spots they enjoyed visiting more than others, they would return time and time again. One of their favorite places was Good Hope Bay, a beautiful bay about 30 miles upriver (or "up-lake") of Bullfrog. The 10-mile-long bay, which was often smooth and glassy and perfect for waterskiing, was almost always devoid of other recreationalists in those early days. There was a nice sand bank and plenty of side canyons to explore. It was here that they began experimenting with pulling a surfboard behind the wake of their new bellboy ski boat (a popular sport today known as "wakesurfing" but back in the 1970s, almost half a century before it was more common, the Bounouses called it "surfing behind the boat"). When windsurfing became popular in the 1980s, the Bounouses would watch for the winds to pick up and then they'd rig up sails and windsurf across the bay.

After about 10 years of using the dingy houseboat, the Bounouses went in on a nicer houseboat shared among six couples—one that was more reliable and had more horsepower. Able to travel greater distances, one of their favorite haunts soon became the Escalante River tributary. The mystique of the Escalante—its winding canyons, secluded coves and beaches, and looming rock walls—entranced the family. They loved listening to the falling desert song of canyon wrens and watching the small birds dive and bank between sandstone and sky. The family would take their speedboat as far up a narrow canyon as they could, and then when they couldn't navigate it any farther, they'd abandon it on the nearest sandbank. They'd then wade and sometimes swim farther up the canyon until they could walk along salmon-colored sand, hiking up shallow, swerving creeks and between lush glades of willows and cattails.

They usually visited Lake Powell at least once every year, if not three or five times (seven was their record). Even after they sold their second houseboat, so many of their friends had houseboats of their own that there was no shortage of invitations to go to Lake Powell multiple times a summer. As years turned into decades, Junior and Maxine became very familiar with the wandering canyons and hidden treasures of the lake, witnessing how the landscape changed depending on the depth of the reservoir. An arch could be visible one year and underwater the next. They might find a beautiful sandstone bay to pull their houseboat up to, only to return the following summer and have the sandstone "beach" be 30 feet up the side of a cliff. They could navigate their houseboat across a shallow channel that acted as a shortcut to certain terrain one year, only to return to a stretch of marshland the next year and have to sidetrack many miles to access the same terrain. Junior and Maxine would take notes of the landscape and the water levels, recording which campsites and features could be visited at which levels.

In June of 2020, my immediate family and a couple of friends had the pleasure of renting a houseboat and borrowing Junior's little yellow speed boat for a trip to Lake Powell. During one of our more memorable excursions, we took the speed boat through a labyrinth of narrow canyons, each of our arms sticking out of the side of the boat in case we needed to push it away from the towering canyon walls. We hit a few dead ends and tried to keep track of the turns so we could navigate back out. There were no other boats in the canyon with us, which was lucky because there wouldn't have been much space for two boats to pass each other. After a couple of maze-like corners, we suddenly came face to face with an arch, the apex only five or six feet above the water and too low to take the boat through. We swam under the arch only to find yet two more arches to swim under, and a mesmerizing cavern after those.

We left the place feeling as though we had discovered some pot of gold at the end of the rainbow, a secret treasure not many others may have seen. Depending on the water levels, the arches might be inaccessible or completely underwater. We described the place to Junior afterward. Before we could even tell him about the arches, upon hearing the description of the canyon he asked, "Did you get to swim under the arches?" He already knew, already had been there many times, already had felt that unique intimacy that we felt as we floated between cool waters and sandstone beams. When we returned during the low year of 2021, which was almost 100 feet lower than the 2020 levels, the labyrinth of canyons was a completely different landscape. Try as we might, we couldn't even find the series of arches.

The last time Junior and Maxine got to visit Lake Powell together was for Maxine's 94th birthday in September 2019. In fact, it turned out to be her very last birthday. It feels very appropriate to our family that she was able to celebrate her final rotation around the sun at a place she loved so deeply, with people she loved—Junior, Randy and Ann MacDonald, and Roger and Margaret Bourke. Junior was even able to surf behind the boat again with Maxine cheering him on from their old, reliable yellow ski boat.

"I found out that before I could join the Bounous family, for my prenuptials, I needed to go 'smurking' in Lake Powell. Junior will take the speed boat to the end of a slot canyon, and then tell everybody they need to don a life jacket and jump in to swim to the end of the narrowing slot. As you proceed into the slot, it gets murkier and dirtier with flash flood debris and floating dead bugs of all kinds. You're swimming through the garbage scene from the original Star Wars movie where you expect a water serpent from below to grab your leg. By the time you persevere out of the slot and back to the speed boat, countless dead bugs and twigs have permeated through your bathing suit. Mild-mannered Junior has figured out how to get all these adventuresome smurking women to 'peel out' before they get in the boat, as we can't tolerate the debris in our suits. That was Junior's welcome-to-the-family smurk!"

— Sue Bounous, daughter-in-law

"One lovely afternoon at Lake Powell, Barry and I were looking for some alone time and took the sail boards across the lake to what we thought was a secluded cove. Apparently Junior became uneasy by our absence and was determined to 'rescue' us. Despite Steve telling him a rescue was not necessary, Junior drove the entire houseboat across the lake. When it came around the corner and I looked up and saw this massive boat looming right there in front of us, a shriek emitted from me that could be heard for miles. I'm afraid It was quite a humorous show of us scrambling for our suits and trying to cover up. Well, we learned our lesson: no more skinny dipping on Bounous trips!"

(Steve and Sue after this event: "Junior, don't you ever try to 'rescue' us.")

— Debra Bounous, daughter-in-law

"Sometimes Junior would organize ski school gatherings outside of the ski season. There was one time when we were at Starvation Reservoir with a bunch of Snowbird instructors. I think this may have been for Junior's birthday one year. We were on this two-story boat, and Junior took a windsurfing board without the sail and had the boat tow him on the board. He pulled himself up with a rope and then threw in the rope and was surfing in the wake. In my mind, Junior started the sport of wake surfing. And Steve did it, too, but nobody else could do it. All these bad boy skier dudes who thought they were big shots couldn't do it, but Steve and Junior could, no problem."

— Joan Berrett, Snowbird Mountain School employee

"He took people on trips . . . and you certainly were challenged, every bit of it—from the morning until late at night. And the next day . . . you had to go up in every canyon, and it's all day long and you're worn out. That's why we call it Bounousabuse."

— Mike Wiegele, Sugar Bowl instructor and
the owner of Mike Wiegele Helicopter Skiing

"Having grown up in Hawaii, when I came to Utah to attend BYU, I wasn't expecting to ever get some surfing time in. Then the Bounous family invited me on a boat trip with them, and I was so amazed that we could surf behind the boat. Barry and Steve were using these little trick water skis, and they were doing all these tricks and stuff.

So then they let me try them, but Steve was driving the boat. And all I remember is that Steve would just gun it, and I'd be up and going and then he'd slow way down. And then he'd gun it again, and I'd be up and going. He was just going fast and slow and fast and slow, trying to get me to fall off, and I was determined I was not going to fall off. I stayed on quite a while till I finally fell."

— Mark Magelssen, family friend

"All of us who have known and shared adventures in beautiful places with Junior and Maxine have memories that are unsurpassed and unforgettable. In the 35 years I have spent at Snowbird in Mountain School—trips to Lake Powell, hiking and camping trips in southern Utah—I was definitely the novice in all the activities. My background in retailing and growing up and working on a family farm did not offer the skills to participate in a lot of the activities, but Junior always encouraged me to 'give it a try.'

As I look back on those times and experiencing the 'agony of defeat,' I must admit I survived somehow, mostly because of Junior's quiet ways. He gave me the confidence and skills to reach goals I would have never accomplished and enjoyed on my own—all of this with his patience through a lot of fun, laughter, and camaraderie from all of the participants at the given time."

— Nancy Kronthauler, Snowbird Mountain School employee

"Junior had plenty of tales of the wildlife that used to frequent Lake Powell when we were there in 2020. He commented on missing the snowy egrets that used to line the banks of the lake when he first started going out there. One morning, after a night hearing barks from nearby dogs and yips from nearby coyotes, we wandered onto shore to check out the animal tracks. We saw the smaller tracks of the coyotes and then what I thought could be

something larger. . . . I called Junior over to look at them, and he confirmed that they were the tracks of a mountain lion. I went off for a hike that day on my own, and after a couple of hours of hiking and wondering if I was being tracked by a mountain lion, I made it back to the boat to find Junior, still out following the animal tracks."

— Courtney Sanford, family friend

"Getting to spend a lot of time vacationing at Lake Powell as a child was very special to me. Hours spent swimming, waterskiing, surfing, hiking, and spelunking are some of my favorite memories of my whole childhood. But my absolute favorite thing about my time in Lake Powell were the early mornings when I'd stumble into Grandpa's boat, curl up in the front in my sleeping bag, and head out onto the glass-like water. We'd head up and down side canyons towing Grandma on skis, and I'd sit and watch for over an hour as she floated on the mirrored reflection of the towering red rock walls. Grandpa would pull her as long as she wanted. His patience and joy at helping people do what they loved is unmatched in my mind. He always just knew that you could get down that steep hill or get up on one water ski or make it to the top, and he'd be right there with you until you did."

— EvaLynn Bounous Bolen, granddaughter

Maxine, as graceful in the water as she is on skis. 1980s.

Maxine and Grant Culley among a very large juniper tree in the Maze District of Canyonlands National Park. 1980s.

Before wakesurfing got its name, Junior and his crew called it "surfing behind the boat." 1980s.

Lake Powell living in the1980s. Bounous, Rowan, and Shane families.

Maxine and Steve on the top of the "Indian Hills" houseboat in the 1980s.

Junior and Steve on a sand dune at Lake Powell. If you look closely, you can see the tips of water skis popping out of the sand in front of Junior's shoes. Junior couldn't get very much speed, but he could "ski" down the sand dune. Steve's method of getting down, riding a finless short-board, was a bit more economical. 1980s.

Exploring a canyon at Lake Powell. The white rock, which is actually red rock that turns white after being submerged underwater, indicates that the lake is at a lower level. Where white rock meets red rock is the high water line.

Junior waterskiing at Lake Powell. Likely in the 1990s.

Junior and Maxine's houseboat at Lake Powell. Not a family to pack lightly or reach for low-hanging fruit, they made their way to Good Hope Bay. The journey was a 20-mile slog from Bullfrog Marina, but with the payoff of very few other people and boats, as well as plenty of toys. (Take note of all of the windsurf boards, sails, and surfboards lined up on the beach.)

Mark Magelssen and daughters Noelle, Joy, and Marie, with Junior and Maxine in front of Rainbow Bridge at Lake Powell. It was an exceptionally high year at Lake Powell, with the water levels reaching the bridge. Late 1980s.

Bill Schwartz and Jo Ann Givan's houseboat near a feature called the Cookie Jar in the early 2000s.

Jo Ann Givan, Maxine, and Junior in a slot canyon at Lake Powell in 2003.

Maxine and Junior with Anne and Bill Loper in front of Delicate Arch. 2010s.

Steve and Junior, in Junior's little yellow boat, passing underneath Gregory Bridge at Lake Powell in October 2021. The water levels had just dropped low enough in the last 48 hours that our boat was able to pass underneath the bridge, which was exposed for the first time since the dam was built and the lake submerged the feature. According to someone who had been camped near the bridge for the past week, if we had tried to do that a few days before, the lake would have been too high. It was quite the experience. The year prior, we had taken our houseboat to this same location and anchored it about 70 feet above where this photo was taken, the bridge still completely underwater.

Junior, Sue, Steve, and Ayja at Cathedral in the Desert. October 2021.

Captain Junior. This was in their "Indian Hills" houseboat, which they shared with six other owners until 2005. This photo was likely taken in the 1980s.

Captain Junior in October 2021.

Chapter 15

Peter Pan of the Mountains

The last few decades of Junior's life—decades that typically involve a quieter and slower lifestyle for the general population—have been anything but boring and sedentary. Even as a "senior," Junior is still a junior. Perhaps the name Junior, which was mostly a mistake, destined him to be forever youthful. For even as Junior's biological clock ticks away, his passion for life and living has not dwindled in the slightest. If anything, Junior's wonder for the world around him and ability to find humor in any circumstance have become richer as he has grown older—proven by the fact that he became a "Junior Ranger" of Canyonlands National Park at the young age of 96.

This is not to say that Junior hasn't been affected by the aging process. Almost a century of a life well lived is certain to have plenty of oscillating moments of joy and hardship, and both Junior and Maxine endured some health trials in the last few decades. For Maxine, these included a tumor in her brain that needed to be radiated, as well as a number of skiing-related injuries that she fortunately always recovered from and which never dissuaded her from continuing to ski into her 90s.

Ironically, almost none of Junior's ailments were skiing related. In fact, he has sustained more injuries falling off or out of things than he has skiing. It seems that Junior has a bad habit of falling from great heights. When he was around seven or eight years old, he fell off the roof of a garage, breaking both arms and probably dislodging a few vertebrae in his back. A couple of years later, he fell out of a pear tree and broke an arm again. Fast forward to his 70s, when he fell off yet another roof while pruning a tree at Maxine's mother's house (which he and Maxine kept and rented out for many years). On his way down, he tried to grab hold of a few branches to break his fall, which instead broke and slashed great gashes in his arm. And perhaps the closest moment Junior had to "meeting his maker" was when he was a teenager mowing hay with a horse-drawn mowing machine. He would often carry a shotgun with him when he mowed hay because as he'd close in the crop circle, pheasants would gather in the center and eventually get spooked out of the crop. But during one ride, the shotgun fell between Junior's feet, hit the mower brace and fired. The bullet ripped a hole in Junior's pants, then grazed his ribcage, leaving bruises and welts. Junior got lucky. The angle of the gun was such that less than an inch in any direction would have produced a much different result.

His ski injuries in comparison have been minimal. While at Sugar Bowl, Junior was running through some slalom gates he'd set up for training purposes. He caught a tip and unfortunately came down on an icy mogul, which knocked his shoulder out of its socket. Another time he overshot a Nordic jump and landed in the flats, twisting his ankle.

His most serious ski injury happened when he was around 80 years old. He had been skiing at Snowbird during an early morning clinic. The clinic leader had been instructing the group to move their inside ski way back as they turned, almost like a telemark skiing technique, but on alpine skis—a technique Junior found to be a bit dangerous. The group started skiing down Chip's Face, which is a long, steep pitch that can be quite firm and sometimes icy. The entire run is likely somewhere between 650 and 700 vertical feet. Somewhere quite close to the top of the run, just as it starts getting steep, Junior fell, hitting his head on the hard snow. He lost consciousness and can't remember falling, but he did gain consciousness a moment later, just in time to realize that he was sliding down Chip's Face on his stomach and headfirst, with the cat track fast approaching and no way to stop himself.

Junior hit the cat track with such speed that it launched him into the air. While airborne, Junior braced himself mentally for a hard landing. But the pitch on the other side was so steep, and he was carrying so much speed, that it was luckily a very uneventful landing—besides the fact that he was now flying down the lower pitch still headfirst, still on his stomach, and now heading toward a glade of trees at the bottom of the run. Junior blacked out again after landing, then regained consciousness as he approached the trees. He spread his arms out in front of his head in an attempt to slow himself and brace for what might be a terrible impact. Luckily there was a patch of soft snow before the trees, and it stopped his momentum completely. He was clear-headed enough to then get himself onto his knees and call up to the group that he was okay. They brought down his goggles, which were packed with snow, and his skis, which they helped him step into.

But Junior was not quite as okay as he seemed. He doesn't remember skiing down to the plaza after the accident. He does recall meeting up at the plaza with Barry MacLean and Dennis Keller, who were his clients for the day. He met them with an all-too-chipper attitude, considering that he had blood running down his face. When Barry said Junior should get checked out, Junior insisted that he was fine and that they should go. Unconvinced, Barry and Dennis called over John Collins, head of risk management at Snowbird and a longtime ski patroller. Collins started asking Junior a few questions. Who was he skiing with? Junior said that he had been skiing alone, which was obviously incorrect, since the clinic group was still gathered around him. Next he asked Junior where he was skiing. Junior said that they were skiing at Sundance today. Recognizing the signs of a concussion-induced delirium, Collins steered Junior down to the clinic and radioed Steve to let him know what had happened.

Junior has a bit of a habit of getting bloody and continuing on his way. When he was more than 70 years old, he competed in a half marathon in the South Fork of Provo Canyon. Near the start, someone accidentally tripped him from behind, and he fell, scraping his legs and his face badly. By chance, a neighbor of his who was a doctor was behind him and saw the fall. He helped Junior back on his feet, helped clean the blood up a bit, and asked if Junior wanted to sit down and get a ride to take him back. Junior said no, he wanted to finish the race. So the doctor ran beside Junior for five minutes or so to make sure he was all right. Junior finished the race a bit bloody, but otherwise fine. A few years later, at 81 years old, Junior would earn first place in his age group in the St. George Marathon, running alongside Barry.

In September of 2021, our family rented a houseboat for a week on Lake Powell. A few of us went for a two-hour hike while Junior held down the fort at the houseboat. By the time we got back, Junior was having a jolly good time. He was wading in the water to his knees tinkering with the boat ropes, had blood running down his leg that he was unaware of, and he was missing a tooth. Grinning through the new gap in his front teeth, he told us that he'd had a grand old time entertaining himself.

The first medical ailment that took an abrupt hit on Junior's life was when he was diagnosed with prostate cancer in his 70s. It happened practically overnight, and his doctor, now a good friend of Junior's named Corbin Clark, advised him to operate immediately. If he didn't operate, they estimated, he'd have only two years to live. The cancer was aggressive enough that even with the rapid operation, Clark gave Junior a seven-year life expectancy. But, over 25 years since that 7-year prediction and no sign of any cancer returning during that time, he's been doing pretty well. In classic Junior fashion, not long after the procedure, he and Maxine planned a trip to hike from the rim of the Grand Canyon down to the river to spend a few nights at Phantom Ranch. Upon hearing Junior's travel plans, Clark strongly advised him not to go, warning Junior that if were to start bleeding while on the 10-mile hike down or 10-mile hike back up, he would likely die. Undeterred, Junior and Maxine had a few lovely nights lulled to sleep by the lapping waters of the Colorado River.

After a life spent sailing more than 100 feet through the air and landing on long wooden sticks, the ailment that nearly took Junior out more than once seemed almost silly in nature. When they were 79, Junior and Maxine traveled to Turkey in the summer. On the plane ride back, Junior noticed a rash developing on his right leg. It didn't improve once they were home, so he visited a dermatologist and started applying cream. Rather than improving, the rash spread up his leg and reached his right hip. It created a burning feeling and reminded Junior of a time when he'd had blood poisoning. Once it reached his hip however, the rash disappeared from his ankle and lower leg, but spread into his left hip, then to his left shoulder, leaving his hips completely. Sensing there was something more devious at work, he sought a specialist to try to figure out what was happening.

The infection moved into his right shoulder and things began to get more painful for Junior. His specialist diagnosed him with a staph infection, a common bacterial infection and relatively harmless when found on the surface of the skin, but very dangerous and deadly if it moves into the bloodstream. Junior became so weak and was in so much pain that he was admitted to the hospital and put on antibiotics. After 10 days or so, he was released from the hospital, just in time for Junior to attend his 80th birthday party in August, which the Keller and MacLean families had planned for him.

However, when Barry picked Junior up from the hospital, he took Junior back to the specialist's office to get him checked out again. Barry dropped Junior into a chair outside so he could park the car. By the time Barry got back to Junior, there was blood all over the ground, coming out of the wound in his arm where the IV had been. Barry immediately got Junior inside, holding his wrist to slow the bleeding. Nurses were able to apply pressure to stop the bleeding, but once Junior's specialist looked Junior over, he told Junior that he needed to go right back to the hospital. He said the insurance company likely had tried to get Junior out of the hospital to keep costs down, but that Junior was not fit to go home yet. Junior headed back to the hospital, and Barry regretfully informed the Keller and MacLean families that Junior's party was going to have to be canceled.

Junior was lucky. His specialist told him that if the infection had traveled down either of his arms, he would have lost them. If it had traveled into his chest, it would have killed him by infecting his heart. For a few months, our family had to hold our breaths as we watched Junior battle the infection, which didn't let up until the end of September. But even the ferocity of the infection didn't stop Junior from continuing to live his life as best as he could. A few weeks after he left the hospital, the Snowbird Ski Team was doing their annual hike up Red Pine to summit the Pfeifferhorn. Despite Junior's weak state, he and Maxine joined them up to the lake.

When they made it there, the athletes applauded Junior, the 80-year-old who had so narrowly beaten death and still could hike seven miles round trip at elevation.

My mother, Sue, was also on that hike. She recalls thinking that Junior was free of staph and, while weak, was completely healthy. That is, until Junior opened his shirt up at one point and she could see that he had a large needle taped to his chest, sticking into the skin above his heart, and a sack with antibiotics strapped to his leg. He still had one more week of antibiotics to go, but he wasn't going to miss the chance to hike up his favorite canyon.

For five years, it seemed as though Junior had beaten the infection. Then when he was 85, his shoulder began to give him serious pain once more. Knowing that this was bad news and he needed urgent medical attention but unable to get in to see his specialist, Junior went to a 24-hour instant care without an appointment. It was a Thursday or Friday, and the staff told him the earliest the doctor could see him was Monday or Tuesday. Junior told them that was unacceptable, and that he would wait until someone could see him. When the doctor did finally see Junior, he told Junior that he was fine and only offered to give Junior medication.

I recall Barry once saying that the only time he's ever seen Junior truly upset and angry was this instance. For those who know Junior well, it's hard to imagine what he must have been like. Throughout his life, Junior has always been more likely to be polite than to push back. Lucky for us, he did push back in this instance. Junior insisted that he would not leave that office until the doctor took an MRI and called in a specialist to look at the results. The doctor gave in and gave Junior an MRI, but then told Junior he should go home and they would get back to him with the results. Junior once again refused, saying that he'd wait in the waiting room until the specialist got in. Once the specialist did arrive, it only took him a minute to see that Junior was again in trouble. He sent Junior straight to the hospital. Another day or two of waiting for an appointment, and Junior might not be here today. The staph infection had indeed returned, but Junior managed to beat it once again.

The final physical hardship that really put a damper on Junior's physical ability to enjoy the places he loves has been sciatic pain. A few years ago, his back was giving him so much grief that he was having a hard time just walking along the path that leads from his backyard up along the hillside where his father planted Italian grapevines over a century ago. It prevented him from skiing as much as he wanted to, as well, and walking in ski boots was almost too excruciating to make the activity worth it. But after a few years of trial and error with physical therapy, Junior has conquered that ailment. Someone might assume that at 90 years old, if you stopped doing as strenuous an activity as skiing you would have stopped doing it for good. Not Junior. Once he started feeling better, he got right back on the hill, strengthening atrophied muscles that were clearly craving to get back on skis. It took only a season or two for them to remember how to connect carving turns and ski powder again. Now at 96, he skies much better and faster than he did at 90.

The hardest part about skiing these days for Junior? He often needs help getting his ski boots on and off. Walking in them can be tiring as well, though once Junior clicks into his bindings, he sheds decades. He once said to me, "I walk like a 90-year-old but I ski like an 80-year-old. Or 70-year-old." Anyone who's skied with him in recent years knows this to be untrue. He still skis better than many 30-year-olds.

What fuels this backward way of aging for Junior (his *Benjamin Button*-ness, if you will) is his outlook on life. The same determined energy that drove him to ski faster and jump farther has translated into making sure he walks every single day, does his stretches, and stays on top of his physical therapy exercises. The pleasure that he gets from doing these things feeds into that energy, creating a positive feedback system that keeps him youthful.

In the spring of 2020, my cousins and their husbands, along with Junior, decided that they were going to build a little fort up in the woods above Barry's house, which they were calling "Grandpa's Hideaway." Junior had mentioned to me that this was a project they were working on, but I was assuming he meant that just my cousins had been working on it for a few years, and really that it was mostly my cousin's husband, Steve Pond, doing the bulk of the work. While visiting one afternoon, Junior gave us a tour.

The trail was a bit sketchy. In fact, far more treacherous than I was anticipating. It was steep, somewhat exposed, and the dirt was loose in places. They had built steps into it using pieces of wood, but it looked like one big rainstorm could cause the whole thing to slide. I was wearing casual sandals and felt unsteady on the steps and grabbed onto tree branches for balance. I was surprised Junior was even trying to walk up it and was even more surprised when he said he had put in these steps here and created another switchback here. I thought I misunderstood him.

"*You* built this trail?" I said in clarification.

"Yep," he said, not even out of breath as he pointed out all the features of the trail. "Steve helped."

We reached the hideaway, and it was a child's dream. I was immediately reminded of the Lost Boys from the movie *Hook*. Steve Pond had moved 20 or 30 large sticks and logs into the ravine to create a large, flat platform around a couple of large trees. There was a plastic slide coming out of one tree above the platform, and their plan was to build little fairy-type structures and to bring in furniture. To me, it completely summed up Junior's unwavering sense of adventure and child-like imagination and wonder.

When Maxine passed away in June of 2020, shortly after we'd visited "Grandpa's Hideaway," I witnessed Junior's youthful air fade for the very first time in my life. Losing Maxine after 67 soulful years of marriage together was incredibly difficult on him, and it was a both sad and scary time for my family for a few weeks as we watched him struggle with the loss. But once he summited the peak of his grief, he knew that she would not want him to call it quits quite yet. She would want him to continue exploring the places and things they loved sharing together, the mountains and desert, the wildflowers and birds, and to continue to raise their family in the heart of the Wasatch. And that's exactly what Junior did.

Junior's 95th birthday was two short months after Maxine's passing. He decided that he didn't want a party. Instead, he insisted that we go camping in the Uinta Mountains, a place that he and Maxine camped almost every year they were together. For a time after Maxine's passing, he struggled to walk short distances along the path behind his house, but by the time he turned 95, he was hiking more than four miles a day in the Uintas at 10,000 feet in elevation. (And drinking margaritas at night!) And he didn't stop there. A few weeks later, Junior drove his RV down to the Needles, where he spent a week camping with Steve and Sue. The weather wasn't quite the ideal autumn desert weather they were expecting. It ended up snowing a few inches on them, but that didn't dampen their spirits. They hiked through the snow, breathing in the approaching winter.

By the time the ski season rolled around, Junior was hiking upward of five or six miles a day. His legs were ready. Before Christmas came, he had skied more than 10 days—more than he had the entire past season. One of my favorite ski days with him was during that time. It was a slow start to the season, and many were complaining about the lack of fresh powder and thin snowpack. After a storm that deposited only a few scant inches of snow, we took Junior out. He hadn't skied off piste in quite a few years, but he began following behind my father as Steve would dart off piste to make a few wedeln turns (more commonly known today as the wiggle turn or hippie wiggle). Junior had been nervous to go off-piste at first, but after letting his legs get used to the motion, he was soon skiing entire runs off piste, wiggling all the way down.

In January 2021, which received almost no new snow, he was practicing carving almost every other day, gaining muscle and confidence and, at 95 years old, skiing better than most people on the slopes. One day, at the end of the day, he insisted on skiing Regulator Johnson, the steepest "groomed" (it was not groomed at the time) run at Snowbird. The run was cut up and our legs, already tired from a full day of skiing, were burning by the time we got to the bottom—not easy conditions for anyone, let alone a 95-year-old.

Then in early February, Junior skied at Snowbird with some old ski school friends. It was a bit of a surprise powder day, and the group spent almost the whole time, from 9 a.m. to 3 p.m., skiing off-piste. I called him that afternoon to see how his day had gone. I could hear his smile as he told me how, for the first time in years, the snow was so deep that he hadn't been able to feel the bottom. For a few glorious turns, his skis touched nothing but deep powder. In his own words: "I hadn't felt that in, gosh, so long. Twenty turns in that is worth my whole day. It felt so good. *I want that feeling. I want more powder.*"

In my first book, *Shaped by Snow*, I tried my best to capture the feeling of powder skiing. It was no easy task; how could you ever truly describe the combination of snow, terrain, gravity, and thrill? But I put pen to paper and did what I could. Junior later told me that section was his favorite part of the book and expressed regret that he would never have that feeling of selflessness while skiing powder snow again—a statement to which I rolled my eyes and said, "Yeah, right."

Between an aggravated lower back and spending more time taking care of an ailing Maxine, Junior's ski days in the past few years had been at an all-time low. My dad estimated that Junior had skied fewer than 10 days in the 2019–20 season, which is dismal when you consider that he was skiing every single day (and that's not an exaggeration) during the winters when he was working as a ski instructor and ski school director. In the 2020–21 season, he had skied 10 days by Christmas. Most people become weaker, slower skiers as they get older. In Junior's case, he started becoming a *much* stronger and faster skier once he hit 95.

Best of all, on that February powder day on Tiger Tail, he experienced the feeling of deep powder skiing, when your body is somewhere between earth and sky, perfectly balanced within the pull of gravity. Junior had the "feeling of the snow turning my skis, not me turning them. I just pointed them where I wanted to go, and the powder did the rest." When all the elements of powder skiing align into one beautiful moment, you leave your body behind and get sucked into that selfless moment of joy and enlightenment. You can taste the way your ski tips cut through the snow, smell the scent of water crystals and pines between the trees, hear the harmonies of mountain and sky and soul.

I want that feeling. I want more powder.

On his 60th day of skiing on April 5, 2021, we loaded him into a helicopter to do another activity he had never expected to do again: heli-skiing. You can always tell when Junior is excited and having a good time by how many jokes he makes. That morning, as we got our gear ready and met the Powderbird guides, almost every sentence coming out of Junior's mouth was a joke. He was on cloud nine. A local sunglass company, Pit Viper, had donated a pair of glasses for Junior to rock that day, and he strutted around the helicopter pad wearing them, giving everyone a hard time. My partner, Colin, decided that he was going to snowboard that day rather than ski, and Junior would not let him off the hook, relentlessly hitting him with jokes about snowboarding. Not even the helicopter pilot was safe from Junior's good-natured harassment.

Despite rapidly warming conditions that led the guides to warn us that we might only be able to get just one run in, we managed four beautiful, albeit challenging, runs. The conditions were not perfect and definitely not easy. Patches of breakable crust and mashed-potato snow haunted the runs beneath us, and it was with a little trepidation that we started skiing, especially Junior. During the fourth run, he hit bad snow that sent him tumbling down the hill.

Have you ever seen a 95-year-old crash while skiing? I'm convinced that it's one of the most heart-stopping things you'll ever see. And what's more, that was not the first fall I had seen Junior take. About two weeks prior to the heli-skiing day, we'd taken Junior off piste into some powder below Devil's Castle at Alta. He skied down a dip that had too much compression for his bindings (for those readers who are avid skiers, his DINs were set only at four). Junior double ejected and went headfirst into the snow.

That was the first time my heart stopped. But Junior had been in nice, soft snow that time. He was fine, though the trickiest moment was getting his boots clicked back into his bindings. It required a few people holding him steady and lifting him out of the knee-deep snow to get there, but he skied the remainder of the day as if nothing happened.

The second time my heart stopped was watching him crash on that heli-ski day. There was no soft snow to cushion his fall that day. Watching your 95-year-old grandpa hit hard snow and have his limbs tossed around like a rag doll is something I wouldn't wish on my worst enemies. He wasn't even wearing goggles—that run, he had decided to wear the Pit Vipers. My first thought was this: "Thank God we have a helicopter right here because he's probably broken all of his ribs, his hips, his collarbone, and the Pit Vipers probably splintered into his eyes, and we're going to have to fly him to the nearest hospital."

But Junior Bounous apparently still knows how to bounce at 95. As he slid to a stop in front of the photographer of the day, Sam Watson, the first thing Junior said to Sam was this: "It was the darn Pit Vipers!" With a little help, Junior was back up and skied the rest of the run. At the time of this writing, he currently holds the Guinness World Record for the oldest heli-skier at 95 years and 224 days.

"After Maxine passed away in June 2020, just a few months shy of her 95th birthday, Junior was heartbroken and went into a downward spiral. He was very weak, and we were afraid we might lose him too. I had just retired, so I made it a point to try to take dad into the mountains as much as I could. As he regained his strength and enthusiasm for life, he started looking forward to the ski season. To help motivate him, we gave him a goal of heli-skiing for a day as a family in the spring if he felt strong enough. Ayja did some research and realized that at age 95, Junior would set the world record for the oldest heli-skier, according to the Guinness Book of World Records. Helping Junior set the world record on April 5, 2021, was an honor we shared as a family and an incredible experience I will never forget." — Steve Bounous

---

By the time the 2019–20 ski season ended, Junior had hit 72 days, just a few days shy of his goal of 75 (Snowbird closed a weekend early due to a melting snowpack, or he would have hit that goal.) He practically lived in his room at the Lodge for much of the season. He was so popular to ski with that it was hard to even get in a day with him at times; when I knew he was staying at Snowbird, I'd call him to see if I could ski a day with him, and he'd already be booked out for the next five days. And as the season continued, he started skiing deeper and deeper snow. (His goal for the 2021–22 ski season was to ski 96 days in honor of 96 years. He made it to 101 days!)

Junior's lively attitude didn't end when the ski season ended. He was such a spry hiker in the 2021 summer that he led my mother and me on some Bounousabuse during a hike around Albion Basin and Cecret Lake that required my mother and me to help Junior scramble up a rock face and bushwack through a ravine. Our friends Roger and Margaret Bourke flew Junior in their plane up to the San Juan Islands for my wedding in August, and he not only ran down the aisle after Colin's aunt Coco (who he claims "left him at the altar"), but he danced the night away for hours, just a few days shy of his 96th birthday. A couple months later, Junior was on what was supposed to be a short hike in the Needles District of Canyonlands in October with my dad, but it turned into six miles of up and down on steep slickrock. There's one thing we know for sure about Junior: he's refusing to slow down.

There was one thing that Junior hadn't done in a few years that we knew we wanted him to get to experience again: exploring Lake Powell. In late September and early October of 2021, we rented a houseboat for a week, with Junior as our captain. The lake was the lowest it'd been since the 1968 lake levels. We were able to witness rock features that literally hadn't seen daylight in 60 years.

One of those features was Cathedral in the Desert—one of the most iconic places in Glen Canyon with a waterfall that hadn't been completely revealed since the water rose. When the cavern and waterfall were initially discovered, they were so named "Cathedral in the Desert" because of their stunning, awe-inducing beauty. According to David Brower, head of the Sierra Club in the 1950s and 1960s, "Cathedral in the Desert was the ultimate magical place in Glen Canyon." In 2020, just 15 months prior to our Lake Powell trip with Junior, when the lake's elevation sat at 3610 feet, my family visited Cathedral by boat, anchoring the boat at the top of the main waterfall and hiking into the upper grotto. Peering into the water beneath our boat, we could see the lip where the waterfall would have begun its cascade to the canyon floor, the cavern below dark and eerie.

With lake levels much lower at 3,545 feet for our trip the following year, Dangling Rope Marina, a key place for houseboats to refill on gas, was closed. Houseboats starting from Wahweap Marina, like us, weren't allowed to venture any farther up the lake due to the likelihood of running out of fuel. This meant that the boat ride to the Escalante arm of Lake Powell, where Cathedral is, would take a few hours in my grandpa's ski boat. So one morning we packed "Old Yeller" (as we referred to Junior's old yellow boat) with enough provisions to last us the day, and we headed northeast. Because so much of the lake was largely inaccessible to most of the houseboats, we had glassy water the entire way through the main channel—something incredibly unique.

I've been visiting Lake Powell every few years for my 30 years of life, and I had never seen the lake look like a river until that moment. The water levels were so low that channel markers were blinking on rocks 100 feet above our heads. Areas that were usually wide expanses of flat water were narrow channels. We were able to take the boat completely underneath Gregory Natural Bridge, a feature that we had parked the houseboat on top of 15 months prior, our boat clearing the bottom of the bridge by a foot. The more we explored, the more it became apparent that the whole notion of Lake Powell being a lake was fleeting—that this landscape was truly formed by a river in the desert.

With it being the second day of October when we visited Cathedral, it wasn't all that warm outside, and since it was still early in the morning, the sun hadn't yet reached parts of the canyon's entrance. Most of us wore puffy jackets and shorts. Knowing the sand would be cold on my feet, I kept my hiking sandals on, as did everyone else in our group. But the first thing Junior did once he got off the boat was take his shoes off, saying, "I want to feel the sand on my toes." The anticipation to see this geologic feature that hadn't fully been exposed since Junior had seen it last in the 1960s was thick in the morning breezes.

It was nearly impossible to get Junior to the main chamber where the waterfall is. In fact, it seemed at times as though he was trying not to make it that far. He would only manage two or three steps before he'd stop to appreciate the reflections in the water or the colorful rocks shining in the shallow creek. He passed through that space with a childlike wonder that, while I was expecting it, nevertheless surprised me with its potency. He was savoring every polished rock, every curve in the little creek, every ripple of water across red sand, every tendril of green maidenhair fern growing out of rock.

Though the Cathedral had been exposed less than a year, it was remarkable to see that plenty of plants had already started growing out of the cracks in the wall where moisture seeped through, creating miniature hanging gardens that Junior was quick to point out to all of us. He recalled the hanging gardens that used to be there before the lake rose, smothering the lower rock walls in dense vegetation. Not expecting how quickly the ecosystem would rebound after just a few months in the desert air, he relished the fact that he was able to see it once more. He never once gave the impression that he thought the "old" Cathedral, the one that existed before the lake rose, was the more special or beautiful Cathedral. He was just thrilled to see the space once more.

Junior zigged and zagged his way through the antechamber, touching the rock wall on one side before veering to the other side to let his toes sink into the deeper mud near the lake shoreline, before backtracking to stand in the shallower running water of the creek. Then he'd stop moving altogether and tilt his head toward the canyon walls, higher than they'd been in over half a century. It must have taken him a good 10 minutes to walk 50 yards. He didn't want to just look at the space; he wanted to move through it completely, touching all that he could. He was like a child playing in a garden.

By then, the rest of our group had walked all the way in to see the waterfall, while I had stayed with Junior through his meandering. I was eager to walk all the way in, desperate to take advantage of the relative quiet of the space before more groups rolled in. But Junior actively disregarded my attempts to steer him to the end, telling me that he wanted to enjoy every moment of this. He assured me that there was no rush. He was going to stretch time as though it were taffy, and there was nothing I could say that would make him move his feet faster, or in a straighter line.

At long last, we made it to the Cathedral. Morning light wove its way through the winding canyon walls, illuminating the rock in various shades of orange high above the waterfall. Peaches and creams in the direct path of the sun mosaicked the higher canyon walls, while salmons and tangerines were illuminated in the antechamber above the waterfall, brilliant in the indirect light from the walls above. The lower rock stood in shades of dark amber and colors that recalled various shades of spice: cinnamon, nutmeg, paprika. The darker shades made it apparent that the lower rock had been underwater not too long ago. Just above the darker water line from a few months ago were smears of green along the walls where bacteria and moss had started colonizing. The rock from where the waterfall emerged looked as though it could have been blown glass, smooth and delicate, yet indestructible, simultaneously looking like it should break at the hammer of a nail and as though it could last through eternity, unfazed as it seemed by being underwater for 60 years. Beneath it was a deep azure pool, looking as though it could hold many galaxies in its depths.

I stood on the edge of the pool with Junior. He pointed at the lip where the waterfall begins its fall and told me about the time he was here once and a man scaled the wall, then did a swan dive off the lip into the pool beneath. With a twinkle in his eye, Junior looked at me and grinned.

"Shall we see how deep it is?"

I didn't really want to get wet. I was quite comfortable being dry. My body temperature was just on the verge of being cold without actually being cold, and any sort of submersion in cold water would quickly change that. But the next thing I knew, Junior was wading into the pool, which dropped quickly and steeply, creating a bit of unsteady footing for a 96-year-old. Junior reached and took my arm for balance, pulling me firmly alongside him as he waded in, not caring that I was quite alright staying dry. It was one of the most special moments of my life, wading into that cold pool with him, watching him witness and interact with this space when he didn't think he ever would again, and witnessing it for the first time. It was perfect. We only wished Maxine could have been here.

To test the acoustics of the Cathedral, my mother, my friend Courtney, and I started singing one of Maxine and Junior's favorite songs, "Edelweiss" from *The Sound of Music*. We caught Junior off guard with the music. He was facing a wall, both hands pressed up against it, examining the lichen growing. He turned around, slightly startled. Then he realized what we were singing. He put his hands to his face and began to cry. As our harmonies came to a close, echoing in the vast chamber around us, holding us within their vibrations, we embraced Junior, our tears joining his in the azure pool.

And we knew that Maxine wasn't gone, she had been there all along, walking alongside us, barefoot in the desert sand.

"What I think is so special about Junior is just his enthusiasm . . . [and] even now at 80, the energy he brings every day to the sport of skiing. There's so many of us that can't keep up with him still. He's so energetic [and] has so much enthusiasm for skiing, but he's so mild-mannered [and has a] low-key personality, and that makes him very, very unique and very special."

— Bob Bonar, Snowbird president and general manager

"During a trip to Lake Powell in 2021, Junior loved living vicariously through us. He was delighted to watch as we all tried our luck with e-foiling and foiling behind the boat, and he was eager to jump in as the driver so he could help create this experience for others. You could tell that he was simultaneously so happy to be supportive of our progress, and also grieving the loss of his ability to be out there trying new things. We decided that we had to get him out there. Using a larger and more stable paddle board with a rope tow, we pulled him from shore onto the water, and he used a paddle for support. [He was] a bit shaky, [and] we were all a bit nervous about him falling, but Junior stayed upright, pulling on the rope tow while balancing above the waves, for a full 10 minutes before a wave unsteadied him and he fell. I jumped in after him, helping him swim to shore, for which he was very grateful!"

— Courtney Sanford, family friend

"My nickname for Junior is Peter Pan, 'cause he never grew up. He never had to grow up. He never gets old . . . that's what his spirit is like and that's what his skiing is like."

— Georgia Clark, Snowbird Mountain School employee

"Just a short time ago, Junior, at 95, took some of us into Tiger Tail and proceeded to thread us through the brush, rocks, and fallen trees in deep powder. My husband, Tom, looked at me and said, 'Where the hell are we?' But once again, we all returned safely. There is a motto to all of this: never try and do what Junior would do without Junior. He protects us with his presence."

— Nancy Kronthauler, Snowbird Mountain School employee

"Being able to ski Pipeline in very tough conditions . . . at nearly 80 is remarkable, and that's probably the ultimate goal for me is at 80 years old to have the same love and passion and excitement and enjoyment out of skiing and be able to keep doing it."

— Steve Bounous, son

"When you live at Alta, it's hard to go elsewhere in the summer or winter. I always feel like I'm stepping down, and not just elevation-wise. It makes you think, 'Why would I leave this canyon?' But Junior and Maxine introduced us to all these amazing places. They always knew that there was so much beauty to be shared. The last time we went to Lake Powell was a few years ago with Junior, Maxine, and Randy and Ann MacDonald. It was in September for Maxine's and Margaret's [my wife] birthdays on September 18, and it was perfect. Not too hot, not too cold, the lake was empty. Maxine was born on Margaret's birthday, and she died on mine. It's a strange intertwining of our lives."

— Roger Bourke, Sugar Bowl instructor

Junior and Steve skiing in New Zealand in the 1980s.
James Kay Photography

Maxine and Junior at Red Pine Lake in 2005. Junior was battling a staph infection and hiked with an IV of antibiotics strapped to him. Maxine had broken her neck in a ski accident earlier that year. Neither sickness nor injury ever truly prevented the couple from doing what they loved.

Junior and Barry running together in the St. George Marathon in 2006. Junior was first in the 80+ division.

Tyndall, Sue, Junior, Steve, and Ayja on the day that Junior set the Guinness World Record as the world's oldest heli-skier at 95 years old. The helicopter and Mount Timpanogos are in the background.

A happy "Birthday Girl" on his 95th birthday in the Uintas. 2020.

Junior after receiving his Junior Park Ranger pin at Canyonlands National Park in 2021.

Junior with his special "Living Legend" name tag the Snowbird Mountain School made for him. April 2022.

Junior and Steve on Junior's 96th day skiing at 96 years old. April 2022. Junior went on to finish the season with 101 days under his belt!

Junior with his award (provided by Mark and Liane Magelssen) for skiing 96 days at 96 years old on April 26, 2022. (Proof that even at 96 years old Junior can still be bribed with chocolate.)

Chapter 16

Among Wildflowers

No matter how much avid skiers pray to Norse snow gods Ullr and Skadi to keep the snow falling, each winter in the Wasatch must come to an end eventually. Fluffy powder settles and compresses into dense corn snow, then shrinks as the sun's light becomes stronger in the spring. This is the life cycle of the snowpack—starting from scant snowfall in the fall and early winter, building throughout the season as the storms keep rolling through the Wasatch, then settling and melting into the landscape it has kept hidden. The snowpack acts like a water savings account for all other times of the year, and as the water molecules, trapped in their frozen state for months, melt and follow the path of gravity downstream, our creeks swell, our reservoirs rise, and the soil in the mountains is exposed to the sun once more.

There is perhaps no phenomenon in the Wasatch tied to the snowpack so beautifully as the wildflowers. Each summer, the hills and basins of the mountains burst into a kaleidoscope of color, as though there were a large glass prism in the sky refracting broken and brilliant light onto the meadows. Spires of mauve lupine create mesmerizing patterns with their closely stacked blossoms. Fiery orange and crimson Indian paintbrushes make the fields look as though they're catching fire. Goldenrod, black-eyed Susans, yarrow, balsamroot, and chamomile complement each other in buttery yellows and whites. Fireweed and elephant's head create pops of color against the greenery with their brazen, bright pink hues, while columbine steals the show with its delicate shape and many tones (determined by the acidity of the soil) of blues, pinks, whites, and yellows. Brambles of wild raspberry, clusters of azure bluebells, and the amethyst and lapis hues of larkspur add the final flourishes to the seasonal swing into summer.

The timing of the wildflower blooms and their abundance is determined by the quality of the snowpack in the winter. The thicker the snowpack, the longer it takes to melt and expose soil where seeds have lain dormant since the previous fall. The farther this process is pushed into summer, the more blooms arrive. A late arrival of flowers means that buds are likely to emerge after the risk of a late season frost has passed, resulting in healthier plants. It also means that species that are usually staggered throughout the summer are compressed into a tighter flowering time frame. While there might be relatively empty spaces between wildflowers when the plants are staggered across a longer amount of time, every inch of soil will be covered by thick groupings of wildflowers during a late-blooming wildflower season.

As residents of the Wasatch mountains for almost a century, Junior and Maxine have observed this intimate link between snowpack and wildflowers during all types of snow years. They've enjoyed so many summers, but one wildflower season stands out in particular. The snowfall in 2011 was memorable; Alta reported more than 700 inches of snowfall (with some claiming it may have hit the 800-inch mark after 10 new inches of snow fell over Memorial Day weekend), and Snowbird's last day of skiing was July 4. While July is often the start of wildflower season during a low snow year, the snowpack stubbornly remained in the mountains through the end of the month. When the wildflowers finally arrived, it was right when folks would normally be visiting the mountains to see the fall colors, rather than flowers.

On Maxine's birthday that year, September 18, Junior and Maxine hiked along their favorite trail in Mineral Basin to witness the explosion of color. The wildflowers were rampant, all vying with each other for soil and light and space. They were packed so thickly along the trails that there were hardly any trails to follow. Together, Junior and Maxine walked through the fields and meadows, stopping every few feet or so to appreciate their surroundings or to name the species of wildflowers as they saw them.

Some of my earliest memories are of my family hiking with Junior and Maxine. They taught us how the landscape was all the entertainment we needed. Natural spaces were our playgrounds, rather than actual playgrounds, and my three cousins, sister, and I were well versed in the adventure story lines we could craft in the red rock deserts, among the cherry trees between our grandparents' and Barry's houses, and within the many aspen groves in the Wasatch. The five of us became superheroes, each with a different power associated with an "element": earth, wind, fire, air, and heart. In other words, we were our own version of the animated television series *Captain Planet and his Planeteers*. Our powers came from harnessing the elements within the landscape around us. Trees, rock, wind, creek beds, and flowers became energy sources from which we could draw our powers to battle whatever evil force decided to cross our path.

Junior was the Captain Planet to our Planeteers. He may have not been squishing himself into rocky crags or rolling around in the sand with us, but he was our fearless leader whom we exemplified in our stories. And he gave us the ultimate weapon in our games: he taught us the names of the flowers, of the trees, of the birds. He was our teacher, and knowing these names gave us our ability to feel as though we could control these things and use them to our benefit, even if it was just in our imaginations.

Whenever we went exploring with our dear "Baqui," as we always called him, Junior would stop to point out aspen bluebells along creek beds in the canyons, apricot globemallow along washes in the desert, Steller's jay and black-capped chickadees flitting between the pines and aspens on the shorelines of mountain lakes. He notices animal tracks in freshly fallen snow, muddy desert creek beds, and in the sandy shorelines of Lake Powell. In the fall he becomes mesmerized watching pikas creating their winter haystack homes among small granite boulders. His intrigue with the natural world isn't confined to wilderness spaces; visit Junior at his house in Provo and he'll point out the family of quails that take shelter in his hedges, or the narrow space between the wall of the house and a bush where he saw a red-tailed hawk dive through at full speed. And Junior credits his love and knowledge of birds and wildflowers to Maxine, who always carried a field guide with her on hikes to identify whatever they saw.

It is a certain type of person who takes the time to learn the names of the things around them. Plenty of folks will never learn the types of trees that grow around their house, or the names of the birds that flit in and out of the bushes in their backyard, or the species of flowers that catch their eye on the side of the road during certain months of the year. It's quite easy to go through life without having a gnawing curiosity to be able to call these things by name. But for those who do have that curiosity, not knowing the nonhuman life forms that we share our beloved spaces with is simply not an option. A bird watcher, rather than watching the road like most car passengers do, will constantly watch telephone poles for hawks, or spot birds perched on the tips of tall grasses in marshes. A wildflower hunter will stop often on their hikes to look more closely at the shape of a petal, the color of a leaf, or a pile of dried vegetation that marks the home of a marmot.

Junior and Maxine's love for flowers and birds grew by learning from others who loved them as well. A friend from their Alta days, Janis Levitt, collected, pressed, and identified over 100 wildflowers in a book she kept over many years. Her husband, Bill Levitt, was an avid birdwatcher. Warren Balsevian was also a birdwatcher, and his wife Sue collected wildflowers. Carl Boyer, a geologist who accompanied Junior and Maxine to the Maze one year during the spring, took photos of all the flowers they came across, wrote the name of each flower on the back of the photo, and then gave them all to Junior. As a newlywed living at Alta, Maxine would pick and dry wildflowers to be placed on the tables in the dining room at the Rustler Lodge. She and Junior would then collect the seeds and scatter them in places around Alta where the soil had been disturbed, returning beauty to the land.

Taking the time to notice and identify plants and animals, often overlooked by the rest of the population, is a quality I've come to associate with living an intentional lifestyle. It's a shimmering light on the surface that speaks to the deeper truth about who a person is. It shows curiosity for the world around us, a capacity to feel wonder, appreciation for finding beauty in unexpected places, and empathy toward all things alive. It's recognizing that it's the land—wildflower petals, bird song, and crystalline snowflakes—that ultimately teaches us all.

In the 1960s, Junior and Maxine's lives crossed paths with a man named Al Davis, who worked part time for Junior at Sundance before following Junior to Snowbird. A naturalist at heart, Al had been a football coach at the local high school but transitioned to heading up a program that took students hiking, fishing, and skiing in the Wasatch. Al brought on other teachers, like a geologist and an English teacher, to assist him, so students would gain a variety of knowledge while on their excursions, creating a multidimensional curriculum that became wildly popular among both students and the community.

Al's love for the Wasatch infiltrated anyone lucky enough to hike or ski with him, including Junior and Maxine. Al even began inviting Maxine to participate in the high school classes he taught, which Maxine absolutely adored. Pretty soon, Maxine, Junior, Al, and his wife, Beth, were cross-country skiing up South Fork, hiking Mount Timpanogos, and camping at Albion Basin together. Fervent lovers of the outdoors, Junior and Maxine found themselves relishing the light Al emitted when they were in the mountains together. With Al, they developed that type of friendship that infiltrates you to the bone, where you share so much that you can't imagine what your life was like before them.

Junior and Maxine were with Al on his last hike. Plagued with a heart disease that killed both his brother and his dad in their 50s, Al tragically passed away quite young. Their group was hiking from the base of Rock Canyon to the top of Squaw Peak—a hike Al had done countless times with no issue. On this day, Junior remembers Al lagging behind the group and telling Junior that he felt weak that day, but not to worry about him. He made it up to the peak and back, but the next day, he was rushed to the hospital with a failing heart. Junior and Maxine went to the hospital room to visit him, thinking that he was going to be alright. Al passed away the very next day.

"My father became pretty sick and had to go to the hospital for his heart. And all of us were concerned. He was 52—someone that age doesn't die of a heart [issue]. His father had problems, my grandfather had problems, [and] as we said, 'Dad, I love you and we'll see you after the recovery room, and everything's going to be okay,' the phone rang. It was Junior Bounous. He was the last person to talk to my father. And he said, 'Al, you know when they put you under you start dreaming a bit . . . and I know you're going to be dreaming about climbing those mountains. If you start up, just make sure you come down.' My father didn't make it through surgery. And at the funeral when I saw Junior, I asked him about the conversation. And he relayed what he had said to my father. And after a moment of silence, he looked at me, and he said, 'Nance, looks like he found a great mountain to climb . . . He's okay.' And wow, everything was okay after that."

— Nancy Davis Thoreson

"Self fulfillment begins when self pity ends. Go for it."

— Words from Al Davis' memorial Junior strives to live by

In many ways, our lives are like trees with an infinite number of branches. Our lives begin at the base of the tree. With each opportunity we are given and with each choice we make, our lives are directed to a certain branch, while the infinite number of branches we don't end up taking remain invisible to our three-dimensional selves. The branch that we do end up following until our lives come to a close is determined by a myriad of things, not just opportunity and choices, but by the places we experience throughout our lives and the folks we meet along the way.

There are people we encounter in our lives who pull us from the path we may have been on, starting us on a new branch, a different direction. A song from the musical *Wicked* describes these encounters using these words: "Like a comet pulled from its orbit as it passes the sun/ Like a stream that meets a boulder halfway through the wood . . . Like a ship blown from its mooring by the wind off the sea/Like a seed dropped by a sky bird in a distant wood . . . I have been changed for good." For Junior and Maxine, Al Davis was one such person whose friendship nudged them from their current branch and made a lasting impact on them—the teacher who taught the teachers.

Teachers don't just simplify the complex and show us the new; they often change the trajectory of our lives. I began writing this biography with the intention of trying to demonstrate how many people Junior has taught, and I hoped to accomplish this by including others' stories in these pages. I wanted to show how Junior was a force that changed people's trajectories, how he guided them onto new branches of life. Through the writing process, I realized that I had it backward. Junior and Maxine are who they are because of those who left impressions on them. The people in these pages, and many who aren't in these pages, made this story possible. Some of them are no longer with us, but they are beside us as footprints in the desert sand or wildflower seed scattered on the wind; some are still here and hopefully are reading these words. As much as this book is a dedication to the wonderful mosaic of a man that Junior is, it is a dedication to all who helped him become who he is.

Junior became such an incredible teacher because, from day one, he was surrounded by them. Levi, whose tireless work ethic, pranks, and intuitive knowledge about water and soil helped Junior realize the essential bones necessary for a successful life. Jennie, who preferred hiking barefoot through the mountains over completing house chores, gave Junior his empathy and ability to love deeply, as well as his first pair of skis. Alf Engen's guidance during those impressionable years changed the course of Junior's life forever. And the teachers of the natural world—the Wasatch, the desert, the forests and the ocean, the soil and sky and snow which Junior came to worship—taught him how to live in harmony with himself and those around him.

For many who knew them, Junior and Maxine will always be associated with the winter. They're local legends, the Ullr and Skadi of the Wasatch Mountains. Like Ullr, Junior was a skilled hunter, and like the giantess Skadi, who married the sea god Njord but left him after becoming homesick for the mountains, Maxine (albeit the opposite of a giantess), returned to the Wasatch after living by the ocean. I, however, will always associate them with wildflowers. Winter will always be their most formative season, where their athleticism and enthusiasm and passion is displayed, but wildflower season is when the depth of their personalities really shines through, when they walk slowly and deliberately and call the flowers by name.

It is widely regarded within our society that the seasonal rhythm begins with spring. Spring is when seeds sprout under the darkness of soil and make their initial journey into the light. The sight of fresh green tendrils poking out of soil, pink buds on bare trees, and sun on our cheeks certainly make spring feel like the ultimate beginning. Plants mature as summer carries on, fading along with tree leaves once the temperatures cool and the intensity of the sun's rays lessens. The arrival of winter storms signifies the end of the season's cycle, when foliage dies, animals go into hibernation, the sky darkens, and the pace of life slows.

In the Bounous family, however, we measure our lives by the snowpack. Those winter storms that mark the end of the typical seasonal cycle mark the beginning of ours. Each storm brings a flurry of encounters, which begin to stack on each other like snow crystals on a landscape, layering our experiences, our relationships, our hopes, and our challenges—the snowpack of our lives. The further we progress into winter, the thicker our snowpack becomes. The sun might be at its lowest in the sky at the start of our winters, but we are blessed with magnificent sunny days after a storm. With maturity comes the arrival of the spring equinox, and as we grow old, our snowpack melts into the surrounding mountains, snow fading to flowers.

Maxine passed away in June, as spring was transitioning to summer and the final snowfields in the mountains were shedding their water. On the day of her memorial service, near the end of June, we awoke to fresh snow in the Wasatch. Skadi graced us with her presence once more; we knew Maxine was up in the canyons skiing powder. The wildflowers were exceptionally beautiful that season.

The thicker the snowpack of one's life, the more beautiful the wildflowers that grow after that snowpack has melted. Junior's snowpack is exceptionally thick, and not just because he is nearing 100 years old. His life has been layered with beautiful relationships, weather-worn hardships, and so much joy that it can't be contained and just radiates from him. He's the water master of the Wasatch, who has stashed immeasurable wisdom within the layers of his snowpack. As he progresses into the spring of his life and his snowpack melts, his teachings seep and spread into the landscape, filling our creeks, our reservoirs, and our soil, and exposing those wildflower seeds of wisdom.

Those who have been lucky enough to cross paths with Junior Bounous have his wildflowers within them. As he's shared his teachings, his smiles, his jokes, and his compassion with us, we absorb them, making his joy part of who we are in turn. We are the students of Junior Bounous, born from the deep snowpacks of the West, rooted in Wasatch soil, raised beneath an alpine sun. May we grow our own wildflowers with his wisdom, his friendship, his laughter, his kind words, the twinkle in his eye, and a little dash of Bounousabuse.

Junior skiing at Alta in the 1950s.

Junior and Maxine hiking through abundant wildflowers on Maxine's birthday on September 18, 2011. A thick snowpack meant that the wildflower blooms got pushed many weeks back from their average time frame.

Junior during an autumn hike up Rock Canyon—one of his favorite places to witness fall foliage.

Skiing in the sun at Snowbird. Early 1970s.

Junior sharing a little snack with a chipmunk near Catherine Pass at Alta. 1980s.

Forever love birds.

Junior following Fast Max down the Baldy shoulder at Alta. 1950s.

Maxine's favorite kind of day: bluebird powder. Somewhere in Canada. 1990s.

Junior and Maxine with Yosemite Falls in the background. Late 1980s.

Maxine and Junior at friend Meryl Matzinger's 100 year birthday party. 2000s.

Maxine and Junior appreciating the horizon in matching tracksuits, somewhere off the Jasper Highway in the Canadian Rockies. Late 1970s.

Junior and Maxine among wildflowers in Mineral Basin, perhaps during Maxine's last time hiking in this favorite haunt of theirs. Around 2018.

Acknowledgments

Where do I even begin? This biography has been on my mind for a long time. There are plenty of people who you might meet in your lifetime and think, "Wow, this person should have a book written about them." It's a strange thing to realize that the book will never be written unless someone actually sits down and puts in the work to write it. In my case, I realized that if I didn't write that book, perhaps no one would. In order to commit to this project, I had to act like I was jumping off a cliff into water: close my eyes, take a breath, (plug my nose because I'm a wimp), and leap. I knew once I started, there would be no turning back.

This being my second book, I had an idea of what I was getting myself into—the possibility that an entire day's research might result in just two paragraphs or sometimes a meager two sentences, as well as the probability that writer's block at some point would prevent me from crafting a single decent sentence for weeks. What I did not anticipate was how much harder this book would be than my first. Writing a book about someone else's life is incredibly intimidating, and not just because the life I was to write about spans almost 100 years. In addition to that, I was going to write about one of my favorite humans on this planet, my mentor, my hero, one of my best friends—my grandfather—the man whom I strive to make proud, whose smile always brightens my day no matter my mood, whose example I yearn to follow both in life and on skis (especially through tree runs). I am struck often by how lucky I am to have been born his granddaughter, to have his blood running through my veins, and to share the last name Bounous with him.

The significant task of writing Junior's biography remained daunting throughout the entire process, yet here it is. And while it is by no means a comprehensive account of Junior's life and likely contains many errors, it is, to this date, the accomplishment of which I'm most proud. I hope Junior feels like I was able to do his story justice.

So many thank-yous are in order to the multitude of people responsible for pushing me over the finish line and facilitating the writing of this book.

Thank you to all the folks who donated to the Junior Bounous Biography project way back in 2019. Your donations helped get this show on the road, and here's the book to prove your donations were worthwhile.

Thank you to everyone who called, emailed, left voicemails, sat with me on chairlifts, or chatted with me during dinner to tell me stories about Junior. You wouldn't believe how much I enjoyed listening to them. I soaked them up. They made me laugh, cry, and feel so overwhelmed by Junior's expansive influence and the love and respect so many people have for him.

A sincere thank-you to Roger and Margaret Bourke, who provided many of the photos and article clippings and helped jump-start my momentum, and to Sal Raio and Jerry Warren for their additional time and energy in helping complete this book.

Thank you to many, many folks up at Snowbird for a variety of reasons—to Snowbird management and Dave Fields for helping Junior accomplish his goals and keep skiing, to the marketing team for sending me photos, to the Lodge employees who help Junior make a home for himself at the Bird. You all are amazing.

Thank you to Madeleine Brown, my editor and friend. Without your patience and gentle persistence, this book may never have left my laptop and made it into print. You were my personal cheerleader who rallied me back to writing when I was feeling uncertain or stagnant. You've helped me accomplish a goal that at times I wasn't sure I'd be able to accomplish. For that you deserve a million thank-yous!

A special thank-you to Colin Gaylord and Courtney Sanford. You may not have been directly involved in the writing process, but you listened to my rants, distracted me when I needed distracting, and helped me unwind from a long day at the computer by making me cocktails. Caravanserai forever <3

Thanks to my sister, Tyndall, for letting me call you many strange nicknames and for being my tree roots when I find myself in a storm.

Thank you to my uncle, Barry Bounous, for your patience while answering all my erratic emails and texts, for being my unofficial editor, fact-checking every word I wrote, and helping me track down photos, names, dates, and plenty of random gems! You have been an irreplaceable well of knowledge and resources while writing this book.

Thank you to my parents—without your unconditional love and support, I would not be a writer, and without your generous contributions, this book wouldn't have been possible.

And finally, thank you, Baqui, for trusting me to tell your story. Thank you for spending countless hours talking, answering questions and more questions, reading and rereading and rereading and editing and answering more questions and rereading some more. Thank you for dredging up details from memories long buried by the decades and for sharing many intimate moments with me. It has been a pleasure to learn about your life and an honor to share it with the world. I feel so lucky to be able to call myself your granddaughter, and I cherish all the time we spent working on this book together. Thank you for teaching our family how to love, how to live our lives full of empathy, respect, and kindness, and—of course—how to ski.

Junior and Maxine in their Snowbird Mountain School uniform around 1975. This classic orange jacket was the second-ever Snowbird Ski School uniform.

Steve, Ann and Randy MacDonald, Sue, Junior, and Nancy and Tom Kronthaler in the Uinta Mountains on Junior's 95th birthday. 2020.

Junior and granddaughter EvaLynn, gnawing on a lilac branch in the Provo Cemetery. Memorial Day. Mid-1980s.

Left to right: Margaret Bourke, Steve, Roger Bourke, Junior, Ayja, Sal Raio, and Sue at Alta in 2019.

Junior at granddaughter Ayja's wedding on San Juan Island in August 2021.
Tyler Rye Photography

Junior waterskiing in the 1980s.

Maxine being the ever supportive partner and taking Junior's sweatshirt as Junior competed in a marathon in St. George in the 1980s. Junior's time was 3 hour and 20 minutes (his fastest marathon) at 60 years old.

Tyndall, Junior, Sue, Ayja, and Steve at the SBSEF 50th anniversary barbecue in April 2022.

Junior, Bonnie Wiegele, and Maxine on a hike in the Canadian Rockies.

Junior enjoying time with granddaughters Ayja and Tyndall. Sometime around 1993.

Bill Levitt and Junior on the sun deck at Portillo Ski Area in the mid-1950s.

Mike Wiegele, Elfriede Shane, Bonnie Wiegele, Maxine, and Junior in Blue River, Canada. 1990s.

Maxine practicing her tree-climbing in Fiji in 1984.

Maxine with the TOLs ("Tough Old Ladies" from Vail) when Maxine was "inducted" into the TOLs. Maxine, in the middle in all blue, is wearing an early Snowbird ski school uniform. Mid-1970s.

Junior with some Snowbird ski instructors on the night he carried the Olympic torch in 2002.

Junior skiing hand-in-hand with Suzy "Chapstick" Chaffee at Snowbird in the 1970s. (She got her nickname after appearing in ChapStick commercials.) Suzy, often credited with helping start a skiing technique known as "ski ballet," was an Olympic downhill ski racer, fitness guru, Title IX advocate, and the first woman to serve on the US Olympic Committee's board of directors.

Maxine and Grant Culley in Nepal in 1987.

Herb and Helga Lloyd with Maxine and Junior in Ishpeming, Michigan, for Junior's US National Ski Hall of Fame induction in 1997. (He was nominated in 1996 but attended the ceremony in 1997.)

Dennis Keller, Junior, and Barry MacLean during the 2002 Winter Olympics.

As demonstrated in this photo, Junior was always much more flexible on skis than he was without skis. Early 1970s.

Junior and Alan Engen skiing at Alta in the 2000s. Alan, taking after his father, Alf Engen, became a great ski jumping competitor and instructor. He has continued to contribute to Utah's ski industry by becoming a renowned ski historian, including coauthoring *First Tracks: A Century of Skiing in Utah* with Gregory C. Thompson, which served as valuable research for this book.

Steve jumping off the Cirque Traverse at Snowbird for a Salomon ad in the 1980s.

Photographer Jimmy Kay, Junior, and Steve in Gad Valley for Junior's 90th birthday celebration in 2015.

Maxine floating through fresh spring powder in April 1976.

Junior ripping some powder at Snowbird in the early 1970s.

A photo of the Snowbird Ski School for Junior's semi-retirement in 1990.

EvaLynn, Debra, Barry, Suzanne and Grant Culley, Sue, Steve, Maryly Culley, Maxine, Junior, Robyn Culley Ihrke and Ray Ihrke during Steve and Sue's wedding at the Cliff Lodge in April 1985.

The Bounous family with their many awards in the early 1970s. Junior had recently won the Alta National Gelande Championship cup, the farthest trophy on the left. Others include art from Disney movies and signed by Walt Disney himself, which were won while the family lived at Sugar Bowl.

Junior teaching Steve about the joys of skiing at Sugar Bowl in the early 1960s.

Junior showing how much angulation an 80 year old can get. Early 2000s.

Steve, Maxine, and Junior in the 1980s. Apparently it was cool for men to rock blazers longer than their shorts back then.

A helicopter ski trip Junior attended on the shoulder of Mount Timpanogos, above Stewart Cirque in the 1960s. Helicopters were later banned from landing on the peak.

Junior shaking Alta president Chic Morton's hand after winning the Alta National Gelande Championship in 1971.

Junior and Maxine at a Halloween party in 1979.

Maxine and Junior in front of Rainbow Bridge at Lake Powell. 1990s.

Eddie "Mo" Morris, Junior, Jean Huber, Alf Engen, and Ted Johnson after being awarded the Alta Diamond pin for powder skiing around 1960. Note Junior's crew cut and his Sugar Bowl sweater. He had recently been named Sugar Bowl's ski school director.

Maxine and Junior with two Sugar Bowl ski school instructors at a party in 1964.

George Jedenoff and Junior in 1999 with a copy of *For the Love of Skiing*, a book about Alf Engen. At the time of this writing, George is 104 years old and also still skiing.

Frank Hirst (best man), Junior and Maxine, and Lorraine Lindey (maid of honor), during Junior and Maxine's wedding on December 12, 1952.

A young, stoic Junior. Likely around the time he graduated high school in 1945.

Liane and Mark Magelssen and Junior in Cathedral in the Desert. October 2021.

Abe Waterhouse, Junior, and Maxine in Aspen in the 1960s.

The Deep Powder Dipsy

By JUNIOR BOUNOUS

Ski School Director The Sugar Bowl Norden, California

"Powder!"—Is there a skier alive who has not thrilled at the mention of the magical stuff? — who has not dreamed of frolicking down an untracked slope, waist-deep in soft white spray?—skiing effortlessly through a sea of feathery snow-dust?

In a sport so strongly influenced by the Austrians, the Swiss, the French and the Scandinavians, the American skier understandably adopts a submissive attitude towards the European origins of his sport. Skiing was born in Europe, was nurtured there, its techniques developed there. Thus the American tends to accept his relatively youthful status in an older world of skiing.

Except in deep powder snow.

For here, in powder skiing, one finds the single outstanding contribution of Americans to the techniques of the ski sport. As James Laughlin put it (SKI, November, 1960), ". . . when it comes to deep snow skiing, it is fair to say that something approaching an 'American' style has been evolved. Our powder stylists have something to show which often makes the Europeans sit up and take notice . . . there is a kind of rhythm, a graceful floating and knifing in deep snow which perhaps we may proudly claim as our own."

And perhaps no one has done more to develop this deep powder style than a former cross-country champion from Provo, Utah, named Junior Bounous. A disciple of veteran Alta skimeister Alf Engen, Bounous is recognized as the nation's leading powder exponent; his interest and understanding of powder skiing are inexhaustible, his teaching gospel. We present, on the following pages, his own account of his efforts to develop a style to help skiers master the not-so-easy art of skiing deep powder snow. THE EDITORS

Deep Powder technique is a strictly American style. Here's how a leading expert skis it

48

An introduction to an article written by Junior about how to ski deep powder. Likely published for *SKI* magazine in the 1960s, while Junior was ski school director for Sugar Bowl.

Junior posing with his awards after winning Alta's National Gelande Championship in 1971.

A key to successful powder skiing is a deliberate pole plant, like Junior is demonstrating here at Timp Haven around 1968.

Junior at Snowbird on his 96th day skiing, which was on April 26, 2022.

Junior working on his "spread eagle." From an unknown magazine in the 1960s.

Sally Deavers, Max Marolt, Spencer Eccles, and Junior Bounous with their Snow Cup awards at Alta in the early 1950s. Junior claimed the bronze, proudly wearing his ski school sweater with his name stitched on the breast.

Junior and his horse, Neg, while Junior was in high school. Mid-1940s.

Steve and Junior hiking the Pfeifferhorn together in Little Cottonwood when Steve was a teenager. 1970s.

Maxine and Junior at the Lodge at Snowbird around Christmas. 2000s.
Mitch Bolen

Maxine and Junior, just a few months shy of their 80th birthdays in 2005.

Maxine and Junior during their time working at Alta in 1954. Maxine had what the couple referred to as her "breakable crust" hairdo, given to her by Junior's student Bill White.

Family photo time! From left to right: Henry Pond, Steve Pond, Eleanor Bolen, Christine Bounous Pond with Junior Jensen Pond in arms, EvaLynn Bounous Bolen, Mitch Bolen, Junior, Barry, Debra, Jennie (granddaughter), Aurora Bounous, James Bounous, and Kayla Smith Bounous. 2020.

In 1961, Fred Lindholm organized a group of skiers to board a helicopter and ski on Mount Timpanogos for the first time. The skiers traversed across the slope and then all started skiing at the same time. Maxine lived up to her nickname, "Fast Max," and quickly outpaced the others. From left to right: Maxine, Elfriede Shane, Junior, and Jim McConkey.
Fred Lindholm